Richard T. Ely

Problems of Today

Richard T. Ely

Problems of Today

ISBN/EAN: 9783743388802

Manufactured in Europe, USA, Canada, Australia, Japa

Cover: Foto ©Suzi / pixelio.de

Manufactured and distributed by brebook publishing software (www.brebook.com)

Richard T. Ely

Problems of Today

PROBLEMS OF TO-DAY

A DISCUSSION

OF

PROTECTIVE TARIFFS, TAXATION, AND MONOPOLIES

BY

RICHARD T. ELY, Ph.D., LL.D.

PROFESSOR OF POLITICAL ECONOMY AND DIRECTOR OF THE SCHOOL
OF ECONOMICS, POLITICAL SCIENCE AND HISTORY,
IN THE UNIVERSITY OF WISCONSIN.

NEW EDITION
REVISED AND GREATLY ENLARGED.

NEW YORK
THOMAS Y. CROWELL & CO.

PREFACE TO THE THIRD EDITION.

THE present edition of the Problems of To-Day contains three new papers, which I have placed together and called Part II. As each of these papers was originally prepared for a special occasion, and as they deal with related topics, a certain amount of repetition was inevitable. I have, however, made no effort to remedy this, because I regard it as an advantage, in a popular economic work like the present. My experience as a teacher and a writer shows me that it is necessary to come back, again and again, to simple principles, and view them from many standpoints, before they can be fully grasped by those who are not trained economists.

RICHARD T. ELY.

JOHNS HOPKINS UNIVERSITY,
BALTIMORE, January, 1890.

PREFACE.

THE present work consists of a series of papers written originally for the Baltimore *Sun*, and only slightly revised and enlarged for republication. When I began my articles for the *Sun* I had no thought of gathering them together in book-form, and it is only after long hesitation that in response to requests from many people in different parts of the country I have consented to do so. Did I have sufficient time to subject the articles to a thorough revision, there would be less cause for my hesitation, but I have not the requisite time at present.

Every one knows the conditions under which articles are written for a popular newspaper. · They must appeal to " all sorts and conditions of men," to the bank president and merchant prince as well as to the artisan, to the mechanic, and to the unskilled day-laborer.

The space to which one is entitled limits the length of an article quite as much as the nature of the subject. An occurrence like the death of the late German Emperor, having no possible connection with the topics discussed in this volume, will nevertheless cut short a newspaper article on tariffs or monopolies. The chapters in this book, then, are not so rounded out and complete as they would have been if originally intended for publication in book-form. On the other hand, I have been advised that there is a certain advantage in the form which these papers have taken, and that it would be of doubtful utility to rewrite them.

Some of my learned friends may think that a university professor ought not to write anything quite so popular in form and style as this work. Perhaps they will say that I ought to have placed over these remarks the title "An Apology." It seems to me, however, that this implies a mistaken view of the functions of our higher institutions of learning, for I believe that to an ever-increasing extent they ought to assume a democratic character, to attempt more than ever before to elevate the masses, and to guide and direct their thought. I believe, moreover, that such experience as we have warrants us in thinking that this sort of effort will react on these institutions themselves and improve them in many respects. The only air congenial to the highest intellectual life is true democracy — which is the same thing as true aristocracy.

However, I will frankly confess what finally decided me to publish these papers in book-form, for in so doing, I shall best explain my purpose. On one day I received letters from three college presidents, each of whom spoke of my *Sun* articles in the most gratifying terms. On another day I learned that nearly all the employés of one of the largest corporations in Baltimore read the articles as they appeared, and invariably discussed them during their dinner-hour.

When I was further informed that, inconvenient as news-papers are for such purposes, the articles were being used in two college class-rooms, I felt warranted in republishing the articles even without a thorough-going revision.

My thanks are due to the Baltimore *Sun* for consenting to the present use of these articles.

RICHARD T. ELY.

Johns Hopkins University,
Baltimore, May, 1888.

TABLE OF CONTENTS.

PART I.

PART II.

PART I.

PROBLEMS OF TO-DAY.

CHAPTER I.

INTRODUCTORY.

I HAVE been asked to write a series of articles on various problems of the day, some of them relating to national life, others to state affairs and still others to our own city. It gives me pleasure to comply with this request.

It is well that the reader should at once understand the character of this proposed series of articles, of which the present is the opening one. First, then, it must be borne in mind that an exhaustive treatment of the subjects discussed cannot be expected; that such a treatment is not contemplated, for the topics are too large to admit of it even with the generous limits allowed me by *The Sun*. I intend rather to elucidate certain elementary principles in the simplest language at my command, and to make a few suggestions in regard to such questions as the nature of commerce, the balance of trade theory, the policy of protection, its connection with monopoly and its bearing on the welfare of labor, the treasury surplus, taxation in state and city, and natural monopolies. I shall not play the part of an advocate and say certain things merely because they are calculated to produce an effect or annoy an adherent of opposing views; rather, I shall endeavor to help my readers to get at the truth about many vexed questions which are much obscured by partisan controversy. Few statistics will be used, because statistics both as a science and an art is still in an unsatisfactory condition, and the data it furnishes are largely unreliable ; further, because " nothing lies like figures " — in other words, it requires a trained mind to pass judgment on statistical arguments, and it is very easy, by a sort of hocus pocus, to make statistics prove whatever you please.

It is particularly easy to prove what you please, with statistics in respect to international trade, for our statistical knowledge is at present so imperfect, that it gives us comparatively little assistance in discussions concerning the consequences of restrictions on the movements of commerce or of the removal of such restrictions. Statistical information is of more value than anything else even now in discussions on some topics of the day, like municipal public works ; but they are not usually so complicated and so many classes of facts are not involved. It may be on this account that those political economists who have begun their serious studies with an examination of the principles and practices of protectionism, or who have been led to devote themselves to political economy on account of their interest in controversies respecting free trade and protection, have often repudiated altogether the statistical and historical method in practical economy, and have cultivated exclusively abstract and deductive reasoning. They have thus fallen into gross error in other fields of political economy than commerce, and have brought discredit upon their science. While deductive-reasoning seems especially applicable to the subject of international trade, and while statistics are imperfect and must be used with caution, every aid which statistics can give must be warmly welcomed.

Let us take as an example of fallacies in statistics one

which has carried great weight with it. I refer to the argument about our increase in wealth and its connection with a protective tariff, in Mr. James G. Blaine's celebrated letter in which he accepted the nomination to the presidency of the United States. Mr. Blaine states that the wealth of the United States in 1860 amounted to $14,000,000,000 ; that "after 1860 the business of the country was encouraged and developed by a protective tariff," and that at the end of twenty years the valuation of our property had increased to the enormous aggregate of $44,000,000,000. An Englishman, however, immediately comes forward with a statement to show that there has been an equally marvellous increase in national wealth in his country since 1846, when free-trade principles were introduced, and he attributes this prosperity to the policy of free trade. Both are wrong, though their arguments are plausible. While I was walking down Baltimore Street yesterday, a merchant sold ten thousand dollars' worth of goods. The two events happened together, but was one the cause of the other? Manifestly you want some other proof than the fact that the two events were contemporaneous. It is equally necessary to ask, both in the case of Great Britain and the United States, what other forces besides tariff laws were at work to increase the wealth of each nation, and merely to ask this question shows that these laws, whether wise or unwise, after all played only a minor rôle. The opening up of new territories, the improved means of communication and transportation, the further application of steam to industry, a host of new inventions and discoveries, accompanied by a population rapidly growing in numbers and increasing in intelligence and skill, — these evidently are the main causes of the augmented national wealth of the United States; and whether the doctrine of protection is true or false, the tariff, after all, was only one factor, and a minor one at that. But let us examine this statistical argument more at length. Forty-four billions ! That is truly an enormous sum, but how much of that have you, my reader ? Have you more than you want ? How many of us, in fact, have enough to satisfy our rational wants ? How many of us could advantageously expend more than we have in food, clothing, improved dwellings, books, music, travel, wholesome recreation ? Certainly most people in my circle of acquaintance ; and the question may well be raised whether what we have as a nation is desirably distributed, and whether certain alarming tendencies to concentration of wealth and monopoly in business are wholly unconnected with our tariff legislation. Many more similar questions are pertinent, but they will not be raised in this place. It is hoped that what has been said will suffice to show the necessity of caution in the acceptance of alleged statistical proof. Statistics are useful, and the formation of an International Statistical Institute to improve statistics, both as a science and an art, is to be hailed with unqualified satisfaction, but the place of figures in a series of papers like this is limited. It is proposed rather to base what is said on facts which can be observed by everybody, and on principles of common sense and well-attested experience.

The subject of national revenue is the first to occupy our attention, because nearly all national problems involve sooner or later questions of national finance. There are various sources of revenue, as land, productive enterprises, loans and taxation, and some local and central governments defray a large portion of their expenditures by profits on certain lines of business entrusted to them. Berlin, for example, meets more than eighteen per cent. of its expenses from the net revenues of its gas-works, although gas is sold below one dollar a thousand ; the profits on state railways in the various German states more than cover the interest charges on their public debts, and four of the German states, — Baden, Bavaria, Prussia, and Saxony, — provide for over half their budgets by returns on enterprises of one kind and another. Richmond, Virginia, and a few other American cities derive profits from gas-works. The revenues of the gas-works of Philadelphia, for example, amounted to nearly three millions of dollars in 1887, out of a total municipal income of $17,-584,255.71. Our federal government, however, is almost exclusively dependent upon taxes. But it must be remembered that taxes are of two kinds, direct and indirect, the former on property and income, the latter on commodities. The taxes imposed upon us by the federal government are, however, exclusively indirect taxes. We have then to ask this question — What are the peculiar features of indirect taxation in general, and what special characteristics pertain to indirect taxation in the United States? An attempt will be made to answer this question in the following chapter.

CHAPTER II.

DIRECT AND INDIRECT TAXATION CONTRASTED.[1]

INDIRECT taxes are chiefly taxes on commodities ; in other words, taxes on what we eat and wear and consume in other ways, or on raw materials and implements used in manufacturing goods for purposes of consumption. They are called indirect taxes because they are usually paid in the first instance by one person and shifted by him to another. The importer of salt, sugar, and coal, pays taxes on these commodities when they enter the territory of the United States, adds them to the price of his commodities, sells them to some one else, perhaps a wholesale dealer, who in turn disposes of them to a retailer, having added the tax and a profit on the money which he advanced in payment of the tax. The retailer finally sells them to you and me, but by this time the tax has been turned over several times and has grown like a snowball rolling down hill. To the retailer the tax has become an indistinguishable part of the price which he pays, and on which he must derive a profit from us, the consumers. Thus indirect taxes roll up, and roll up every time one person shifts them upon another, until finally the augmented burden rests upon the shoulder of the taxpayer. An indirect tax is thus a tax which vio-

[1] A large part of this chapter has been printed in my "Taxation in American States and Cities." The difference, however, between this chapter and the one bearing a similar title in the other book, is too great to allow me to call it simply a quotation.

lates one of the celebrated four canons of taxation, for it takes from the pockets of the taxpayer far more than it puts into the public treasury. It is a wasteful kind of taxation. This is not mere theory. It is a fact of which any one can satisfy himself by conversation with intelligent merchants who understand the operations in which they are engaged.

INDIRECT TAXES VIOLATE THE PRINCIPLE OF EQUALITY.

Another accepted canon of taxation is that its amount should be measured in each case by ability or the revenue which a citizen of the commonwealth enjoys. This is what is called equality of taxation. Government should exact equality of sacrifice of us all. An income tax honestly assessed and honestly collected, meets the requirements of this canon. How does the case stand with indirect taxation? This is taxation of consumption; but does consumption of taxed commodities vary with income? We import salt and tax it nearly fifty per cent. of its value. Does the rich man consume more salt than the poor man? Do you increase the amount of salt in your soup with an improvement in your financial condition? It is said that, on the contrary, the amount of salt consumed by the poor man is greater than that consumed by the rich man, because the latter uses other condiments, while salt is often the only seasoning the former enjoys. We have in a tax like this what is called a regressive tax, a tax which increases as income decreases — the worst kind of a tax and the most unjust. The tax on sugar is over seventy-five per cent. on value, and from it a large part of our revenue is derived. It is similar in principle, although there is a difference in rates according to value of sugar, so that higher grades pay more, and it is true that people of large means consume more than poor people. But the difference in rate and in quantities consumed by no means corresponds to differences in incomes. It may be doubted whether a man with ten thousand a year consumes less than one with fifteen thousand, and he certainly does not consume an inferior quality of sugar. A man with two hundred thousand a year will not consume twenty times as much as one with two thousand a year, much less will he consume one hundred times as much. Here we still have the regressive tax. But take even taxes on imported silks, which yield fifteen millions a year, and appear to be among the fairest of indirect taxes. The rate is almost fifty per cent. Silk can hardly be called an article of superfluous luxury at the present time, and a lawyer who supports a family on three thousand a year is taxed out of all proportion higher than the plutocrat whose income is three hundred thousand dollars. It is needless to continue illustrations. With the progress of democratic thought, the idea of progressive taxation meets — rightly or wrongly, that need not be discussed here — with increasing favor, and some of the states where the principles of democracy are carried farther than anywhere else in the world, the Swiss cantons, have recently introduced progressive taxes on property and on income, but our federal government relies wholly on a system of regressive taxation ! One would think this in itself would be sufficient to check the ardor of protectionists who are at the same time working-men ; but this is by no means the whole story. Take up any treatise on taxation and read the arguments in favor of indirect taxation, and what is the first thing to attract your attention ? It is, that with the present calls upon civilized governments, and with the unwillingness of people to pay direct taxes, and the resistance which men of means offer to high direct taxes levied in proportion to income, it is practically impossible to maintain the modern government without large contributions from people of limited resources, and the only way to tax them is by indirect methods; in other words, mingling taxes with prices paid, so that goods cannot be bought without paying taxes. It is, too, worthy of notice that the English system of indirect taxation, which we have inherited, originated in the corrupt reign of Charles II., about two hundred years ago. Then the burden of government rested upon the land held by feudal tenure, but the Parliament of Charles II., "by a majority of two only, divested the landed gentry of all their feudal obligations to the crown without touching their privileges, and as compensation to the state imposed an excise duty upon beer, spirits, wine, tobacco, and numerous other articles. . . . It marked the dawn of our modern system of indirect taxation; and the emancipation of the aristocracy from special burdens on land thus accomplished, helped to alter the whole current of our later fiscal history." These are the words of an English writer on finance.

Perhaps one of the best tests of the true character of a government is the nature of its system of taxation. If we turn to Russia we shall find there taxes such as we might naturally expect under a modern despotism. The Russian budget for 1881 exhibits revenues of 118.75 millions of rubles from the land and poll tax, and 19.26 millions of rubles from the taxes on business, and these are the only direct taxes. The indirect taxes in Russia yielded 376.59 millions of rubles. It is to be noticed further that of the 118.75 millions from the land and poll taxes, about one-half was the revenue of the poll tax — the most iniquitous form of direct taxation.

INDIRECT TAXATION AND PAUPERISM.

There is a connection between indirect taxation and pauperism which is worthy of notice. All direct taxation places a limit below which it will not go. This is too low in Maryland, — at any rate lower than elsewhere, — but even with us a man must have at least a hundred dollars before he can be taxed. Indirect taxation does not discriminate between the last dollar of the poor widow and the dollar which is only one in an income of a million. It raises prices, reduces the value of income, and forces some who are already near the awful line of pauperism to cross it, and thus puts to death higher aspirations in a class of citizens and lowers the level of civilization. But the absurdity of the thing is seen in this, that when the tax has destroyed the value of a man as an industrial factor in the community, what has been taken away is given back in alms !

INDIRECT TAXES OBSTRUCT TRADE AND FOSTER MONOPOLY.

The cost of collection of indirect taxes is high, and necessitates an army of spies and informers. They thus interfere with liberty of movement and obstruct trade in a thousand ways. Thus, again, indirect taxes take out and keep out of the pockets of the people more than they yield to the treasury of the state.[1] Indirect taxes foster monopoly and discourage the small producers. On account of indirect taxes a larger amount of capital is required to enable one to begin business than would otherwise be necessary, while in the administration of indirect taxes there is almost

[1] Statistics representing the cost of collecting direct and indirect taxes may be found in my work, " Taxation in American States and Cities."

always something which favors the man producing on a vast scale. The federal government requires bonds from producers of taxed commodities, and a poor man is not always able to secure bondsmen. Federal taxes are paid in stamps and discounts are given to those who purchase large quantities at a time. Indirect federal taxation has concentrated or monopolized the production of the chief domestic articles which it has touched : namely, matches, tobacco, and intoxicating liquors. The monopolistic feature of indirect taxation varies very greatly in different times and different places, but in some form or another it almost invariably exists.

INDIRECT TAXES CONGENIAL TO DESPOTISM AND ARISTOCRACY.

Indirect taxes are imposed on people without creating so much discontent as direct taxes and without causing so close a scrutiny of the method in which the proceeds of taxation are expended, because the mass of men do not realize that they pay taxes every time they purchase dry goods or groceries. They are an underhanded kind of taxation. It is not, then, surprising that they are in the minds of many identified with despotism and aristocracy, while there is a growing opposition to them on the part of enlightened democracy — an opposition which undoubtedly goes too far at times. In the United States it should be remembered that while national revenues flow from indirect taxes, state and local governments are supported chiefly by direct taxation. National revenues are about as large as the revenues of all the states and all the local political units put together, so that we pay less than one-half of our total expenses of government by the proceeds of direct taxes, and over one-half by the proceeds of indirect taxes. There would be great opposition to an extensive system of direct federal taxes, because the face of the federal tax-gatherer in our states is not a welcome sight. Of course he is now every-where, but he keeps out of sight of most of us, and so we do not realize it. A good deal of this feeling against direct taxes has been properly called "puerile," and among a people sufficiently moral, patriotic, and enlightened, indirect taxation might perhaps be abolished. We must, however, take people as we find them, and at present its total aboli-tion is out of the question. Of course it is an undoubted advantage to be able to pay one's taxes in small amounts from time to time, when one buys a few pounds of sugar, a little tobacco, or an article of clothing. Our indirect fed-eral taxes are of two kinds, tariff duties and internal revenue taxes ; the former laid on commodities imported into the country, the latter on commodities produced within the country. Now there is a peculiarity about the revenues which flow from taxes on imported commodities, and that is, that those taxes are in the United States not laid for the sake of revenue, but for quite another purpose. The aim of the tariff taxes is to render it more difficult to bring com-modities into the United States, and thus either to remove competition from those Americans engaged in the produc-tion of commodities which some of us want to import, or at any rate to serve as a breakwater, and to modify the power of competition. The revenue which these taxes af-ford is merely an incidental matter. The purpose of the next chapter will be to consider certain peculiar features in our financial situation caused by the fact that taxes are laid on commodities for other than revenue purposes.

The following table, taken from Paul Leroy-Beaulieu's "Traité de la Science des Finances," shows the amount of indirect taxes raised in nine of the chief countries of Europe in 1876 : —

Countries.	Population.	Internal Revenue Taxes on Commodities in Thousands of Francs.	Customs Duties in Thousands of Francs.	Total Product of Indirect Taxation.	Per Capita Contribution in Francs.
Germany . .	42,727,360	264,375	151,351	415,726	9.72
Austria-Hungary } .	36,882,466	352,840	49,000	401,840	10.89
Belgium . .	5,403,000	51,269	22,139	73,408	13.53
Denmark . .	1,903,000	5,251	28,254	33,505	17.60
France . . .	36,643,000	954,059	264,351	1,218,411	33.25
Netherlands .	3,865,456	77,986	12,186	90,173	23.32
Switzerland .	2,759,854	979	12,376	13,356	4.83
England . .	33,093,439	671,000	505,000	1,176,000	35.50
Italy	27,500,000	368,146	100,958	469,104	17.06

CHAPTER III.

REMARKS ON THE PRINCIPLES OF A SOUND SYSTEM OF FEDERAL FINANCIERING.

THE principles which should control public expenditures differ in marked manner from those which should govern private expenditures, and the failure to recognize this fact explains many mistakes which have been made in American financial history. It is not necessary in this place to elaborate all the differences between private financiering and public financiering, but in any discussion of current financial problems one should be clearly grasped. It is this: Private expenditures should be governed by revenues, while in the case of a public body it should first be determined what one wants to spend, and then receipts should be made to correspond to public needs. The private man brings his receipts up to the highest point: in other words, he endeavors to obtain as large a profit from his business as possible, or to derive as large an income from his occupation as circumstances will permit. After he has found that his income is $500, $1,000 or $5,000, as the case may be, he then — and, if a prudent man, not before — decides what he can spend. Unlike a private party, the representatives of the people ought first to decide that it is necessary to spend certain sums of money for the public good, and then ask the people to provide the means, laying taxes to meet expenses; or, if part of the expenses are defrayed by profits on public works and revenues from other sources, laying taxes to meet the deficiency in receipts. This is a well-tested principle of public financiering. Strict adherence to this principle brings order and harmony into public accounts, while its violation produces confusion and waste. It implies that taxes are wholly, or to some considerable extent at least, laid for revenue purposes.[1]

When we begin an examination of our federal finances, we are struck by the disproportion between the needs of government and the revenues for meeting these needs. Sometimes the revenues are too large and sometimes too small, and when it is noticed that they are apt to be plentiful when there is comparatively small call for expenditures, and distressingly small when our needs are large and urgent, it is a not unnatural conclusion that there is a radical defect in our financial system. Such is the case, and the defect is the one mentioned, that taxes are not laid for revenue purposes. When taxes are imposed upon a people to defray the expenses of government, it will be ascertained what those expenses properly are, and the rate of taxation will be so adjusted as to raise enough money, neither more nor less. This is the plan pursued by the mayor and common council of Baltimore, and the tax rate is designed to vary, and to be $1.50, $1.60, or $1.70, according to our actual needs. It can readily be seen, however, that the moment one loses sight of the object of taxation, which is revenue, and lays taxes for other purposes, it would be surprising if revenue should correspond with the need for revenue. That there should be this correspondence implies not only that taxes should be laid with a view to the probable revenue from them, but that the system of taxation itself should be a

---

[1] This does not imply that no other purpose than revenue should be associated with the financial system of a country. A part of the taxes at least ought to be purely for revenue.

flexible one in at least some of its essential points, so that revenue may readily be lowered or raised without an acute disturbance of business relations. The English government finds flexibility in its income tax, which is raised or lowered from year to year, according to estimated revenues from other sources and estimated expenditures. If it is required to raise large sums for the prosecution of a war, the proper minister at once brings a bill into Parliament to raise the rate of the income tax. Gladstone originally intended to defray all the expenses of the Crimean War by taxation without loans, and Parliament, with that end in view, raised the income tax considerably. This tax involves no disturbance of business relations, for it is not a tax on business or property, and it requires much of those only who have much to give. Thus, entirely apart from the fact that this method makes the influential classes feel their responsibility for the course of government, this English income tax, so far as it goes, assures a condition of sound public financiering. It is not meant in this place, and at this time, to raise the question of the desirability of an income tax. Even the friends of an income tax are very properly inclined to regard it as better adapted to state than federal purposes, but what is said illustrates my point, namely, that it is necessary to establish a system of taxation which in some of its parts at least shall be flexible. Now, it is manifest that our federal government never has had a system of taxation which answered the requirements of national financiering. Our chief source of revenue has been taxes on imported commodities. When are these likely to yield large returns? Manifestly during time of peace and prosperity. When are they likely to yield little? Manifestly during periods of foreign complications and wars. But it is during periods of the first sort that we need little, and during periods of the second sort that we need much. Two periods in our history are specially instructive on this point, and these are the periods covered by the War of 1812 and the late Civil War. Mr. Gallatin was forced to rely upon loans during the first war, and these could be placed only under conditions disadvantageous to the public, because there was no adequate basis for them in public revenues, for these consisted of duties on imported commodities, and the war, which called for increased expenditures, diminished imports. Mr. Dallas, in 1814, said: "The plan of finance which was predicated upon the theory of defraying the extraordinary expenses of the war by successive loans, had already become inoperative," and he ascribed the collapse "to the inadequacy of our system of taxation to form a foundation of public credit, and the absence from our system of the means which are the best adapted to anticipate, collect, and distribute the public revenue." Mr. Dallas uses the following instructive words in his "Report on the Finances for 1815": "It certainly furnishes a lesson of practical policy that there existed no system by which the internal resources of the country could be brought at once into action when the resources of its external commerce became incompetent to answer the exigencies of the time. The existence of such a system would probably have invigorated the early movements of the war, might have preserved the public credit unimpaired, and would have rendered the pecuniary contributions of the people more equal as well as more effective. But owing to the want of such a system, a sudden and almost exclusive resort to the public credit was necessarily adopted as the chief instrument of finance."

It seems scarcely necessary to remind my readers of the results of the financial policy of the late war. Secretary Chase, in his first report, in 1861, estimated revenues from customs duties at $57,000,000, and at the end of the first quarter found it necessary to reduce the estimate to $32,000,000. There existed no system "by which the internal resources of the country could at once be brought into action," and before this machinery could be created and rendered effective, the war was nearly finished. The result was a vast and demoralizing public debt, on part of which it was necessary to pay twelve per cent. for money received, and return $100 in gold for $50 lent to government; further, the creation in time of haste, confusion, and dire need of a tax system, which may be called a monstrosity.

Our tax system now yields surplus revenue, and it is difficult to reduce it because it is framed for the benefit of private interests, and these resist its reduction. "The full realization of self-government requires a delicate adjustment of budgetary machinery, but surplus revenue acts as a weight which throws that machinery out of balance." These words are from H. C. Adams's "Public Debts," as able a work on finance as has ever appeared from the pen of an American.

Now it is not true that this surplus revenue could not be advantageously expended. There are many uses to which it could be put which would be highly beneficial. The construction of proper coast defences is one; the construction of great artificial water-ways and the improvement of natural water-ways and harbors of really national importance is another; the purchase of the telegraph is a third. These are given simply by way of illustration.

It is not pleasant to pay taxes, but it may be doubted if the ordinary man invests any money which yields so large a return as that which he pays in taxes, provided always that it is expended by honest and intelligent public officials. This is often not appreciated because there is too general a fail-

ure to recognize what is due to good government. But the
moment the machinery of government begins to move unsat-
isfactorily or to exhibit signs of breaking down, even the most
confirmed tax dodgers do not hesitate to utter cries of alarm
and indignation. Perhaps the anarchistic agitation has done
some good in calling attention to the importance of good
government. Mayor Latrobe, it occurs to me in this connection, made an excellent point in his recent address before
the West Baltimore Improvement Association. He admitted
the burden of taxation, but put the question, "Does any
one regret the issuing of a single loan made heretofore
for public improvements, such as the Gunpowder Water-
works, the new City Hall, Druid Hill, Patterson, and River-
side Parks, the opening of Cathedral and German streets?"
Certainly no one regrets these expenditures. It is doubtless true that the needs of the United States government
may in the future require enough more than now to consume all our present annual surplus, for Secretary Fair-
child's report shows that the ordinary federal expenditures
increased over thirty millions from 1884 to 1887, yet it is
also true that in a matter like this we ought not to proceed
faster than is warranted by the enlightenment of public opinion. This should crystallize about a measure and demand it
before revenues for carrying it into effect are provided. To
provide revenues before it is decided for what we need them
is putting the cart before the horse. The surplus revenue
could be usefully expended, but there is every reason to fear
that it will not be. Rather than inaugurate any public work
designed to benefit the entire public, but which is not as yet
demanded by the public, timid Congressmen are more likely
to grant money to clamorous private interests, with the idea
of winning their support. Moreover, such a public measure
as the appropriation of public money for the removal of

illiteracy —one of the dangers to the republic — cannot be discussed on its merits so long as an enormous surplus exists. Its advocates are suspected of improper motives, very likely of trying to get rid of the public money to bolster up war taxation, and it fails to receive the fair, impartial discussion which it deserves. The so-called " Blair Bill," which aims to distribute seventy or eighty millions, more or less, among the states for the promotion of education, and to base this distribution on relative illiteracy in the various states, may or may not be a proper bill. The character of this bill is not involved in the present discussion. The proposed measure simply illustrates the difficulties which attend even the discussion of any popular measure so long as our present methods of financiering continue. Free traders are in too many cases becoming fanatical in their opposition to any government undertakings on account of their desire to prevent expenditure of public money, and thus by means of an alarming surplus in the treasury to force tariff revision upon the country. Protectionists, on the other hand, are too inclined to become demagogues and to favor extravagant and iniquitous expenditures, provided they are calculated to " catch votes."

As it is seen that duties on imports are not satisfactory as an exclusive source of federal revenues, and can only form part of a system of federal taxation, the question arises : What have those to offer as a substitute who wish to abolish our present internal revenue taxes ? Unless the revenue reformers keep these various points in mind they are likely to be outwitted. The ten per cent. tariff reduction of 1872 was repealed in 1875 on account of deficiency of revenues, and if internal revenue taxes are abolished, and there is nothing to take their place, every future fiscal emergency will serve as an effective plea for a higher tariff. If we desire

once for all to break with our high and complicated tariff
system, to avoid financiering of such a nature as to produce
violent fluctuations in business affairs, and to bring business
down to a natural basis, we must be prepared to maintain
and establish a system of taxation capable of meeting the
varying demands on the public treasury.

CHAPTER IV.

THE NATURE AND PURPOSE OF COMMERCE.

THE design of our present tariff laws is to regulate commerce, and they are based on a certain theory respecting the nature and purpose of commerce. This fact should be fully grasped, for no one is qualified to speak on protection and free trade who has not clear ideas in regard to the part which commerce plays in modern industrial life. The free-trader finds favor with the mercantile community because he looks upon an extension of commercial relations with satisfaction, and thinks that restrictions and regulations of commerce do more harm than good. When an ancient French monarch called an opulent merchant to him and desired his advice in regard to measures suitable for the extension of commerce, the merchant simply replied, "Laissez faire," which, interpreted into plain English, means: "Let us, the merchants alone. We ask nothing more. We ask no assistance. We only desire that you should not interfere with us." It was then quite natural that an early American free-trader — Condy Raguet — who, in 1829, published the once well-known "Free-Trade Advocate and Journal of Political Economy," should take as the motto of his periodical "Laissez nous faire." The protectionist on the other hand, looks with distrust upon foreign commerce, for he fancies that the interests of the home producer may thereby be endangered. He therefore advocates restrictions upon commerce that he may diminish its magnitude. Occasionally one is found who even wishes that a wall of fire surrounded the United States, so that nothing might be imported. Coupled with the apprehensions concerning the home producer one frequently finds disparaging views concerning the real utility of commerce. These are partly traditional, and are found from the earliest times to the present. The ancient Persians held commerce to be a school of lies. Cicero and the Roman philosophers despised commerce, Cicero going so far as to say a merchant could never make anything unless he lied in the most atrocious manner. St. Chrysostom believed it scarcely possible that a man could be at the same time a Christian and a merchant.

There can, I think, scarcely be a doubt that the influence of these old views lingers on after commerce has changed materially its nature. Commerce originated in robbery, and in early ages it supplied chiefly articles of luxury. The Phœnicians and Greeks were pirates before they were merchants, and piracy played an important rôle in the development of English commerce in the sixteenth century. Nomadic people first robbed caravans, and only at a later period became guides and protectors of them, and thus assistants in the creation of a legitimate commerce. Piracy and robbery are no longer aids, but only enemies to commerce, which is as a rule now found on the side of law and order.

An error of a different sort is still unduly current. It is that commerce is not productive. Benjamin Franklin said there are three ways for a nation to acquire wealth : "The first is by war. . . . This is robbery. The second by commerce, which is, generally, cheating. The third is by agriculture, the only honest way." The late Horace Greeley used to lament in his *Tribune* the large number of merchants, and to hope that the time would come when ninety-nine men out of a hundred would become real producers.

The truth is that the merchant is as truly a producer as the farmer. The farmer creates no new matter. No one can do that. He simply changes the position of things; puts things in fit places, and thus adds to their utility. He drops the corn in the hill, — changes its place, — puts it in the right place. He changes the position of earth, putting it over the corn. The corn is acted upon by natural forces. Certain elements in the earth, air, water change their positions, and form new combinations. The corn grows, and what was useless becomes useful. The farmer has changed the position of things and created utility or a quantity of value. That is all. No more than the merchant can he add one particle to the quantity of matter in the earth. Now, under the direction of the merchant, the position of things is changed. Goods are brought from a place where they are not needed, and where they could have no value, to a place where they are needed. Thus the merchant creates precisely what the farmer creates: namely, a quantity of utility or value. We may call it "place-value." Likewise the merchant keeps things from a time when not wanted to a time when wanted, and increases their utility. Thus he creates "time-value." And it should be remembered in this connection that commerce, with the aid of the improved means of communication and transportation, has become so effective in the creation of time-values and place-values that famines are now unknown in the civilized world, whereas, even as late as the last century, districts in France and England suffered the horrors of famine, while superfluity could be found within three hundred miles.

It has been stated that commerce previously ministered to luxury. Only articles of high value in small bulk could, in early days, become the object of commerce, for it cost more to transport such commodities as the masses consumed than they were worth.

Grain and bulkier articles were transported occasionally in considerable quantities between seaports only, but the commerce in these articles must in all earlier ages have been comparatively small.

Precious stones, amber, finely-woven fabrics, silks, spices, wine, oil — these are the articles with which early commerce was chiefly concerned. Perhaps nothing can better illustrate the progress of commerce in our century than those passages in Adam Smith's "Wealth of Nations," in which, in 1776, he assures the English farmers that they need never fear the importation of Irish cattle and Irish grain, because they were so bulky in proportion to values as to render so distant a transportation unprofitable. "Even the breeding countries of Great Britain are never likely to be much affected by the free importation of Irish cattle." And a little further on Smith adds : "Even the free importation of foreign corn could very little affect the interests of the farmers of Great Britain. Corn is a much more bulky commodity than butcher's meat. . . . The small quantity of foreign corn imported even in times of the greatest scarcity may satisfy our farmers that they can have nothing to fear from the freest importation." As every one knows, a hundred years later the importation of corn and beef from America, three thousand miles away, has been a cause of alarm to the British farmer.

Two conclusions follow naturally from this : one is that distance is not in itself the barrier against competition which it once was, consequently does not afford the same degree of protection to a given locality ; the other is that restrictions upon commerce now are a matter of concern not merely or chiefly to the wealthy, as once was the case, but may be felt disastrously by the poorest, in raising the prices of articles of daily consumption for the masses. The question of free trade and protection thus assumes a magnitude heretofore unknown. The total foreign commerce of England was estimated in 1355 at 2s. 10d. per capita ; in 1614, at 16s. 6d. per capita ; in 1801, at £4 6s. 6d. per capita ; but in 1880, at £16 6s. per capita.

The per capita value of the exports. of the United States increased from $6.03 in 1801 to $14.93 in 1881. The foreign commerce of Germany more than doubled from 1860 to 1880.

Commerce has gone hand in hand with the increasing national and international division of labor which has made modern wealth and the wide diffusion of comfort possible. In early stages of industrial development, each family was sufficient unto itself and enjoyed a rude kind of independence, but existence was precarious. Dearth followed plenty quickly, and there could be no adequate provision for future contingencies. But as civilization began to advance the division of labor was carried further and further, until at present time each one has some one occupation, perhaps manufacturing the sixtieth part of a shoe. Thousands minister unto his wants, and he in turn ministers unto thousands. To use a scientific expression : Differentiation accompanies social development. But the point of importance for us now is this : This diversity of pursuits, upon which our industrial civilization rests, implies and requires the existence of active commerce. The principle is for each individual to do what he can do best, and for the people of each region to utilize their own relatively greatest advantages. If Minnesota can best grow wheat, and South Carolina cotton, and Virginia corn, it is manifest that the total wealth of society, the products for our consumption, will be more abundant if each locality is devoted to that pursuit for which it is specially adapted.

Precisely the same principle holds with regard to international commerce. If England is specially adapted for certain pursuits and we for others, it must be clear that our mutual prosperity will be promoted by a diversity of pursuits and an exchange of products. Or are there special conditions applicable to a division of labor between nations which are not applicable as between the various parts of the same country? Some will say: If England sends us commodities, our labor and capital will be deprived of opportunities for employment. But how so? If England sends us commodities, must we not send commodities abroad in payment? And will not our labor and capital have more abundant employment in the production of commodities for which they are specially adapted than in those for which they are not specially adapted?

There are those, however, who think that it is a good thing for a nation to send abroad more than it imports, so that it may have a favorable balance of trade. It is imagined that a nation grows wealthy by this means. It is, therefore, necessary to examine the balance of trade theory.

CHAPTER V.

THE BALANCE OF TRADE THEORY.

" HE who attempts to draw any conclusion whatever as to a nation's wealth or poverty from the mere fact of a favorable or unfavorable balance of trade, has not grasped the first fundamental principle of political economy."

When I heard these words uttered with emphasis by one of the most careful living statisticians, some years ago, I must confess that I was a little startled, accustomed as I had been to laudations of favorable balances of trade as indications of increasing wealth. Yet I suppose nothing in the entire range of economic science is more beyond controversy.

Everybody knows what is meant by a favorable balance of trade. A trade between two countries is considered favorable for that one which exports a larger quantity of goods than it imports, and unfavorable for the one which imports more than it exports. Similarly the entire foreign trade of a country is regarded as favorable if all exports exceed in value all imports. The idea is that there is in such cases a balance which must be paid in money, and that a nation, like an individual, grows opulent by the accumulation of money. Let us examine these various ideas with some care.

If our exports exceed in value our imports, what does it mean? It may signify that a number of Europeans own property in the United States, and that this surplus pays their interest, dividends, and profits. We know, as a matter of fact, that many Europeans do own much property in the United States. Englishmen own vast tracts of land in our country, many millions of acres, particularly in our West, and the absentee English landlord has become a prominent feature of American as well as of Irish life. Likewise great blocks of stocks and bonds issued by American corporations, as well as municipal, state, and federal bonds, are held in Europe. Now is it not evident that after we have sent abroad enough goods to pay for goods sent us, we must still send abroad an annual tribute in exports to satisfy the claims of foreigners upon our industry? This accounts for a portion of our so-called favorable balance of trade ; but who will say that it is a cause for national self-gratulation ?

But a favorable balance of trade in the United States may also signify something else. It may mean that we are paying off the capital of the debts we owe abroad. If the surplus is not large enough to pay even interest on European claims, we may become more deeply involved in debt, the favorable balance of trade to the contrary notwithstanding. Let us recall our instructive experience during the late Civil War. We were at that time making heavy demands on European industry on account of extraordinary expenditures at home. Our imports exceeded in value our exports. We were, as a matter of fact, going in debt for current expenses. After the war we began to pay off interest and principal of our foreign indebtedness, and our exports exceeded in value our imports. At that time our favorable balance of trade, in so far as it could be accounted for by the payment of debt, was undoubtedly a good thing.

A favorable balance of trade might be partially explained by the acquisition of property abroad by Americans. I do not say that such is a fact. I simply say it is a possible explanation. If Americans are acquiring property abroad, it is manifestly necessary not only to send out of the country goods in sufficient quantity to pay for goods we import, but a surplus to pay for investments which, on this hypothesis, are being made in foreign countries.

If the balance of trade is favorable, the difference, or a part of it, is sometimes imported in bullion or money.

A favorable balance of trade may, then, denote increasing wealth, or it may denote poverty and economic dependence upon foreign nations. It may denote neither the one nor the other, but simply signify that a nation is holding its own in international relations. The mere fact of a favorable balance of trade in itself tells you absolutely nothing about a country. It is, however, true that a majority of the wealthier nations of the earth have what we call an unfavorable balance of trade.

Let us compare the value of imports with that of exports in a few countries, selecting recent years almost at haphazard, and not taking certain years with a design of proving something.

The value of German imports for 1876 was 3914.8 millions of marks,[1] that of exports, 2551.2 millions of marks ; for 1887 the figures are : imports, 3887 millions ; exports, 2775.3 millions. Precious metals are included, but if they were excluded the proportions between exports and imports would not be radically changed thereby.

The imports into France in 1873 were valued at 4576.4 millions of francs,[2] the exports at 4822.3 millions of francs.

---

[1] A mark is $0.238; for purposes of rough calculation, four marks may be regarded as equal in value to one dollar.

[2] A franc is a little more than $0.18; for rough computations, five francs may be regarded as equal to one dollar.

The figures for 1874 are : imports, 4422.5 millions ; exports, 4702.1 millions ; for 1875 : imports, 4461.8 millions ; exports, 4807 millions ; for 1876 : imports, 4908.8 millions ; exports, 4547.5. Precious metals are included in exports and imports, but as in the case of Germany, they are relatively so small, and are in this case so nearly equal, that the proportions between exports and imports are not materially changed thereby.

The exports from France exceed in value the imports from 1873 to 1875, inclusive, but in 1876 the imports exceed in value exports. A possible explanation would be that France was sending commodities out of the country from 1873 to 1875 to pay for the expenses of the war with Germany, but that in 1876 trade had regained its normal condition.

Hume tells us that over a hundred years ago the English nation was struck " with universal panic " because some one demonstrated that the balance of trade was so unfavorable as to leave them — that is, the English people — without a shilling in money in five or six years. That demonstration was made twenty years before Hume wrote his essay on "The Balance of Trade," but he records the fact that money was then more plentiful in England than ever before. The unfavorable balance of trade still continues in England, and is something enormous — the best proof of England's immense wealth, for this unfavorable balance represents the tribute other people pay to Englishmen. The imports into England in 1874 — to take the statistics in one year only, which answers our purposes as well as a dozen — were valued at £331,143,000, exclusive of precious metals ; the exports, also exclusive of precious metals, at £278,053,000.

Rich little Belgium also has a large unfavorable balance of trade. The imports into Belgium, exclusive of precious metals, were valued at 1448.5 millions of francs ; the exports from the country, also exclusive of precious metals, at 1063.8 millions.

These are wealthy countries, but the United States with its favorable balance of trade is also prosperous.   In the fiscal year 1877–8 our imports were valued at $466,873,000, and our exports at $722,812,000.   But Egypt—poor, impoverished Egypt — has the most magnificent so-called favorable balance of trade to be found in the world !   I mean, of course, in proportion to its entire commerce.   In 1874 the imports were valued at 507,064,155 piasters, the exports at 1,342,347,266 piasters ; the estimate for 1876 was : imports, 561,946,693 piasters ; exports, 1,333,333,408 piasters.

These illustrations, which might be multiplied indefinitely, show how much significance is to be attached to a favorable balance of trade in itself.   However, it is only a wealthy nation which can have a large unfavorable balance of trade as a permanent thing.   What does this mean?   It means that such a nation possesses stocks, bonds, and various kinds of property in other countries, and that the people of those countries are working for it.   It is similar to the case of a man who is able to consume more than he himself produces. It is a sign that others are working for him.   To value a foreign commerce in proportion to exports is to misconceive the advantages of commerce.   Commerce is valuable for what it brings us, not for what it takes from us.

It will readily be understood, then, that I am not able without reservation to join in the self-gratulations of those who delight in our large favorable balance of trade, and that I scarcely think this a strong tariff argument.   Our favorable balance of trade places us in the same category as Ireland, India, and Egypt.

CHAPTER VI.

FURTHER CONSIDERATION OF THE BALANCE OF TRADE THEORY.

THERE are several points connected with the balance of trade theory, as usually stated, about which it is essential that we should have clear ideas. They therefore require further examination.

First. It follows naturally, from what has been said in the previous chapter, that a favorable balance of trade does not signify that the precious metals are flowing into the country. In itself it tells us nothing about the international movements of the precious metals. Gold and silver may be coming to the country while an unfavorable balance of trade exists.

Thus, in 1882 the amount of gold and silver imported into England exceeded in value the precious metals exported, although during that year the balance of trade was against England to an amount exceeding in value one hundred and twenty millions of pounds sterling.[1]

On the other hand, the precious metals may be leaving a country while a favorable balance of trade continues. The commerce of the United States for 1884 serves as an exam-

---

[1] "The amount of bullion and specie which has been imported into England during the ten years from 1867 to 1876 has exceeded by no less than £53,800,000 the amount which has been exported; although during this period the aggregate value of her imports exceeded by no less than £804,000,000 the value of her exports."—*Fawcett, in his "Free Trade and Protection,"* page 135.

ple. The balance of trade was in our favor, but the value of precious metals exported exceeded the value of precious metal imported.

Second. If a favorable balance of trade in the United States were always accompanied by an addition to our store of money, it would not necessarily be a cause for national self-gratulation. People fall into the most obvious errors in this matter because they do not stop to inquire into the differences between those things which make an individual prosperous and those which make a nation prosperous. A merchant says : " If I increase my stock of money I become wealthier." This is true, but it does not follow necessarily that we would all be more prosperous if the total amount of money in existence were doubled. It would, on the other hand, be a misfortune to some people, and to multiply the amount of money in existence twenty times would probably be a universal calamity, upsetting all industrial and commercial relations. This must be made clear. If the money in my pocket is increased twenty-fold it is a good thing for me, because my proportion of the money in the country is increased. I can buy more goods. But if the amount of money in every one's possession is multiplied by twenty, will there not be a corresponding rise in prices? If so, will I be better off than I was before? In one case, I will, namely, if I owe something to some one ; if I am in debt and my debt is to be paid in money. If, on the other hand, sums of money are due me, this increase in the circulating medium impoverishes me. We may look at this matter — and it is of vital importance in these discussions — from another standpoint. Why do we want money? Manifestly for things it will buy. But does the increase in the supply of money in itself increase the quantities of useful things which we wish to buy?

The Spaniards in the sixteenth and seventeenth centuries made the mistake of overestimating the importance of gold and silver to a country, and instead of building up commerce and manufactures and improving their agriculture, seemed to think of little else than the devices by which the largest possible amount of the precious metals could be brought into the country, especially from their American possessions, and once in the country could be kept there. They neglected the most important sources of wealth, and to this day they have not recovered from the disastrous consequences of their mistaken policy.

I am far from saying that it makes no difference whether we have much or little money. A large amount is required to conduct the business of the country and to obviate the inconveniences of barter. An increasing amount is required for our growing, expanding industrial life. A fall in prices, owing to insufficient supply of the precious metals, increases the value of financial obligations incurred in the past and enriches bondholders and other creditors at the expense of the rest of the community. All this I recognize. I simply maintain that no regulation of commerce by protective tariffs is required at the present time on account of our money supply. There are other ways and better ways of providing for a sufficient quantity of money. The international movement of the precious metals is largely automatic. If the precious metals begin to leave a country which is not cursed with an irredeemable paper currency prices will fall, but the moment prices fall it becomes more profitable for foreigners to purchase their commodities, and there is thus a tendency to check the flow of money from the country. This by no means exhausts this large subject, but it is sufficient for present purposes.

Third. I have to remark that as between countries commodities are exchanged for commodities, and that very little money passes from one to the other. If England sends us commodities we do not, as a rule, send money abroad, but we pay for them in commodities. This is a matter so familiar to merchants who have dealings with foreign countries that it may seem to them scarcely worth while to mention it. Yet a failure to comprehend this fact and its bearing is a chief cause of confusion of thought in regard to international trade.

This third point is closely connected with the second. When money does begin to leave a country it becomes more profitable to export commodities than formerly. Thus through action on prices the natural relations between exports and imports are maintained. I send goods to England, and the Englishman to whom they are sent becomes indebted to me. At the same time another Englishman sends goods of the same value to an American importer. So we agree that this importer in America shall pay me, and that the English exporter shall receive his pay from the Englishman who bought my goods. Thus no money leaves England and none leaves America. This all takes place through the medium of bills of exchange, drafts, occasionally postal money-orders, and the like, and the services of bankers and brokers are required, but the principle is the simple one just described.

Illustrations will serve to render this still clearer. In the year 1884 in England it required an importation and exportation of only a little over forty millions of pounds sterling to do a foreign business of over six hundred and twenty millions. It required in the same year in the United States an exportation and importation of less than eighty-eight millions of dollars to do a total foreign business in imports and exports valued at about fourteen hundred millions of dollars.

Fourth. The balance of trade theory grew up at a time when it was imagined that there was a more serious diversity between the interests of one nation and those of another than actually exists. It used to be supposed that what one nation gained another lost, and our protective tariffs can be traced back to that illusion. This must not be misunderstood. This illusion is not a sufficient explanation of protectionism now. It is not in this connection even stated that something may not be said for protectionism. It is simply asserted as a historical fact that protective tariffs can be traced back to this illusion.

Some optimists push the idea of harmony of international interests too far. Unfortunately, complete harmony does not exist — unless, indeed, we view those interests from the highest Christian standpoint. But in the main, in matters of trade, international interests are harmonious, at least to this degree, that each ought to desire the prosperity of all the others. This is so simple that it seems absurd to state it as a scientific proposition; yet the failure to act on this principle has been a fruitful cause of enmity between nations. Do we desire opulent or impoverished customers? Which class does a merchant desire? The case of a merchant's customers is similar to that of the purchasers of a country's products. Nevertheless some people talk as if we had something to hope from the impoverishment of Europe by means of war or otherwise.

What we would thereby gain would be temporary and would be more than counterbalanced by loss in the future. All this has been stated often enough, but one hundred years ago it was as something startling that Hume proclaimed his desire for the prosperity of other nations as consistent with his loyalty to England. These were his words: "Were our narrow and malignant politics to meet with success, we should reduce all our neighboring nations to the same state of sloth and ignorance that prevails in Morocco and the coast of Barbary. But what would be the consequence? They could send us no commodities ; they could take none from us ; our domestic commerce itself would languish for want of emulation, example, and instruction, and we ourselves should soon fall into the same abject condition to which we had reduced them. I shall therefore venture to acknowledge that not only as a man, but as a British subject, I pray for the flourishing commerce of Germany, Spain, and even France itself. I am at least certain that Great Britain and all those nations would flourish more did their sovereigns and ministers adopt such enlarged and benevolent sentiments toward each other."

The balance of trade theory, then, as ordinarily presented must be rejected. It represents it as the purpose of each nation to export more than it imports in values, manifestly impossible as a universal policy, to say nothing of the fact that it misrepresents the true end of commerce, which is imports, not exports. The hypothesis upon which it is based is false, and the conclusions drawn from it are mis·leading.

CHAPTER VII.

THE EARLIEST TARIFF LEGISLATION IN THE UNITED STATES.

I INFER from occasional remarks that some people who have been good enough to read my papers, imagine that I take a far more radical position on the subject of free trade than I should like to assume. I have no desire to attack American manufacturers, and I certainly am not prepared at present to advocate the withdrawal of all protective duties at once. On the contrary, I hold that this would be a grievous blunder and a positive wrong. I am not even willing to call myself a free-trader. I am neither a free-trader nor protectionist in the sense in which these words are often used. I am unable to believe that any one policy respecting international commercial relations is an absolutely correct policy for all times and all places. Nor have I any sympathy with those who attack all protective tariffs on abstract moral grounds. If a protective tariff is a good thing, let us by all means have a protective tariff. But when I say a good thing I mean a good thing for the people as a whole, and not for any one class of the people. At the same time, I am not prepared to denounce protectionism as in itself class legislation. It is quite conceivable that protective taxes may be laid on imported commodities in the interest of the country as a whole, and of course that is always the design of pure-minded legislators. On the other hand, tariff legislation may become virtually class legislation, and I believe one of the most serious weaknesses of the policy of protection as viewed in the light of history is its universal tendency to become this kind of legislation. Special interests are apt to lay their hands on even the best kind of a protective tariff at a very early date in its history and to shape it to their ends in disregard of the general welfare. To explain my position still further, it may be well to state at once that I shall urge no constitutional objections to a tariff. Always provided that protectionism promotes the general welfare, I do not believe that such exist; and it is very certain that nothing is to be gained at the present time by pounding away at this well-threshed straw.

The subject of tariff legislation must be viewed historically in order to understand the merits of the present controversy between free-traders and protectionists in the United States. The men are few, indeed, who would claim that it is rational to legislate on the tariff as if we were going to start from the beginning and frame a new policy for a new land. Our present policy is an historical growth, and as such must be treated. When one sees the jobbery and corruption connected with tariff legislation, the hypocrisy it fosters, and perceives how certain monopolies hide themselves behind it as a safe bulwark, one feels at times moved by righteous indignation to wish the whole thing swept from the face of the earth. But more mature reflection tends to calm one, and to show the impracticability of any such radical measure.

It is impossible to present a history of the tariff legislation of the United States in these articles, for if it were attempted to do that, and to do it thoroughly, new issues might arise in the country, and, indeed, in turn become matters of the past before this series of papers could be brought to a close.

A few main facts should, however, be brought to mind, and a firm grasp kept on them in discussions on the tariff.

Protectionism, whatever proportions it may have since assumed or whatever appearance it may now present, entered our country with the meekness of a lamb. Everybody knows how it happened. It became necessary in 1789 to provide the young republic with revenues. Direct taxation seems to have been rejected without serious consideration as not adapted to our federal government. There was the usual prejudice against direct taxation, coupled with a jealousy of the states against what they would have deemed interference in the affairs of their citizens. Now, as indirect taxes were the only alternative, it remained to choose between taxes on commodities produced at home, internal revenue taxes, and taxes on imported articles, customs duties.

The prejudice against internal taxes seems to have been nearly as strong as against direct taxes, and for somewhat the same reason. Taxation of commodities is in any shape a serious interference in the business affairs of producers, but when commodities are taxed on entering the country in a few great ports it is less obvious. To-day there are, doubtless, persons who fail to see the fact, although it is beyond all controversy, that the taxation of three or four articles of domestic growth or manufacture is an almost incomparably smaller measure of interference in private affairs than the taxation of four thousand and more imported articles. On the other hand, the tax paid by producers at home is more readily visible ; the fact of the existence of the tax is palpable. It was therefore decided to begin our revenue system with customs duties.

The first tariff act was passed in 1789. It was mainly for revenue, while protection was only incidental. Another

motive whicn was prominent, if not predominant, is well described by Prof. Henry C. Adams in his monograph on
"Taxation in the United States, 1789–1816." It was the
spirit of nationality which was so pronounced in the early
federalists.

It was hoped by means of a tariff on imported commodities and by the use of domestic products to weld together
the different states into a strong union. It was this same
animus which prompted public men to appear in homespun
clothing. The difference between this plea for protection
then and the plea we hear now is brought out by Professor
Adams, in these words : "The argument then regarded as
convincing was, 'The sure way to establish nationality is to
exclude foreign products.' Now, on the other hand, we
hear, 'The sure way to become rich is to exclude foreign
products.' "

But what was the rate of taxation imposed by the act of
1789, and what was the character of this taxation? First
its comparatively simple character must be noted. There
was a list of articles subject to specific duties, taxes on
quantities of commodities, and not on values — the simplest
kind of import duties. Then taxes were very moderate.
Nails and spikes, for example, were taxed one cent per
pound, molasses $2\frac{1}{2}$ cents per gallon, boots 50 cents per
pair, hemp 60 cents per 112 pounds, coal 2 cents per bushel.
There were three or four classes of duties, based on values,
or *ad valorem* duties. One class paid 10 per cent., another
$7\frac{1}{2}$ per cent., a small class 15 per cent., while all unspecified
imported goods were taxed 5 per cent. There was a short
free list, including important commodities, such as wool,
cotton, dyeing woods and dyeing drugs, copper in plates,
and all furs. The significance of these rates becomes manifest by comparison with the table of *ad valorem* rates on

dutiable merchandise entered during the fiscal year ending June 30, 1887. In this table we find that the rates vary from a little over 21 per cent. to 154 per cent.

Revenue was insufficient and rates were raised about 2½ per cent. in 1790. The purpose was revenue, and not protection. The truth is, there were scarcely any manufactures to protect at that time except shipbuilding. Agriculture and commerce were the chief pursuits. Revenue was still insufficient, and the tariff law of 1792 was passed, and this was supposed to carry out the intention of Alexander Hamilton as expressed in his celebrated report of the previous year on manufactures. The average rate of duties then became 13½ per cent.

Internal revenue taxation was introduced in 1791, and distilled spirits were taxed, producing the "Whiskey Insurrection" in Western Pennsylvania. Opposition to this tax was manifested in several states, and the grounds of opposition were largely those which make against indirect taxation in general. In 1794 internal taxation was extended, and thus three new sources of revenue were included. The sale of liquors, the manufacture of snuff, and auctions were taxed. Carriages were also taxed about this time, and at rates varying from $2 each per year to $15 each per year. Stamp duties on certain legal papers were added in 1797. Direct taxes on lands and houses were added to the sources of revenue towards the close of the century. Then direct and internal taxes aroused opposition and were one cause of the fall of the federalists. They were all abolished after Jefferson became president. Before that they had not been satisfactorily administered and had not become very productive — to do which requires several years for a new system of taxation.

What was the consequence of this state of things? Precisely what might have been expected. Import duties were raised in 1792, 1794, and 1797 because new demands were made on the public treasury and revenues were insufficient. After internal taxation had been swept away the movement became more rapid. Taxes on imports were raised in 1804, and although this, like previous acts, was regarded as merely temporary, it is significant " that no important duty once imposed, except that upon salt, was ever relinquished."

Well, duties on imports were raised continually until disturbances with England called for such large expenditures that they were doubled in 1812, which, instead of producing more revenue, lessened existing revenue; for, " in the arithmetic of taxation, two and two, instead of making four, often make only one." After all, it was necessary for the same party, which, in response to popular clamor, had abolished internal revenue taxation, to reintroduce it, again going to the expense of building up a suitable machinery for administering the system and waiting for it to begin to produce large returns. The worst aspect of such shifting policy is the disturbance of business, under which the weaker elements, " the small men," go to the wall, thus producing a tendency to monopoly and concentration of wealth. The lesson to be drawn from this is obvious, and corroborates what has already been said. It is essential to public welfare that a system of taxation adequate to meet fluctuating, and on the whole increasing, demands on the public treasury should be maintained. It is not stated at present what this should be. Our internal revenue taxes may be retained or something put in the place of them, but in either case the main fact remains. Our duties on imports will always be fluctuating, will always tend to increase, and will always give opportunity for jobbery and corruption, unless they are based on true, rational principles, and to base them on rational principles is impossible unless other fruitful, easily managed sources of revenue exist.

The duties up to 1816 were for revenue with incidental protection, but in that year Clay spoke in favor of "a thorough and decided protection to home manufactures by ample duties," and his ally, Mr. Ingham, declared the revenue to be only an "incidental consideration." How did it happen that the old standpoint was completely reversed so that the principle of "protection, with incidental revenue," took the place of the principle "revenue, with incidental protection"? The event which led to this change in policy must be described in the following chapter.

CHAPTER VIII.

THE GROWTH OF PROTECTIONISM.

WE have already examined the first cause which led to the establishment of protectionism as "the American system." This cause was a faulty federal revenue system, lacking the first principle of scientific finance, which is flexibility and elasticity. We have seen further that this weakness inheres of necessity in any system of national revenues based almost exclusively on duties levied on imported commodities, because these yield least in every critical juncture. A deficit and debt result therefrom. The question then arises, How shall we increase revenues? But having provided only one source of revenue, we most naturally have recourse to that. But this is not all. Taxation moves along the line of least resistance. Adam Smith tells us that in the days of feudalism, government was so weak that only those were taxed who were powerless to resist taxation : namely, the common people. The clergy and nobility were exempted, and privileged classes arose, as always happens under weak governments. But in the case of taxes on imported commodities there is a line along which they can move without encountering any opposition whatever. Let us express ourselves more accurately. There may be some opposition, but this is opposition on the part of the unorganized masses, — "the forgotten millions," — while there is an organized body of special interests urging an increase of taxation along this line. Government is entreated to tax those things which home producers desire to sell, in order to limit competition. In whichever other way the legislative authority turns for revenue, powerful opposition is encountered, while there is no outside pressure brought to bear to urge it to levy taxes of such a nature as to interfere as little as possible with the pursuits of the people, and to place as small a burden as possible on the ordinary man. The forgotten millions are beginning to organize, and this is the chief significance of bodies like the Knights of Labor. By their very nature they are impelled to watch public measures from the standpoint of the people at large, and not from the standpoint of special private interests. This must not be taken as an indorsement of all the views of any labor organization. It is very natural that popular organizations should hold many mistaken views in regard to the general welfare. But it is believed that the drift of such organization will on the whole and in the long run be in the right direction. The permanent success of such an organization depends on the strength with which it pushes forward to the attainment of purposes calculated to benefit the masses.

However, the line of least resistance for the movement of taxation is manifest in a country which relies for revenue mainly, if not exclusively, upon customs duties. Protectionism was the most natural outgrowth possible of our system of taxation, and I dwell upon this because precisely at this time it is essential that we should understand those principles which underlie our financial development and make it what it is. Otherwise a repetition of past errors is something inevitable.

A second cause, however, was powerful in the establishment of protectionism in the United States, and it was this second cause which led in the first instance to the substitution of the principle of "protection with incidental revenue," for the older principle, "revenue with incidental protection," and an examination of this cause is of prime importance in a study of our tariff history. I refer to the hostilities between the United States and England — and, to a less extent, France — which finally culminated in "the War of 1812." Before these hostilities our chief pursuits were commerce and agriculture, while manufactures were insignificant. There was more or less manufacturing industry, but it was pursued in small shops where the proprietor worked with his own hands, assisted by two or three journeymen and one or two apprentices. There was, for example, always the village carpenter and shoemaker, and the blacksmith at the country cross-roads. But manufacturing on a large scale could scarcely be said to exist, and it was even in Europe only in the early stages of its development, for the "industrial revolution" had but recently begun. Now, during the European wars, which centred first about revolutionary France and later about the person of the first Napoleon, our commerce developed with a rapidity which is said to be without parallel in the world's history. It was unsafe to send goods in European vessels, as all European powers had their enemies, and the goods were consequently liable to capture. America was the great neutral power, and our commerce was for some time tolerated under more or less vexatious restrictions. While commerce was in this troubled period of the world's history pursued with difficulty, the relative disadvantage of our commerce was least. It was estimated that our advantage, as compared with the commerce of other countries, could be placed at twenty or thirty per cent. While this condition of things continued, we naturally absorbed an ever-increasing share of international trade. It was equally natural that our capital and labor should be attracted by the rewards of expanding commerce. The following table will place vividly before the reader the result of the events described from 1789 to 1796.

YEAR.	AMERICAN TONNAGE EMPLOYED IN FOREIGN TRADE.	BRITISH TONNAGE EMPLOYED IN AMERICAN TRADE.
1789	127,329	94,110
1792	414,679	206,065
1794	525,649	37,058
1796	675,046	19,669

The American tonnage engaged in foreign trade increased up to the year 1807, when it amounted to 848,306. A change was then forced upon American industry. The struggle between France and England waxed fiercer, and mutual hatred became more intense. Both determined that there should be no neutrals, and endeavored to force the United States to take sides with one or the other. A series of measures were inaugurated with this end in view. Thus Great Britain in 1806 declared a blockade of all those ports in Europe which belonged to powers allied to France, and Napoleon followed this action by his " Berlin decree," which forbade all vessels from entering any British harbor. England retaliated in 1807 with the " orders in council," aimed directly at American vessels, and forbidding them to enter any European harbor outside of Great Britain and Sweden. Napoleon replied with his " Milan decree," which ordered the capture and sale of all American vessels entering British harbors. What was America to do? There were various things which might have been done, but as to what actually was done, I doubt if any American feels proud of this chapter in his country's history. Low taxes seemed to be valued above everything else, and no provision was made by Congress for maintaining our dignity and our rights as a nation. The penny wise and pound foolish policy was pursued with results even more than usually disastrous. Our Congress decided to withdraw the assistance which our commerce offered to the nations of Europe, hoping thus to bring them to terms. It was a kind of governmental "boycott," which, boomerang-like, reacted most severely on ourselves. The Embargo Act of 1807 forbade the departure of any American vessel for a foreign port, and this was followed by the Non-Intercourse Act of 1809, which prohibited commerce with France and England, but not with other powers. This act expired in 1810, but was revived against Great Britain, which continued its hostile actions until the outbreak of the War of 1812. This war was the most complete kind of protection, for commerce with England was by us declared unlawful, and our ports were blockaded by England.

Our commerce was crippled, and as early as 1808 a marked change in the character of our industrial life was visible. The capital and labor which formerly had obtained employment in international trade was diverted to manufactures. "A commercial war," says Prof. Henry C. Adams, "is always propitious for the establishment of new industries, and in the present case there was developed an intense desire to maintain by law, after the cessation of hostilities, those conditions which secured to industries control over the home market. Then for the first time was it that protection as an independent industrial system forced its way into the history of the United States."

The exports from the country during the years 1808 to 1814 declined from a little over one hundred and eight millions of dollars to less than seven millions, and revenues from customs and tonnage from a little over twenty-seven millions to less than five millions.

"Establishments for the manufacture of cotton goods, woolen clothes, iron, glass, pottery, and other articles sprang up with a mushroom growth." These are words used by Professor Taussig, from one of whose works on the tariff I take the following statistics showing the growth of the cotton industry during the war period. There were but four cotton factories in this country in 1803, when new machinery and new methods began to be introduced. It 1805 the number of spindles was 4500; in 1807, 8000; in 1809, 31,000; in 1810, 87,000, and in 1815, 130,000.

When the war with England was brought to a close our commerce had been in considerable part destroyed. Capital and labor had been diverted to manufactures, but these had been established under abnormal conditions. They had now to face the competition of Europe, and in particular of England, whose stores of commodities, long pent up by war, began to flow over the world, and in quantities in excess of the power to purchase them on the part of consumers. The manufacturers cried out for protection to their "infant industries" against the old-established industries of Europe, and their cry was heard. A possible alternative course of action must be discussed in the following chapter.

CHAPTER IX.

INFANT INDUSTRIES IN THE UNITED STATES
IN 1816.

THE industrial situation in the United States at the close of the War of 1812 was a trying one, presenting problems which required for their successful solution statesmanship of a high order. Now, statesmanship of a high order does not mean merely the ability to lead men, but the ability to lead them in a direction which subsequent events prove to be the right direction. It is, however, possible only for those to forecast with a reasonable degree of probability future events in the life of a nation who have a profound knowledge of the causes at work which are shaping national destiny and making it what it is. We are now speaking of industrial development; and the science which treats of this is political economy, one of the most difficult sciences to master in its various ramifications. We see, then, how much is required in a man to give such character to his political activity that it shall wear permanently the mark of statesmanship. There must be leadership, with all the rare and admirable qualities which that implies; and this must be accompanied by action based on a profound insight into the nature of social and economic forces at work both in the nation and in the world at large.

Great as were the men of the first half of this century, in the light of present events it must be acknowledged that anything which can fairly be called statesmanship was rare indeed among them.

The year 1816 witnessed the firm establishment of the protectionist theory as "the American system."

Protection to manufacturing industries had not come of our deliberate and carefully-formed purpose. First, as we have seen, the thought of our leaders, with Hamilton at their head, was this: We must have revenue; and if, in raising this revenue, we tax imported commodities of a kind produced at home, and make importers pay from five to fifteen per cent. on the bulk of imports, our home industries will receive, merely as an incidental matter, a slight protection; and it is well that they should be thus favored.

This was a mistake; for, granting the principle, a way was opened for its subsequent growth. The principles which distinguish between a tariff for revenue only and a tariff for protection are radical, and it is not easy to combine the two. Perhaps it is not too much to say that any attempt to do so amounts to a victory of the principle of protection.

When the first tariff bill was under discussion in Congress, Mr. Clymer, of Pennsylvania, appears to have been gifted with an insight comparatively rare, for he wished the bill separated into two parts. The one part was to be a revenue bill, and was to be shaped with reference to revenue principles solely. Other matters, such as protection to infant industries, were to be considered by themselves, and on their own merits. This was entirely rational; and if protectionism is desirable, this is the proper scientific method for affording it. The question now involved is not protectionism or free trade; but if protectionism is desirable, how shall we establish it?

The disadvantages of taxes on imported commodities are many. One of the chief of them is that it compels us to

move about blindly in the dark, without power to estimate
fully the consequences of our own acts. We pay taxes to
encourage manufactures; but the extent of the burden we
carry no man knows, because we are operating in violation of that canon of taxation which prescribes that taxes
should take out and keep out of the pockets of the people
as little as possible over and above what flows into the public treasury. We pay a tax which goes to the government
and is returned to us in the inestimable benefits which good
government confers; but we pay another tax in increased
prices of commodities, and we cannot ascertain the precise
amount of this burden. It contains some of the worst evils
of indirect taxation which have been already described. It
is covert; it takes from us in sly, pick-pocket fashion, and
we never know the cause of our diminished fortunes. The
ordinary man simply feels that something is wrong; but he
cannot tell what it is. *The Sun*, in a recent article on "The
Cost of It," gave an estimate to the effect that we pay to
government only one-fourth of the total burden. In other
words, if this estimate is accurate, for every dollar we pay
into the federal treasury we pay three more to home producers, in higher prices than would otherwise be necessary,
and instead of an apparent burden of $217,286,893, we are
bearing an actual burden of $880,000,000.

The second false step was made in the establishment of an
inadequate system of federal finance already sufficiently
elaborated in these articles. It is only necessary to remind
readers of the fact that its nature was such as to compel
a recourse to customs duties for the increasing demands of
government.

The manufacturers of 1816 wanted protection, and pleaded
for their infant industries, and this argument told, for the
protection afforded them was originally limited to a short

period. The duty on cotton and woollen goods was, for example, raised to twenty-five per cent., but this was to hold only until 1819, when it was to be reduced to twenty per cent., which was about the average rate under the act of 1816. Calhoun defended this protective measure on the ground that infant industries required the fostering care of government. It is contended, however, by free-traders that real infant industries never get any protection; but in the tumultuous clamor of special private interests, only the powerful can hope to receive government aid. There is much in our history which, so far as it goes, tends to substantiate this view. Every one knows that instead of gradually lowering the duties levied for the sake of infant industries as they progressed toward adolescence and maturity, the protective duties were raised. The more they got, the more they wanted; and the twenty per cent. duty of 1816 would be scorned in 1888.

Yet we must not lose sight of the facts of the case. What was to be done? Two false steps taken by Congress have been mentioned; but more powerful was the War of 1812, with the preceding events which led to it. This war period was in itself the strongest kind of protection; and manufacturers grew up under this protection, which came not by our action, but in spite of ourselves. Should these manufacturers be allowed to perish, their capital to be destroyed, in part, at least, and should the labor which they afforded employment be cast adrift? Congress replied, "No"! Protectionists say, "Yes; your free-trade theory will be all right when you have established perpetual peace between nations, but that Utopia has not yet been attained; and until human institutions are radically changed, war will from time to time interfere with the plans of you free-traders and disturb that international division of labor upon which you predicate their beneficence. Yes. When you can guarantee perpetual peace we will become free-traders; in the meantime we will adhere to protection. Free trade is cosmopolitan and visionary. Protection is national and practical."

This is about the way Frederick List argues in his "National System of Political Economy," and he strikes me as the ablest of the protectionists. The proposition of Mr. Clymer shows one possible alternative to the course actually followed by Congress. It would have been entirely practicable to have separated the question of revenues from that of protection. We could have afforded protection by bounties to home manufacturers, and have encouraged them by awards of large prizes of one, two, three, or even four hundred thousand dollars for improved industrial processes and for superiority of product. This is a plan which could be more easily carried out than our tariff system, and if protection is desired, the more carefully it is examined, the more it must commend itself to the impartial student. Foreign producers would not be excluded, but the bounty could be made to equal the disabilities of a state of infancy. We would pay it with open eyes, and would know precisely what our infants cost us, and could balance this burden over against the advantages which they confer upon us. We could watch the progress of manufactures from the state of infancy through youth to full maturity, and make bounty at every period proportional to its own weaknesses as compared with the strength of foreigners; and we could do this with full consciousness of what we were about.

Or we might exempt all manufacturing establishments, like federal bonds, from all taxation, national, state, and local. As all foreign manufacturers are staggering under a heavy load of taxation, this would be an immense help to home producers. This would have been probably bettei than the bounty system. If, in 1816, manufacturers had been relieved of all taxation, it would seem that they could scarcely ask for more assistance, for, at that time, the cost of transportation was so high that distance itself was a great protection. It must also be remembered that profits of manufacturers had been abnormally high during the war period, and they had no right to complain if obliged to work for a time without profits. Finally, it must not be forgotten that protectionism itself raises the cost of many things manufacturers use, and in so far defeats its own end. It is probable that manufacturers were unduly alarmed in 1816, and that many of them could have survived without any increased protectionism. We could in this case also ascertain the exact amount of our burden. We might assess all manufacturers so exempted from taxation every year, and by calculating what they would pay if not exempted, we would know how much assistance we were giving. Prices would not be raised by this sort of protection to infant industries.

These devices are mentioned as possible and practicable alternatives. It is not intended to recommend them, nor is it desired to condemn them in this place and at this time.

Still another possible alternative in 1816 was to let the manufacturers shift for themselves, like other people, and adapt themselves to changed conditions as best they might. More will be said about this plan hereafter.

It is undoubtedly true that free trade does not bring the advantages to any nation which it would could perpetual peace be maintained for all time. International industrial relations are disturbed by war, and great suffering ensues. Our late Civil War affords an instance. The employés in the cotton mills of the north of England suffered terribly because the manufacturers could not obtain their supplies of cotton from our South. This produced a so-called cotton-famine. Such things are liable to happen, so long as war continues among men, and this is a real, substantial argument for international arbitration. It is not easy to see, however, how high protective tariffs are going to remove the evils of wars. If each country makes itself self-sufficient industrially, it will lose the advantages of international commerce, and will be carrying a part of the burdens of war permanently.

International trade has not accomplished what Cobden and others hoped for, — peace between nations ; still there is reason to believe that, on the whole, it makes for peace ; and we may, in the United States, reasonably hope that we will not often, or during long periods, be called upon to suffer the horrors of war.

CHAPTER X.

THE INFANT INDUSTRY THEORY OF PROTECTIONISM FURTHER CONSIDERED.

I SAID in the last chapter that the proposition of Mr. Clymer favoring a separation of revenue measures from other political schemes showed that there was one possible alternative to the course actually followed by Congress in the firm establishment of protectionism in 1816. There were, in fact, several alternatives described. One was the bounty system, and the other the plan of special exemption from all taxation, either of which, it was argued, was preferable as a scheme of protection when looked at in the light of reason. It still remains to be considered whether it would not have been better to have refused any interference in behalf of manufacturers, and to have allowed them to adjust themselves to new conditions as best they might, as other people are forced to do, and thus to have established with respect to manufacturers in general the policy of non-interference.

This is a matter of present interest because the question of general policy is coming up again, and is certainly to be raised repeatedly in the near future. First, it must be remarked that a liberal policy with respect to trade and non-intervention in general has been injured by those extremists who claim too much. Doctrinaires say government should do as little as possible, and that is the best government which governs the least. Yet when we see the English laboring classes elevated by factory legislation protecting the

laboring classes by restricting the labor of women and children and prohibiting " pluck-me stores " and payment in
kind, and thus the theories of radical socialists like Carl
Marx discredited, for they say that the workingmen have
nothing to hope from the present state ; when we witness
somewhat similar beneficial effects in Massachusetts and
New York, and when we reflect on the inestimable benefits
of our free public school system even when viewed exclusively from the standpoint of material wealth ; when we learn
that, doctrinaires to the contrary notwithstanding, municipalities are to an increasing extent supplying themselves with gas
without the intervention of corporations, and that with the
most satisfactory results ; when we contemplate all these
things, we are too inclined to reject the entire policy of non-
intervention and favor government interference everywhere.
It is necessary to discriminate.   One law governs those
pursuits which are monopolies, another those which are
always subject to the steady, constant pressure of competition, while yet a third principle prevails with reference to
labor, and in general it may be said of pursuits which are
strongly competitive that competition is in the main a sufficient regulator, and that, so far as they are concerned, that
government is best which governs least.

   " During the present century," says a discriminating
writer, " two great discoveries have been made in the
science of government.   The one is the immense advantage
of abolishing restrictions upon trade, the other is the absolute necessity of imposing restrictions upon labor."   He
would have expressed his meaning more clearly if he had
said " upon labor in behalf of labor," for he had in view
regulations increasing real freedom.

   While, then, only an extremist will support the proposition
of non-intervention as of universal application, the impartial

student of American affairs can hardly fail to see his inclination strengthen in favor of letting commerce and manufactures take their own course without legislative interference, the more minutely he examines our present condition and its historical antecederts, for he will find that the best-laid plans for fostering infant industries and building up a barrier between American labor and the so-called "pauper labor" of Europe come to naught. It is scarcely possible to carry them out, and in the end the hard-working, thrifty, industrious class of employers and employés alike are hampered in their efforts to gain a livelihood, while enormous trusts and syndicates are formed, crushing as with an iron hand the independent manufacturer, and grinding down American labor by bringing into competition with it ignorant and lawless European hordes, which have been brought into the country free of all duty.

The infant industry theory of protection finds its classical statement in these words of John Stuart Mill's treatise on political economy : "The expenses of production being always greatest at first, it may happen that the home production, though really the most advantageous, may not become so until after a certain duration of pecuniary loss, which it is not to be expected that private speculators should incur in order that their successors may be benefited by their ruin. I have, therefore, conceded that in a new country a temporary protecting duty may sometimes be economically defensible ; on condition, however, that it be strictly limited in point of time, and provisions be made that during the latter part of its existence it be on a gradually decreasing scale. Such temporary provision is of the same character as a patent, and should be governed by similar conditions."

This is precisely what during the first half of our national existence we proposed to do, and, as has been stated, tariff laws were limited to a few years, and laws have actually been passed contemplating a gradual reduction of tariff duties, with the intention of entering upon a permanent free-trade period. But our history has been of such a character as to lead one to doubt the practicability of the infant industry theory. A tariff law passed for two years is extended and duties raised before we scarcely enter our national existence, and the fate which thus overtook Hamilton's " temporary " increase of duties has been repeated again and again. It is true that a rational system of federal financiering might have helped matters somewhat, but even if we should be led to adopt better financial methods, have we reason to hope that experience in the near future will be different? The theory of our institutions is that municipal councillors, state legislators, and federal congressmen meet to discuss the public welfare calmly and impartially, and to pass such laws as they may regard beneficial to the people. The truth is, the initiative in legislation in general does not come from the legislator, but from the pressure of some powerful external special interest. Go to an ordinary legislature or city council with a measure, and you will be asked who is back of it, who wants it passed, and what is the consideration? If you simply come with the general welfare at heart, and have no great organization with votes at your back, your reception will be a cold one. Now so long as this is so, how can it be expected that governmental aid will be withdrawn just in proportion as those who receive it grow strong? That is the theory; but on the contrary, the pressure for aid increases as strength increases. Can one instance in all the history of the American tariff be adduced where protection was offered to aid in the establishment of an industry not already in existence? I think not one, yet this is what the theory calls for. The idea is that after canvassing the situation, congressmen say : " Our natural resources are such that we ought to have a beet-root sugar industry, for example. Yet not a trace of such industry exists, on account of the enormous difficulties in the way of its establishment. Let us, therefore, tax imported sugar to give our would-be producers a chance."

The actual practice is this : Representatives of powerful establishments go to Washington and say : " We have large paper mills in the Connecticut valley or elsewhere, and we wish to be protected against foreign competition." It will readily be seen how akin this is to the monopolistic spirit, for monopoly means simply absence of competition.

Several things are proved by this brief sketch which any one specially interested will find more amply demonstrated in Taussig's " Protection to Young Industries." One is that protective tariffs did not give us our manufactures. They came into existence without it. The question of free trade *versus* protection is not at all a question of manufactures or no manufactures. Nor is it a question of a diversified or homogeneous industrial life.

We see, further, that protective duties once established tend to increase, and that a treatment of the tariff in accordance with scientific principles is at least very difficult, if not impossible. A recent careful writer says that the theory of protection is not altogether erroneous could it be applied, but he holds that no modern parliament or congress can be trusted to apply it, and on that account he rejects protectionism in practical politics.

Why is it that the more protection one has, the more one wants ? The reason is this : Manufacturers may be divided into several classes with respect to profits. There are those advantageously situated and skilful and energetic — great industrial leaders. These men require no special help, and they belong to the first class. There are those whose profits are a little smaller on account of inferior natural advantages or inferior mental qualifications. These are manufacturers of the second class. So profits descend until in every pur-suit you find those "on the ragged edge" who but just live, who barely "keep their heads above water," as we say. Prices are high enough to enable these manufacturers of the lowest grade to live, and the profitableness of another business is measured by the differences between its cost of production and the cost of production in those establish-ments which just keep alive; so the lower the scale of inef-ficiency, the higher the profits of the favorably situated. Let these lines represent the various grades of manufactures in the United States : —

Profits of class 1 will be measured by the distance be-tween 1 and 6. Now, if you wipe out 6, it must be by lower prices, and thus will the abnormally high profits of class 1 fall. Now, under a system of free trade, the opera-tions of those advantageously situated will be extended and those working inefficiently will be compelled to exert them-selves and produce better and cheaper goods or to change their occupation. The question, then, at issue is this : Shall we have only manufactures of a high degree of efficiency, or shall we also raise up and keep in existence an inferior class of men? Manufactures we are certain to have, for we are more advantageously situated than other countries with respect to some branches of industry, and there is probably scarcely any line of manufactures which could not be pursued in some favored spot by some one.

Now it must be manifest that the more efficient the labor and capital of the country, the more we will all have to enjoy and the greater our opportunities for leisure. What is produced now is not sufficient by any means to satisfy all rational wants of all men. Much more must be produced for that purpose, and if what is produced is often not consumed, owing to the absence of purchasing power on the part of the masses, this is another matter, and the difficulty cannot be remedied by protective tariffs.

The extension of aid to manufactures in 1816 accustomed us to look upon it as our duty to tax ourselves for the benefit of certain pursuits; whereas, if they are natural to the country and desirable, they can be profitably established without help. The pauper spirit has been nourished and it appears to have worked like free soup-houses on the poor. Some business men, instead of bending all their energies to the production of cheap and good commodities, are always plotting to get something from the public purse. Thus towns are induced to bid against one another for railroad facilities, and our federal government has been pursuaded to part with the heritage of the people " to encourage " railroad building; whereas it would seem desirable, if we, the people, pay for the roads, that we should own them.

When changes in productive processes injure skilled workingmen, we say they must suffer quietly and be content, because the general public gains. If a type-setting machine should render the skill of type-setters superfluous, it would produce immense suffering, but we would not subsidize them from the public treasury, or levy a tax for their benefit of one hundred and fifty per cent. on those using the machine.

Workingmen, on the contrary, are severely rebuked when they resist improvements.

When the elevated railroads in New York injured property-owners, the claim for damages was resisted on account of the public good. So, at the close of the late war, thousands upon thousands of farmers were well-nigh ruined, and many of them completely so, by the contraction of the currency, which lowered the price of their farms and raised the value of all existing mortgages until often the mortgages equalled the value of the farms. Yet farmers were not indemnified on account of their loss.

Is it not, then, better to exclude favoritism in legislation, and to let each industry stand on its own bottom?

CHAPTER XI.

PROTECTIONISM AND LABOR.

AS time went on, the plea that protection should be afforded to the "infant industries" of the United States grew ridiculous, and its advocates began to cast about for an argument which would meet with some other reply than a sarcastic smile. Manifestly the period of infancy must end some time, and the infant industry argument is based precisely on the hypothesis that protection is merely a temporary need.

The infant industry plea is not often heard now, and may be regarded as decidedly antiquated. Yet occasionally echoes of the old war-cry of the protectionists are still heard. Although they are so feeble as scarcely to deserve notice, it may be well to devote just a word to them.

First, one hundred years of protection ought to have developed our industry beyond the stage of infancy if protection ever can do it.

Second, the arguments which make for protection to industries in a young and enterprising but poor country, and which, indeed, in such cases, if intelligently applied may justify it, no longer hold in the United States. Protection is needed, it is said, because the pursuits, although naturally remunerative, cannot become so for several years, and men want immediate returns. This is true in a new country, but it is not true with us. We have many men in the United States whose purses are as long as those which can be found

anywhere, and whose minds are as shrewd as those of foreign capitalists.   If it is a mere question of who is able to
hold out longest in a competitive contest, American capitalists need no assistance.   They are quite competent to look
out for themselves.   Nor is it true that immediate returns
are desired.   Almost unlimited money can be obtained in
the United States for enterprises which promise only after
years to yield large returns.   Let us examine a few evi-
dences of this fact.

Why is it that long-time loans are more valuable than
short-time loans?   It might be supposed that if a federal,
state, or municipal government owes me some money, I
would want it at once, and say, "The sooner I am paid, the
better."   But the contrary is the case.   I say, "The later
the date of payment, the better pleased I shall be."   It is
because capital is so abundant that people are glad to part
with its use for a long term of years if they can be guaran-
teed a small annual payment.   Look at the readiness with
which people advance money for canal schemes and other
great improvements, in the hope that they will after years
become profitable.   A few concrete instances will help to
make this plain.   Once, when I was conversing with a great
capitalist, he mentioned to me incidentally in connection with
a certain scheme : "I told H. that if he wanted to do a good
thing for himself and the country, that was a good opportunity.   I told him that he must expect to lose money for
ten years, but that then he would begin to make money."

A company in New York — and it practically, I am told,
consists of one man — has been preparing a great dictionary
of the English language for publication for years.   It has
spent thousands of dollars, and I am inclined to think even
hundreds of thousands, already, and has not received one
dollar in return, because the work has not yet seen the

light. Nevertheless, it continues to spend money by the thousand, and seems perfectly satisfied in the prospect of a large future profit.

When I was travelling in the North once I met a gentleman from Virginia who was managing a large farm in that state owned partly by himself and partly by two capitalists. The arrangement was that he should manage the Virginia farm, receive a certain cash sum every year, spend whatever he might deem desirable in improvements, and then divide the surplus. It so happened, however, that this gentleman also owned a farm in New York State, where he had formerly lived, and to which he was anxious to return. Now, as it had been agreed that in case of dissatisfaction the dissatisfied party must buy the other out at an appraised valuation, he decided to spend so much in improvements every year so that there should be no surplus to divide. This he did year after year; yet the two capitalists, who occasionly visited the farm, always expressed perfect satisfaction with the management. As a matter of fact, they did not care for any revenue, but were content to see their property grow in value. These are merely typical cases. The truth is, if at the present time the natural conditions are such as to make any branch of industry profitable, there are men keen enough to see it, shrewd enough to hold their own against competition from abroad, and rich enough to await its development until it yields revenue. We, as a nation, are rich and powerful, and blessed with natural opportunities such as no other country enjoys; and however it may be elsewhere, as, for example, in Japan, the infant industry theory is an absurdity in the year 1888 in the United States.

Nevertheless, appetite grew with what it fed upon, and the call was for increasing protection. How justify it? As I said, protectionists began to cast about for another special plea, and they found it, and from about 1840 up to the present we have heard a new war-cry : namely, protection of American labor against " the pauper labor of Europe."

It does not seem difficult to account for this new plea. A political labor party arose about the year 1825, and soon acquired some influence. George Henry Evans, whose name may be remembered by some of my readers, was one of its leaders, and among its organs may be mentioned the *Workingman's Advocate*, the *Daily Sentinel* and *Young America.* Its platform contained twelve demands, among which were the following : —

" The right of man to the soil ; ' vote yourself a farm.'

" Down with the monopolies, especially the United States Bank.

" Freedom of public lands.

" Homesteads made inalienable.

" A lien of the laborer upon his own work for his wages.

" Abolition of imprisonment for debt."

A " workingman's convention " met at Syracuse, in New York State, in 1830, and nominated a candidate for governor, who received but a few votes. In New York City, however, they were more successful, for, joining forces with the Whigs, they elected a few members of the legislature. These men finally entered the Loco-foco party and were captivated by " Old Hickory," whose nomination and election they attributed to their influence. The Democratic party, under Andrew Jackson's leadership, re-echoed some of the war-cries of the workingmen's party, and seemed finally to have side-tracked this early labor movement, and to have brought it safely into the fold of Democracy.

Plainly the laboring classes were beginning to acquire a consciousness of their own existence as a distinct class in industrial society, and wily politicians thought it time to throw the workingman a sop. Hence, about 1840 we find the watchword " Protection to American labor against cheap foreign labor " taking the place of the former rallying cry, " Protection to our infant industries." No doubt for party purposes it was an immense improvement. It proceeded upon the hypothesis that the American employer must pay more than his European competitor for labor, and that difference must be made up to him by a tax on foreign competitors ; some, indeed, with a nice air of accuracy claiming it as a scientific principle that duties should be precisely such in every instance as to equal the difference in cost of labor. It is assumed that if duties fall, American labor must also fall in price, and, like European labor, become pauper labor. One manifest superiority in this new plea is that it does not advocate duties as something temporary, but as something to endure as long as American labor is " dear " and foreign labor is " cheap." Another is the benevolence wrapped up in it, and not merely benevolence. It is benevolence of a superior and unique sort ! Benevolence often means sacrifice on the part of him who exercises it, as when I wear an old coat that I may help educate the orphan child of an old friend. Not so the benevolence of the protective tariff, for it is warranted never to take a penny from the pockets of its most devoted adherents. They may live in palaces, eat the choicest cuts of roast beef, drink champagne, and be merry while their bank accounts swell ! Have they not done their part ? Are they not the representatives of protection to American labor ?

But is American labor, after all, protected ? Let us at once go to the heart of things. If I have anything to sell, it is conceivable that I may be helped in two ways by government. To say that I want to sell a thing means simply that I want to get something else for it. I sell that I may buy. Money simply comes in as a medium. A farmer sells corn for money, and with that money buys shoes. Corn is really exchanged for shoes, and money is used as a medium merely to facilitate exchange. Now, if government in some way can increase the supply of those things which I wish to buy, I may be benefited. More will be offered me for what I have to sell. On the other hand, if government can diminish the supply of the article I want to sell, I can get more for it, and I am benefited. How stands the case with the wage-receiver? What has he to sell? The commodity, labor, and nothing else. With that commodity (labor) he must purchase all other things. Now what is government doing for him? Is government rendering labor scarce and commodities plentiful? On the contrary, no duty is put on labor. Labor comes in free. Not only that; our protectionists are helping to increase the supply of labor and to keep its price down. Do not federal consuls encourage emigration from Europe to America? Do not states and territories send agents abroad to aid and abet foreign labor in its purpose to fill up the supply of labor in our own market? Do not the protectionist employers themselves keep their agents in every part of Europe to help swell the throng of those coming to our shores, and, in case of demand for higher wages, to take the place of the discontented? Strange! Yet it is all true! Every word of it, and the organs of the protectionists gloat over the increasing supply of labor in our markets. *The commodity which the laborer has to sell is not protected. All that government does is to help increase its supply and thus reduce its price.*

But then it must be that government is trying to increase the supply of those things which workingmen want in exchange for their commodity, labor! God forbid! It is taxing them and rendering them scarce! It looks as if government were working against labor, doesn't it? A funny world, isn't it?

CHAPTER XII.

TRUE PROTECTION TO AMERICAN LABOR.

OUR last chapter showed that while labor was not protected by tariff laws, the commodities which labor
received in exchange for its part in production were taxed
and rendered dear. We saw that in consequence of this
fact government had worked against labor in two ways, for
it had on the one hand encouraged the importation of labor
free from all charge, and on the other it had discouraged
the importation of those things which labor requires for the
maintenance of life. The reader should keep a firm grasp
on those facts in all discussion on the bearing of a protective
tariff on labor. It is easy to see what would have been done
by sincere and intelligent advocates of governmental protection to home labor. I do not now raise the question as to
the desirability of such protection. I simply propose to
answer this question : Assuming that it is the duty of the
federal government to aid labor by taxes, how should these
taxes be laid ? It is proposed to help labor to secure high
wages, and it is therefore necessary to raise the price it com-
mands by diminishing the supply. What can be simpler
than the solution of the problem? Tax the commodity
labor by taxing every foreigner landing on our shores, and
encourage, on the other hand, a plentiful importation of
goods. This would necessarily alter the relation between
supply of labor and demand for labor, and supply of commodities and demand for commodities. in the interest of

labor. Now, how high a tax should the sincere advocate of protection favor on each able-bodied emigrant from foreign lands upon his entrance into an American port? We must find out the value of a workingman, viewed simply as a producer — not as a husband or father or citizen, but simply as one who produces things which have value in the world's markets. Now, calculations of this kind have actually been made, and $1000 may be taken as a low valuation. Taxes on some imported commodities are as high as one hundred and fifty per cent., and a tariff devised in the interest of labor ought to put the highest tax on those who supply the commodity labor. We may say, then, that a tax on each foreign able-bodied emigrant of $1500 is not excessive as compared with other taxes on imports. Females might be taxed $1000, and children $500. If this would not give a certain advantage to home labor, then two and two do not make four.

It is to be noticed further in this connection that distance in itself is not the protection to labor which it once was, for the transportation of emigrants is so cheap now that the employer practically has a free world-wide market in which to procure the commodity labor. Thus the saying is literally true, the laborer sells his commodity in a free market and buys in a protected market.

It may be well to say a word more about restrictions on immigration, for this is now a live question, and my opinion has recently been asked. I cannot at present favor restrictions on immigration of the kind above described, although . they are simply the logical conclusions from principles which, it is claimed, we are now trying to apply in the interest of labor. It seems to me there are other and better ways for advancing the interests of labor, foremost among which is a thorough, systematic training of each boy and girl born on

American soil for the actual duties of life. These duties are both public and private, and preparation for them must include training designed to fit one to become a worthy member of a family, a worthy citizen, and a useful member of industrial society. In other words, each child ought to be so trained as to discharge honorably its future duties with respect to the family, the state, and, furthermore, to render an honest equivalent for those economic goods which are needed to support life in decency and comfort, or, still more simply expressed, to get a living. This preparation falls in part to the church, and with her functions we are not now concerned. Largely, and to an increasing extent, it must fall to the school, because old-fashioned methods, especially as seen in the apprenticeship system, are becoming antiquated. They are burdensome alike to employer and employé, for the former is often as much opposed to them, and frequently more opposed to them than the latter. Probably General Francis A. Walker, the head of the most successful Massachusetts Institute of Technology, is as well qualified to speak on this subject as any man, and of apprenticeship he says this : "As it exists to-day it is an advantage to neither party. The apprentice can only learn a narrow specialty, so narrow, as a rule, that its only value to him is the meagre pittance which he can earn from day to day, but at the sacrifice of any further educational advantages." The schools, then, need both extension and improvement, and that in several directions. One is in respect to practical ethics, for along this line our schools have been lamentably deficient. Practical ethics are required to prepare for a worthy life in the family and in the state. Second, practical training for the business of life in the industrial sphere is a necessity. We need industrial training in general, and, in particular, we need more professional schools, using that expression in its broad-

est sense. At one time it was thought by many that special
schools were not required for lawyers, preachers, and physicians, but now the mistake of this has been demonstrated by
actual experience. Well, the mechanic needs special schools
as well as the lawyer or preacher. Our girls ought to learn
how to cook and sew, and our boys to handle tools and keep
accounts in schools.

Third, the present branches of study should be better
taught, and this requires a higher grade of teachers. The
profession of teacher should be elevated in rank and its
rewards increased.

What has this to do with the tariff? Everything, because
we are discussing protection to labor, and I am pointing out
in what true protection as distinguished from spurious protection consists. Protection to labor consists in rendering it
highly qualified.

Do I need protection from inferiors? On the contrary, it
is the superior man who may drive me to the wall. So if
American labor by suitable training of youth is rendered
more highly qualified than foreign labor, it will find itself
better protected than by any tariff walls which human
ingenuity can in the year 1888 erect about the United
States.

Labor may rightfully demand that laws should be passed
to keep out a low and degraded class of emigrants, who tend
to lower our civilization and to throw upon us the burden of
their support as paupers or criminals; and here again we
come to an actual burden which rests upon our entire
industry, weighing down employer and employé alike. Protection from the scum and offscouring of Europe and Asia
may rightfully be demanded by all. Dr. Edward W. Bemis,
a former student of mine, has made some recommendations

which seem to me worthy of commendation.[1] He advises that the passport system be introduced as an effective method of controlling immigration, and that only those be allowed to enter our country who can bring a passport duly signed by an American consul. No passport, however, should be granted to those assisted to emigrate by any charity organization or governmental agency. Transportation to America costs so little that local European authorities find it cheaper to unload their poor and degraded upon us than to keep them at home. Already our burden for public alms is heavy, for it is estimated that one in a hundred receives charity in the United States even at this early period in our history, and the proportions of the burden will be realized by those who reflect that even the great German army includes less than one in a hundred of the population. I would say that the passport ought not only to set forth that the one to whom it is given is not aided in emigration by charity, but that he has not been a recipient of public charity for the preceding twelve months.

. No passport should be given to those assisted by the agents of any land-grant railroads in the United States, or, in fact, by the agents of any corporation.

Passports should be granted to those over sixteen only in case they can read and write. These restrictions are the most important which occur to me. Any attempt to limit immigration so as to exclude those who hold dangerous *opinions*, is a suggestion at once so absurd and impracticable that I hope no one who reads this book will require a demonstration of its folly.

The poorer quality of a large proportion of European emigrants in recent years is seen in the sections of country from which they emigrate. Formerly German emigrants came to

[1] See his article on Immigration in the *Andover Review* for March, 1888.

us from the Rhine, and the prosperous, enlightened country in the west of Germany. Now they come from the eastern parts and Polish frontiers, the most degraded part of the "Fatherland." Similarly, it is said that the poorest parts of Ireland are now sending us their surplus population, and that the Irish now coming to America are inferior to the earlier Irish emigrants.

If it is said that this sort of protection to home industry is an injustice to European countries, it can be replied that it is not improbable that we shall be able to do most for the advancement of human civilization in America if we do not load ourselves down with a too heavy weight. America has her part to play in the world's history, and if this is to be a beneficent part, it is essential that we should amply protect our own people and allow our institutions to develop naturally from within, without violent assault from alien influences. On the other hand, there are many questions which European governments must sooner or later settle for themselves, and I am not sure that we benefit humanity by receiving the worst elements they send us, and thus enabling them to prolong the existence of ancient abuses.

CHAPTER XIII.

AMERICAN LABOR NEEDS NO SUBSIDY.

I THINK it was a French king who asked his wise men to explain why it was that if you should put a large fish into a pail filled with water, the water would not run over. This puzzled them all greatly, until some one suggested that it was not a fact that the water would not run over. The king, indeed, had not stated that it was a fact. I am reminded of this story when I hear some of the current discussions on the tariff.

It is said, for example, that the American manufacturer must receive higher prices because labor costs him more than it costs his European competitor, and that these higher prices must be secured through the action of a protective tariff. But is it a fact that labor costs the American manufacturer more? I doubt it. Wages may on the whole be higher, although even here, on account of unsteady employment, the difference is not so great as many imagine; but wages and the cost of labor are two quite different things. The cost of labor depends upon two things — first, wages paid; second, the efficiency of labor. Will the practical man, who pays $2 a day to his employés engaged in some manufacturing enterprise in Massachusetts, at once remove his business to Georgia if told that employés can in the South be procured in abundance for $1.50 a day? By no means. He would be a fool to do it. He will first ascertain many other things about business, and he will institute a diligent inquiry into the relative efficiency of Northern and Southern labor. He will say: "The vital question with me is not how much I pay a day, but how much will it cost me to get a given piece of work done." *Now when we thus compare labor cost in Europe and America, it appears that in a large portion of the industrial field the American manufacturer has a decided advantage over his foreign competitor, for it costs him less to get a given piece of work done.* The American receives higher wages, but does so much more work in a day than the European that his services are cheaper and more desirable. Is not this plain? Suppose I employ two men, A. and B. A. receives $2 a day and B. $4 a day, but B. accomplishes three times as much in a day as A. Who is the cheap laborer? Here, as so often happens, the current saying, "the best is the cheapest," holds true. An American bricklayer receives more per day than a Dutch bricklayer, but he receives less per brick laid. The same holds with regard to wages per day and wages per piece in certain grades of spinning, and one who is familiar with the details of manufacturing in Europe and America can give examples in abundance. Mr. Schoenhof has looked carefully into this matter and made a report to the Department of State, which was noticed in *The Sun* in its issue for December 21, 1886. It appears that in the manufacture of silk in an English mill the average earnings of the employés were $2.25 a week, while they were $5.50 a week in an American mill with which Mr. Schoenhof was acquainted. Nevertheless, the American operatives did so much more work that the results were cheaper in our country. A factory near Frankfort-on-the-Main in Germany pays 21 cents per pair for making the uppers for ladies' high top button gaiters, while the price paid labor for the same services in Lynn, Massachusetts, is only 11 cents. A pair of boots can be manu-

factured in Lynn and laid in boxes for 33 cents, which is far
below the German cost, although the German laborer receives $3.38 per week, on the average, and the American
$9 per week.

It is not true, by any means, in all industries in this
country, that the cost of labor is less, but it seems probable
that, on the whole, we are quite capable of holding our own
in this respect. As a rule, high-priced labor is cheap labor,
and labor for which little is paid is worth little. I have
often been impressed with this fact in observing the effectiveness of servants in those parts of the North with which
I am acquainted, as compared with the effectiveness of
Virginia servants. A house servant may be procured readily
in the small towns in Virginia for $5 a month, whereas in a
New York village you would be very likely compelled to pay
$10 a month. Nevertheless, the Northern servant accom-
plishes about three times as much, and is in reality the one
to furnish the cheap labor. A "social protective tariff" has
been more or less discussed by political economists in recent
years. A "social protective tariff" means simply a tariff
designed to compensate the manufacturers for increased
labor-cost in a country where laborers receive high pay for
few hours, and enjoy other exceptional advantages. Something can be said on theoretical grounds in favor of this
proposition, but the difficulty in applying it is found to be
the fact that it is the laborers with long hours, low pay, and
few privileges who seem most to require protection. England is the country most dreaded in international competition, but nowhere in Europe are wages so high and the
number of hours' work per week so small. The English
workman has, in some respects at least, the advantage over
the American. He works only fifty-six hours a week, and
his labor organizations are so strong that they can afford

him better protection than American organizations. Labor organizations in England have, in fact, passed through that stage of existence in which American organizations still find themselves, and are no longer obliged to struggle for the right to exist. They are accepted as a settled fact. Arbitration is more successful in England than with us, and factory legislation is more highly developed. " Pluck-me " stores were prohibited in England in 1833, whereas a Pennsylvania judge, — and Pennsylvania is a state where the American system of protection is strongest, — in the year of grace 1887, actually declared the law prohibiting payment in kind unconstitutional, and that on the ground that American workmen must be protected in their freedom of contract! The father of one of my colleagues is an English manufacturer of cotton, whose employés, to the number of twenty, I believe, came to America to seek their fortunes, and they all, without a single exception, returned to England convinced that they fared better where they were. This is not meant to depreciate the advantages of our country, for on account of our still undeveloped resources there are openings here, and particularly for the gifted, which can be found nowhere in Europe. It does prove, however, that our superiority for the workman is not a clear case, and the country we most dread in international competition is the one where, with the exception of our own, wages are highest, and where workmen actually toil fewer hours per week than they do in our own. Some of the countries with the lowest wages in the world are not at all felt in international competition.

After all, it seems a strange thing to contend that a country with superior advantages cannot compete with one with inferior natural gifts. It is like claiming that a man who raises one hundred bushels of corn per acre will be driven out of the market by one who raises only fifty. Yet this is actually what some claim. What is the reason why wages are high in the United States? It is simply because Nature has lavished her gifts as never before upon an intelligent, enterprising, and industrious people. Labor and capital, when government does not force them into unnatural channels, yield a larger return than in Europe. If you invest a capital of say $1000, and an amount of labor equal to 1000 days' work, in America, you will receive a greater product, more bushels of potatoes or wheat, or pairs of shoes, than in a country like Germany. There is consequently more to be divided among all those who take part in production than in the Fatherland, and of this greater plenty labor receives a share in higher wages. There is nothing so veils the real nature of trade as the use of money as a medium of exchange, and if one imagines transactions to take place without the intervention of money, it helps wonderfully to clear up many things. A farmer and two laborers, let us say, produce, with a given investment of labor and capital, one thousand bushels of potatoes, whereas a German peasant, with his two hired laborers, produces only six hundred bushels. Manifestly, there is less to divide between labor and capital in Germany, and profit and wages are both small. Now, there are those who want to tell us that men working under superior conditions cannot hold their own against those working under inferior conditions. Is any one disposed to dispute the fact that our conditions are more favorable for the creation of wealth? A little travel and careful observation in foreign lands must be sufficient, I should say, to convince any fair-minded person that our natural facilities are superior. Barren hillsides are cultivated in Germany which would in America be neglected. Why is this so, if not because the American farmer

can do better than to expend his labor and capital on bar-
ren hillsides? Take railroad building. The grand opportunities for investments in railroad construction have in
Europe already been seized, and new investors are obliged
to be content with small returns on insignificant branch
lines. Go into an English or a German town, and you will
find capitalists and laborers eager for opportunities which
Americans would despise. Why? Simply because the grand
opportunities in old countries are very few. This may be
looked at from a still different standpoint. Will it be disputed that the total wealth created in the United States is
large in proportion to our capital and our population? If
not, then the entire point is conceded. The tariff laws
create no new wealth, and our larger wealth creation can
only be traced to our better advantages.

I desire, as soon as possible, to tell my readers what I
think ought to be done at the present time with respect to
the tariff, but I must beg them to be patient, because so
much ground must be cleared of undoubted fallacies before
it is possible to take a rational view of the protective tariff;
and when the word "fallacies" is used, reference is had to
things which no man can believe when he once turns them
over in his mind and carefully analyzes them. These fallacies, in fact, frequently amount to absurdities, and all the
absurdities by no means proceed from the protectionists.
However, I desire now to call attention to the fact that
England and Germany could not ruin all our industries,
even if their advantages were in everything superior to ours.
Many will say if foreign countries can produce more than
we with a given amount of labor and capital, they will drive
us out of the world's market, and even capture our home
markets. But how is this possible? Will they supply us
with commodities and take no return for them? If that

were true, the backward nations of the world would indeed have an easy time of it, for other more highly developed nations would supply them with commodities for nothing on account of their inferiority. If, however, something is taken in return, then the production of that something will furnish opportunities for labor and capital. Perhaps, it will be said, they will take their pay in money. If they do this, the precious metals begin to leave us, prices will fall in our country and rise elsewhere, and it will thus become profitable for foreigners to buy our commodities, which would again turn the stream of precious metals back to us.

The truth is simple. It is relative advantages, and not absolute advantages, which determine the course of international trade. If England can with ten days' labor produce either one hundred bushels of wheat or two hundred yards of woollen cloth, and with the same labor we can produce seventy-five bushels of wheat or one hundred yards of woollen cloth, England will not on account of her superiority furnish us with both wheat and cloth. She will furnish us with that commodity in which her advantage is greatest, and we will send her that in which our inferiority is least; in other words, we will exchange our wheat for English woollen cloth. Both England and America will gain thereby. Each will do that for which nature has best fitted her. This is the way exchanges naturally take place between nations. One may be superior to others in well-nigh every branch of production, but each one will seek to find those pursuits in which it has relatively greatest advantages. The wealth of the world will thereby be increased. Had England accepted our offer of reciprocal free trade in 1783, and had free trade always obtained, we would have had manufactures; but it is doubtless true that a larger portion of our labor and capital would have been devoted to agriculture, and farming would be a more flourishing pursuit, for it is in agriculture that our relative advantages over European countries are most conspicuous.   While not prepared to join without qualification in Jefferson's laudation of agricultural pursuits and his condemnation of manufactures, I cannot but think we would fare quite as well if our change from an agricultural people to a manufacturing people were not proceeding with such a hot-bed rapidity, and if our cities grew in size with a more regular and less feverish haste.   Has not, indeed, this unprecedented increase in the population of cities been one of the chief causes which have made them so corrupt and depraved that they are regarded as a menace to our civilization?

CHAPTER XIV.

THE IMPORTANCE OF A WIDE DIFFUSION OF ECONOMIC KNOWLEDGE, WITH A FEW INCIDENTAL REMARKS CONCERNING A GOVERNMENT TELEGRAPH.

IT was seriously proposed a few years ago to introduce the study of political economy into the public schools of Belgium, and there can be no doubt that in a country ruled by popular vote it is of the first importance that the people should receive some training in early life in the elements of that science which is concerned with the fundamental conditions of national prosperity. A very little knowledge of practical economics would make us a happier and a still more prosperous people, and it is not necessary for one believing this to hold exaggerated notions regarding the achievements of political economists. Political economy, if it were more generally understood, could not prevent all strikes and lockouts, but even a slight knowledge of the nature of industrial society would do away with many of the senseless controversies between labor and capital which are so great a loss to us all. Political economy is not in a position to give an absolute and unqualified answer to the question, Shall we have a government telegraph service or a private service in the United States at the present time? Familiarity, however, with such discussions on the part of the people would make much that we hear on the subject impossible, and force the advocates of various measures to confine themselves to valid arguments, and thus to help us to arrive at a rational decision. A presentation of the claims of the Western Union Telegraph Company at Washington a few weeks ago has attracted a great deal of attention, and yet this presentation involved an error which to one who knows anything about the principles of the telegraph service is as palpable as the assertion that three times six are nineteen is to one who knows the multiplication table. Nowhere else, it was maintained, can a message be sent so far for so little money. But what has distance to do with proper telegraph charges? Why should more be charged for sending a message a long distance than for sending one a short distance? Does any one imagine now that anything is carried? There is a slight difference in cost between messages sent for a long distance and a short distance, especially if it is necessary to "forward" or re-telegraph the message, and the greater length of lines involves a small additional investment of capital. Nevertheless, the difference is a minor matter, and, with the exception of Russia and Turkey, every country in Europe disregards it, and has one charge for all domestic telegrams regardless of distance. It is like the case of the post-office. Rowland Hill introduced his celebrated reform, the penny-postage system, by analyzing the expenditures for carrying letters and presenting the results of his investigations to the public. It costs something for the post-office to receive letters, cancel the stamps, sort them and send them on the way. It costs something at the other end of the route to sort and deliver the letters. Here are two elements of the total cost, and the third is actual transportation, and this Hill showed was on each letter so insignificant that it could advantageously be neglected altogether. Thus cost was seen to be nearly identical for all letters, and the true interests of all

were promoted and administration simplified by one uniform charge. Similarly, we have one uniform charge in
most countries for telegrams, and this is 12 cents for 12
words in England; in Germany, 17 cents for 10 words; in
Belgium, 9 cents for 10 words. Germany's charge is the
highest, I believe, in Western Europe. Now, what about
long-distance telegrams? No European country outside of
Russia has any long distances like ours, and when a telegram is sent three or four thousand miles in Europe it becomes an international telegram, and charges on international telegrams are based on different principles, and are,
very properly, higher than for domestic telegrams. The
receipts on international telegrams must be divided between
two or more countries, and are higher on that account, as
well as for other reasons, on the same principle that it
usually costs more to send a parcel a given distance when
it passes through the hands of two express companies than
if it is carried the whole distance by one.

It was further asserted that the telegraph service was a
loss to England. It was not mentioned that this is due to
two simple facts : One is, that England paid an exorbitant
price for her telegraph, and that the interest on this outlay
is reckoned among expenditures ; and the other, that there
had been a recent reduction of fifty per cent. in charges,
and, like post-office reductions in charges, the first effect
of such a measure is sure to be a loss, although in a few
years a profit results therefrom. Neither was it mentioned
that other countries derive a profit from their telegraph service. All these are a few simple elementary facts, and yet,
through ignorance of these, a people may be easily deceived.
The Sun recently mentioned a matter in this connection
which is worthy of serious consideration, and that is, the
increased patronage. *The Sun* did not commit itself, but

simply called attention to the matter.   Other newspapers
have, however, spoken of it as an insuperable obstacle in
the way of a government telegraph.   Yet familiarity with
economic discussions ought to show one that there is another aspect to the case.   Our federal civil service is bound
to increase, and there are those among my readers who will
live to see it double its present dimensions.   This is inevitable, because the expansion of the country must bring with
it increased federal business, unless, indeed, all government
business, army and post-office included, is handed over to
private corporations !   Now, it strikes me that the real
danger is this : that our civil-service force will gradually and
imperceptibly grow until we have 100,000 more federal
employés than at present.   That is precisely similar to what
has happened before.   A danger which creeps upon us
unawares is a serious one.   Should, however, our federal
employés be increased by 18,000 at once, that would force
upon the attention of the people the principles of sound
administration, and the danger of an abuse of political power
for partisan ends.   The result could hardly fail to be most
salutary.

Although this is a somewhat longer digression than I intended, I do not regret it, for there are certain aspects of
the tariff question which can be profitably treated in connection with other problems of the day, and they will be so
treated in this and some of the succeeding chapters.   The
whole topic of the desirability of a wide diffusion of economic knowledge was suggested by the receipt of a protectionist campaign document while I was writing my last
chapter.   This was addressed " To the Laboring Men of the
United States," and is so full of popular fallacies that it
requires a somewhat lengthy treatment.   It is one of the
things which are only possible because in industrial affairs

people have not yet got so far as the multiplication table, and do not know that three times six are eighteen — not nineteen. It is not the question of free trade or protection, but the question of valid arguments, and rational action must proceed from such arguments. Again, it seems necessary to protest that no one contemplates any action which will overthrow manufactures that have grown up under a protective tariff. There are reasons why that should not be done, and why all the industrial interests of a country would suffer if that were done. These will be presented in due time. Now we are concerned with the campaign document which lies before me.

"The receipts of the government," it is stated, "are more than necessary to pay the expenses, consequently they must be reduced by the enactment of new tariff laws. The Democrats propose to lessen the receipts by reducing the tariff, and this will flood the country with foreign goods made by the pauper labor of Europe, and must necessarily take that much labor from our American workingmen. The Republicans propose to reduce receipts by abolishing the internal revenue tax laws and raising the tariff on foreign goods to such a point as to prevent them coming into our country, and thereby give to our workingmen the right and privilege of making goods to supply our home markets. Every article brought into this country that took ten days' labor to make it, takes just ten days' labor from our people ; this fact is too plain to be contradicted. The free-trade capitalist wants the tariff reduced, because his money will then buy more of the products of labor. In other words, he says to you, ' I want the privilege of buying wherever I can buy the cheapest, and with free trade you must work for the same wages now paid the pauper labor of Europe, or I will buy European goods.' With a tariff that will protect our American industries, there will be such a demand for labor that legally organized labor can demand of their employers fair and just wages ; but with a low tariff you render it impossible for your employers to pay you good wages, because they must sell their products in competition with the products made by the low wages in Europe. In the first nine months of 1887 there were about 1,500,000 tons of foreign iron brought to this country. Now, if this iron had been made here, it would have given out $32,000,000 of wages to our own workmen, and that would have employed during that time 80,000 men. This is but one article of manufacture, and so it is with a multitude of other articles now coming into this country, but which your votes can keep out. This country should make laws to protect our own workmen, and not the workmen of England and Europe."

This opens up a great question, the ramifications of which affect our daily life in a thousand ways. I mean the relation which exists between spending money and giving employment to labor. This will be considered in the next chapter.

CHAPTER XV.

THE SEEN AND THE UNSEEN.

SHALLOW as he was, Frederic Bastiat undoubtedly said many good things, and is entitled to our gratitude for having cleared up, as no one else, some of the first principles of economics. Perhaps one of his happiest efforts was his exposition of the difference in industrial society between that which is seen and that which is not seen. A worthy shopkeeper, Jacques Bonhomme, is enraged because his careless son breaks a pane of glass, while the spectators who gather about the scene offer the father this consolation : "It is an ill wind that blows nobody good. Everybody must live, and what would become of the glaziers if panes of glass were never broken?" Who among my readers has not heard similar expressions of opinion? And how many of them are there who do not feel that there is a certain justice in the view of the indifferent but good-natured spectators? I remember a report which reached me three years ago that a warehouse in Baltimore was destroyed by fire. I was in a small company at the time, and a young woman, of at least average intelligence, made the remark, "It is time the old building did burn down, and give workingmen a chance to get employment. It has been standing the last fifty years." Some time previously a good friend of mine, a lady of considerable means and a devout member of one of our leading churches, told me that she considered it the duty of the wealthy to spend money on dress, in order to give employ·

ment to labor. A clergyman whom I esteem was recently reported as raising objection to the Charity Ball on religious grounds, but admitting that, after all, it was a good thing for dressmakers and other employés who were engaged on the elaborate toilets, as well as for the merchants, who sold thousands of dollars' worth of goods.

At the close of the last chapter I made a quotation from a high-tariff campaign document to the effect that 1,500,000 tons of iron brought to this country from Europe ought to have been produced at home, as in that case $32,000,000 would have been spent for wages in our country and 80,000 men would have received employment for nine months. Let us examine these various opinions with some care, for they are all closely related. Certain phenomena are seen in each instance. The glazier receives six francs for putting in a new pane of glass, and he is happy because he has an opportunity to earn some money. The warehouse burns down, and bricklayers, carpenters, and masons are employed for several months in putting up a new building. The wealthy lady spends $200 for a single dress, and the merchant who sells the material, and the dressmaker, are both pleased, precisely as those are delighted who minister to the wants of the belles at the Charity Ball. The high-tariff people shut out foreign products and point to our busy workmen engaged in manufacturing those things which, but for the tariff, would be imported. All these things are seen and observed of all men, but there are other phenomena of equal importance which pass unnoticed. Jacques Bonhomme, the shopkeeper, was just on the point of ordering a new pair of shoes for his wife, for which he expected to pay six francs. These shoes he is now unable to order on account of his loss, and the shoemaker misses his opportunity to earn six francs. This is that which is not seen, but it is beyond all controversy that no additional employment has been given to labor because the careless son broke the pane of glass. The shopkeeper's wife is, however, put to the shame and mortification of wearing old and patched shoes ; and from all this we see that society is poorer on account of the broken pane of glass. There is a smaller quantity of commodities to be enjoyed by the various members of the community than there would be otherwise, and suffering ensues. So it will likewise be discovered that loss and waste in the other cases are simply loss and waste, and no amount of sophistry can make them anything else.

We see the men putting up a new building on the site of the old, but that which is not seen is a decreased expenditure somewhere else, and yet there is scarcely a doubt about this. Possibly the insurance company which sustains the loss decides on that account not to construct a new building for its own use as it had intended, and thereby the demand for labor is diminished. It is more probable that it is obliged to refuse a loan which some builder desired for the purpose of carrying forward improvements. Or, the company may be obliged to lower dividends, and on account of diminished means people buy fewer hats, shoes, coats, and other things which they need. My good friend who spends $200 on a single dress sees employment given. She does not perceive that if she had given twenty calico dresses to as many poor old ladies, quite as much work would have been given to sewing-women. Extravagance finds no justification whatever on the plea that it gives employment to labor. A possession of money simply means that a person has control over a certain amount of labor and capital, which may be directed in any channel one pleases. I may so use my money that labor and capital shall minister to my wants and to my pleasure, or so that labor and capital shall minister to the wants and pleasures of others. When I do the one I show that I love myself; when I do the other I show that I love my neighbor. One man spends $200,000 on a private house; another, $200,000 on a public library building. Labor is employed in either case, but in the one an individual derives a selfish advantage therefrom, and in the other the advantage is generously conferred on the public. I know a school in which poor ignorant people are trained to useful occupations at the same time that the mind is instructed. The sum of $1500 endows a permanent scholarship and keeps one person there for all time. That $1500 furnishes directly as much labor as the same money spent in a feast, and indirectly it furnishes a thousand times as many opportunities for employment, because graduates go forth from this school skilled, intelligent, and honest laborers, increase the wealth of the country, and help to organize industry on a solid basis. I have known $1500 to send one hundred boys from the slums of New York City to the West, where most of them — not all of them, but the great majority — become honest, respectable, hard-working citizens, who all their lives long furnish opportunities for labor in the commodities which they purchase. When the boys were taken West, the $1500 gave employment to labor on railroads and hotels and boarding-houses, just as much employment as the same money spent on Charity Ball costumes would have given, and thereafter it furnishes a thousand times as much employment. The faithful, conscientious person, who will take the trouble, finds endless opportunities to spend money so as to help others, to lift them up and prepare them for useful careers, and needs never spend money on self to give employment to labor. My friend may be right in spending $200 on a dress. She must answer for that to her own conscience; but she spends it, if she understands the consequences of her own acts, simply because she wants a beautiful dress, and considers it in this instance justifiable to prefer her own happiness to that of others.

Now let us return to the tariff. We see 1,500,000 tons of iron enter the country. That is seen. We fail to notice that in payment for this 30,000,000 bushels of wheat leave the country, and that the farmers find a market for their produce which would otherwise be closed. Our business men are talking about foreign markets, but is any one insane enough to think that we can sell to foreigners unless we import from them? And what would be the object in such proceedings — in always sending goods away from the country and never receiving any? The thing which is not seen is that if we stop importing we must stop exporting, and that if we stop exporting we deprive our own home labor of employment, and transfer employment which American labor might have to the so-called pauper labor of Europe. Ought it to be necessary to dwell on this in Baltimore? Would we not have a flourishing trade with South America in our own city did not the tariff render it impossible to import goods from South America? And is it not true that because we cannot import goods from South America we cannot export them? For how can shipping thrive unless it has cargoes both ways? And as we cannot export to South America, are we not depriving American labor of employment?

Is there any one who would like to see us abstain from all dealings with foreign countries? If it is good for us to keep all our money at home, why is it not good for one single state to abstain from all dealings with other states? And if good for a state, why not for a city? Let us build a high wall about Baltimore, and shoot the man dead who comes in or goes out. That would keep our money at home. But why should not each family be sufficient unto itself, and keep all its money at home? I am a practical farmer. Is it not foolish for me to send money away from home for butter, eggs, potatoes, chickens, hams and the like? I could raise them if I desired. Why not do this? Because my time is worth more for other purposes. It is only in a state of complete barbarism that each person is sufficient unto himself and avoids exchanges with his neighbors. Now if it is profitable for an individual to find out those things for which nature has adapted him, why is it not advantageous for the people of a city or state or a nation to find out those things in the production of which the Almighty has given them facilities, and to exchange surplus products with the surplus products of other cities, states, and nations? Surely it is thus that the most abundant opportunities will be offered to labor to find employment; not merely that, but the largest possible returns for its services will thus be secured.

CHAPTER XVI.

THE BASIS OF THE CLAIMS OF POLITICAL ECONOMISTS.

"A FAULTY political economy is the fruitful parent of crime." This is one of the wisest of the many wise sayings of Dr. Thomas Arnold. Everybody acts upon some theory of political economy, for it is impossible for a rational man to play his part in industrial society without having some reason for his actions. A man who acts without reason for his actions we call either an insane man or a fool. But as soon as a man puts his reason for an industrial action into words, he explains the economic theory which underlies the action. Everybody must in the nature of things be more or less of a political economist, and consequently more or less of a theorist, for to act without theory and without reason are one and the same thing. Of course, the reason given for an action may be valid or it may involve all sorts of fallacies. Equally, of course, the theory of industrial action in a given concrete case put forward by a business man may or may not be sound; but the moment he begins an argument he becomes a theorist. Economic theory treats simply of the principles which govern action, and in its last analysis is based upon experience. A newspaper published within a thousand miles of the Baltimore City Hall has of late had much to say about free-trade theorists and professors of political economy, who are teaching their classes free-trade doctrines. I propose to make no

special comment on these various squibs, which are both
amusing and entertaining ; but it may be well to say a word
about the claims of political economists in general, and
about the basis on which they rest, for these are involved
sooner or later in all economic discussions.   Political economy is concerned with the facts of industrial life which it
attempts to arrange, classify, and explain.   This involves a
treatment of past industrial life, the forces which have been
at work and which have made it what it is to-day ; finally,
an examination of those forces now at work, and which are
shaping the future.   But why, it can be asked, should political economists presume to instruct business men about the
facts of industrial life when business men are all the time
engaged in industrial life and make it what it is?   Let us
see.   You converse with a business man in Pittsburg, Pennsylvania, about those aspects of business which concern the
public, and he will very likely give you a theory which he
will claim is impregnable because it is based on facts with
which he is thoroughly familiar.   No political economist can
convince him, he will tell you, that his theory is not· sound,
for he *knows* that it is.   Very well.   Now go to New York
and converse with a business man, and he may dogmatically
lay down exactly the opposite theory, of which he is quite
as positive, because, as he says, he knows the facts.   This
may suggest an explanation of the functions of the political
economist ; and, when even in the same city you find business men of different occupations holding the most contra-
dictory opinions, it becomes evident that it would be desirable to have a class of men with a larger acquaintance with
facts to stand between these jarring factions.   This is precisely what political economists attempt to do.   A thoughtful business man must often feel that he is in the position of
a man in a dense forest who, as the proverb has it, can only

see the individual trees and not the forest at all. A political economist is rather in the position of a man on an elevation who overlooks the entire forest and gets a better general view than one in the midst of it, and can better tell him
how to escape from the forest. But this also suggests something else. The more minute and detailed knowledge of the
man in the forest itself is of importance. Should he without
reflection follow the directions of the man on the hill-top, he
might find himself hopelessly stuck in a quagmire which
could not be seen from a distance. Both the general and
the special knowledge are required; and political economists who fail to accord due respect to the special information of the man of affairs fall into most grievous error.
Mayor Latrobe acted with a full appreciation of this fact,
as it seems to me, when during his last term he selected the
members of the recent city tax commission, for he chose a
representative of business, a representative of the law, and
a representative of the science which deals with taxation.
Industrial society, or, if a more popular term is desired, the
business world, is a thing which grows like a plant or an
animal; and careful observation, coupled with accurate in-
ductive and deductive reasoning, enables us to discover the
laws of its growth, its health, and its disease. No organism
is, however, more complex; and political economy is still in
its infancy, and while worthy of attention, its teachings must
undoubtedly be accepted with more or less caution. Political economists, it is true, differ in important particulars; but
I suppose these differences are not more radical than those
of physicians, or, in fact, than those of many other scientific
men, while it may be said that those respects in which there
is substantial harmony among them are still more important
than their differences. Now when, as is the case in the
general view taken of commerce, there is something ap-

proaching substantial unanimity among economists, it is not
unreasonable to claim that this view deserves at least as
much attention as it receives.   When a political economist
sets forth his opinions, it should be remembered that these
are not merely his individual opinions, but opinions formed
in the light of a science which, if it is still in its infancy, has
nevertheless been pursued for one hundred years, and has
received contributions from some of the brightest minds of
modern times.   Nor, when it is considered that the science
which deals with human beings living in society and consti-
tuting a living organism is the most complex and difficult
of all sciences, can it be claimed that its progress has not
on the whole been encouraging; while it is probable that
this progress is at the present time more rapid and more
hopeful than it has ever been before.   It is further noteworthy that political economists have not been " mere theorists," if by that is meant men who have had no practical
experience outside of their own specialty.   I have, on the
contrary, been struck by the fact, in reading the biographies
of political economists, that they were as a rule good business men, some of them winning great distinction in pursuits
which are ordinarily called " practical."   There is Ricardo,
for example, who on the English stock exchange outstripped
all his competitors and won so large a fortune at an early
age that he was able thereafter to devote himself exclusively
to intellectual pursuits.   Few men have done more for
economic science, though strange as it may seem, this practical business man was the most purely abstract and theoretical — using that word in an ordinary sense — of all
political economists, and did harm in leading political
economists away from a careful observation of actual experience.   Then in England we may also mention Henry
Fawcett, professor of political economy in the University of

Cambridge, probably the best postmaster-general England ever had. Robert Owen, extremist and radical though he was, made, it seems to me, some important contributions to economic science ; and he was for a long time regarded as the most successful cotton manufacturer in Great Britain. He was often spoken of as a " cotton prince," just as we call certain men railway kings. One of the most excellent works on banking was written by J. W. Gilbart, formerly director and general manager of the London and Westminster Bank, one of the greatest banking houses of London. " Lombard Street, a Description of the Money Market," is one of the standard works in economic literature, and it was written by Walter Bagehot, who was a practical financier, as was the author of "The Theory of Foreign Exchanges," the Right Hon. George J. Goschen. When we turn to Germany we can find scarcely one economist of note, I think, who has not taken some practical part in the government of his country, or of some of its local political units, and that, so far as I have learned, with uniformly beneficial results. Political economy has until very recently been in a backward position in our own country, but it is now rapidly taking a better position as a practical science. One of the American contributions to economic science is the work " United States Notes," by Hon. John Jay Knox, whose reports as Comptroller of the Currency are among the best things written on our banking system. As president of " The Bank of the Republic," in New York, it will be admitted that Mr. Knox is now doing the work of a " practical " man. Our national banking system itself, one of the best which the world has ever seen, is to no inconsiderable extent due to Dr. McVickar, formerly professor of political economy in Columbia College. Gen. Francis A. Walker is to-day one

of the most distinguished political economists, and as he
has, in addition to other services, brought the Massachusetts Institute of Technology into the front rank of such
institutions, he ought to receive the respect of the community as a practical man; for I will venture to say that to
manage successfully a great institution of learning requires
as profound a knowledge of men and affairs as it does to
build up a great commercial or manufacturing establishment.
Dr. James, of the University of Pennsylvania, has written the
best treatise in the English language on "The Relation of
the Modern Municipality to the Gas Supply," and by his
opposition to the sale of the municipal gas-works of Philadelphia has saved that city millions of dollars, and this
strikes me as an extremely practical thing to do. The best
treatise on public debts in any language is the work of Dr.
Henry C. Adams, professor of political economy in the
University of Michigan; and to write an excellent work on
so practical a topic is certainly practical.

The truth of the matter is, political economy is a body of
knowledge as yet incomplete and imperfect, still of vast importance, which has been built up by the labors of those on
the one hand who were primarily business men, and secondarily political economists, and on the other hand by those
who were primarily political economists and secondarily
business men. While it may be true that political economists have often failed to give due weight to the special detailed knowledge of those who are exclusively men of affairs,
it is equally true that we have suffered serious loss — a loss
amounting to hundreds of millions — because business men
have so often failed to master general economic principles.
Business needs political economy, and political economy
should diligently appropriate the teachings of business.

Dr. Arnold said — to return to my text — " A faulty politi·

cal economy is the fruitful parent of crime." More might have been added, for it is not only the fruitful parent of crime; it is the most fruitful parent of folly and consequent misery. The last chapter in this work dwelt upon the importance of phenomena not readily seen. It seems that a few points are not yet clear. It is said "it is after all better to spend one's money in extravagance than to hoard it up." Money "hoarded up" and "locked up" is something about which we hear every day. What is meant by these expressions? Who hoards up money? No one in these days — at any rate very few. Money is put in banks. Does any one of my readers imagine it stays there? By no means. It is used in business and gives employment to labor. Take our savings banks. In one of them there are deposits of over sixteen millions of dollars. Is this money hoarded up? By no means; it is all used. You see money employed in building in Baltimore, and you say it is a good thing, for it makes business and gives employment to labor. Where did that money come from? If any reader of this article will talk with practical builders and practical bankers, I think he will soon be convinced that that is precisely the money which is in popular parlance hoarded up or locked up.

One of the first things which ought to be taught in schools is that what is saved is spent. To save money does not mean to spend less. It simply means to spend money in such a way that something is left to show for it. Take two mechanics, each receiving high wages, say $4 a day. One spends his money in having "a good time." People like him; they smile upon him — while his money lasts, but no longer — and say he "keeps money in circulation." The other mechanic is careful, self-denying, frugal. "He hoards his money," but he builds him a home. So it is seen when one goes below the surface of things, that the money saved has after all been spent, and just as much employment has been given to labor. At the end of ten years your "good fellow" is very likely impoverished and broken down, and the thrifty mechanic has shown himself after all the better man, the better father, the better citizen.

I know of nothing more pernicious in its consequences than these shallow judgments which we hear about spending money and "keeping it in circulation." It is the faulty political economy which makes the man more popular who spends ten thousand dollars on a feast than his neighbor who "saves" ten thousand and builds six homes for workingmen's families. It was this faulty political economy which made the third Napoleon, the curse of his country and of his generation, so popular in his extravagance, while the frugal court of the Prussian monarch was setting his people an example of industry and thrift which are now making them both wealthy and mighty, dreaded by England in the industrial field as much as by France in the military field. It was this faulty political economy which led the same newspaper to which I have already referred to suggest that a great and grinding monopoly was not so bad a thing after all, because its head men spent their money "royally."

CHAPTER XVII.

THE DIFFERENT KINDS OF MONOPOLIES, WITH SOME REMARKS ON THE LAND QUESTION.

I HAVE dwelt upon the importance of political economy, and have endeavored to show that political economists are practical men. I may add that political economy, as it is pursued to-day, is a most interesting study. " Every beginning is difficult," says the proverb, and this holds with reference to political economy; but when one once conquers the difficulties of the beginning, no intellectual pursuit can be more fascinating than that which is concerned with an examination into the nature, the development, and the desirable constitution of industrial society. It may be doubted, however, whether any one of the many topics with which it deals is of more absorbing interest than monopolies, while it scarcely admits of controversy that no economic topic is less understood.

It is necessary in a discussion of monopolies to divide them into classes, for the principles which hold for one class will be found inapplicable to another, and any effort to lump all monopolies together, and to treat them all alike, will produce confusion, both in theory and practice. Monopolies are now discussed daily in the press in their connection with the tariff, and trusts, and syndicates, but it cannot be said that the discussion produces a great amount of light. It is, however, accompanied by growing indignation as the evils of certain monopolies are more and more keenly felt, but this indignation is as likely to produce harm as good, unless it can be directed into proper channels. While it may be claimed that the indignation is righteous, it is indeed a bold man who would be willing to say that it is enlightened.

Monopolies with respect to ownership and management may be divided into two classes, public and private. The post-office is a public monopoly and is a national blessing. The telegraph is a private monopoly, and the fact that it is so is nothing less than a national calamity. Private monopolies are odious. They are contrary to the spirit of the common law and of American institutions, and wherever or whenever they exist, are a perpetual source of annoyance and irritation. Public monopolies, on the other hand, are productive of vast benefits when confined to their own proper sphere. Modern civilization would give place to anarchy should all public monopolies be abolished. The army and navy and police are public monopolies, and when we see great corporations, as in Pennsylvania, employing private armies of their own, mercenary troops engaged of a citizen of another state, thinking people look upon it with alarm as incipient anarchy of the most malignant type. We must, then, draw a sharp line in all our discussions between public and private monopolies.

But monopolies may be divided into two different classes from another standpoint. Certain pursuits are monopolies on account of their own inherent qualities. These we call natural monopolies. Legislation neither makes them monopolies nor can it prevent them from becoming monopolies. All that legislation can do is to recognize the fact that they are and must remain monopolies, and to act upon it. There are other pursuits which are made monopolies by legislation, and these we call artificial monopolies. Patents throw around those engaged in the manufacture of certain articles a barrier which shuts out competition. The production of a new American book is an artificial monopoly, rendered such by a copyright. Legislation could, if it were thought desirable, abolish both patents and copyrights, and thus do away with those monopolies which they create. Switzerland is an example of a country which does not grant patents, and thus does not create by means of patents artificial monopolies. Tariffs, which shut out foreign competition, sometimes enable home producers to form gigantic combinations which crush in a grasp of relentless cruelty every attempt at competition within our own borders. These combinations could rarely embrace the entire civilized world were every feature of protectionism removed from our tariff legislation. These pursuits are, therefore, also artificial monopolies, and they are daily increasing in number to the consternation of the public. Perhaps I ought to make an exception when I say that the increase of monopolies of the artificial sort is viewed with alarm by the public. Socialists view it with satisfaction, because they believe that competition in industry is an evil which ought to make way for complete and perfect monopoly in every pursuit. Socialists see in trusts and syndicates nothing but the remorseless march of monopoly, which they have long predicted will never cease until concentration of business becomes complete. The last stage in this evolution, according to their doctrine, is the transfer of monopolized business to public control and the consequent inauguration of the socialistic state. The capitalists engaged in these combinations are hailed by socialistic writers as fellow-socialists, and the socialistic tendency in trusts and other artificial monopolies admit of no doubt. When we come to a discussion of artificial monopolies, we, in fact, touch the only really dangerous socialism in the United States. Those who spend energy in fighting the socialism of the doctrinaires who write books and deliver lectures are, in my opinion, simply Don Quixotes attacking windmills. "The game isn't worth the candle," and that is the reason why — if a personal explanation is in order — I have never spent much time in criticism of the socialists. I have believed there were certain truths in the teachings of scientific socialism which it is well enough to notice, but the prospect of professed socialists ever gaining an ascendency in America has seemed to me so remote a contingency that I have never thought it worth while to spoil pen and paper and waste ink in exposing their errors. The results of years of study, reflection, and investigation have convinced me that the only dangerous socialism in America is monopoly controlled by private greed. This is sufficiently important to justify us in giving some attention to the views of one of the most rational socialists, who sees the approaching triumph of his faith in the "trust." I refer to Laurence Gronlund, who, in his new work, "Ça Ira, or Danton in the French Revolution," speaks of the socialistic tendency of business in America in these words: "Of the movements by individuals, the most significant is that toward *production on a large scale.* By 'production' should also be understood transportation and commerce, for they add value to the product, just as well as does the labor of the operatives on raw materials. All that is necessary here is to note this tendency, for all admit that production everywhere — the most trivial as well as the most important — is being concentrated in the hands of richer and richer employers, of larger and larger corporations.

"But there is one feature of this concentration that deserves special mention because it is novel, and as yet it seems confined to the United States, where the capitalist system is more unfettered than anywhere else. It is what is called the *Trust*. This is monopoly in its most concentrated form. Suppose the presidents of all the incorporated companies in a given branch of industry in the whole country assembled, and one of their number in whom they all have perfect trust — hence the name — selected to perform the function of *absolute* manager, with power to determine, autocratically, how much each company is to produce, and consequently its share in the proceeds, and you have the 'trust.' It differs from a 'pool' in this, that none of the parties can withdraw. The individuality which the law confers on each company by the act of incorporation is merged in the 'trust,' over which the State has not the least control; indeed, the whole arrangement is kept as perfect a secret, as far as the public is concerned, as possible. . . . It is easy to see, that, when these 'trusts' become general, and that is only a question of very short time, they will revolutionize our present system, for they mean the destruction of competition, which then will be utilized simply to crush their weaker rivals. Some of our newspapers, on getting wind of these 'trusts,' have become alarmed, seeing in them terrible future dangers to the State, and that, indeed, they would be; they would institute a new slavery, the most formidable slavery that ever existed, if evolution would stop there. But it will not. That is why this movement is at the bottom, an *unconscious* one; the capitalists engaged in in it are, unconsciously, the greatest revolutionists in the world.

"Now this concentration shows us what is going to be one important feature of the new social order — shows us that *production* on the *largest possible scale* will be *the only practical mode of production in the future*."

It is not necessary to dwell longer on the tremendous practical importance of a discussion of monopolies. No problem of to-day is so pressing, and it is, indeed, as a part of the general growth of monopoly, both a cause and a consequence of monopoly that protectionism is most deserving of attention.

We will begin the discussion of monopoly by a treatment of natural monopolies, because that will help to clear the field and render the characteristics of artificial monopolies more readily comprehensible.

There is one natural monopoly which stands apart by itself with peculiar qualities. It is land. Land was not made by man, but was given to man ready made. It was a gift of nature, or, if you please, of God. But so much was given, and no more. The amount that man can add to land or take away from it is so utterly insignificant as to be unworthy of notice. The most tremendous practical consequences flow from the fact that land is a natural monopoly, and the so-called land question deserves all the attention it is receiving. It deserves even more attention than it is receiving. I would gladly take up this question and discuss it carefully, were it not so large a question. It would, however, require all the remaining papers of this series even to sketch it in outline. It may be said, too, that important as this question is, the amount of land in proportion to our needs is still large, and it is a problem of to-morrow rather than of to-day. However, it is sufficiently a question of to-day to warrant indignation at the way in which our public domains have been squandered and empires of valuable lands have been conferred on private corporations. The more vigorous efforts — inadequate as they are — to guard the interests of the public against land plunderers are encouraging. It is to be hoped that a further step will be taken and that the Pre-emption, Timber Culture and Desert-land Acts will be repealed. The Homestead Act should be the only settlement law of the country, and even that I should like to see amended, although I will not take time to describe the desired amendment here. Unfortunate as have been some of the phases of the agitation of Henry George, I cannot but think that the world owes him a debt of gratitude for placing in a clear light before the masses the fact that land is a natural monopoly. The ugly feature of his agitation is his proposed confiscation of the rent of land ; but the view which Cardinal Gibbons — if current reports may be trusted — takes of his contemplated measure seems to me most sensible. I do not believe it will ever appear to the American people a just thing to take the property of land-owners without compensation. I do not believe that the moral sense of the American people will ever tolerate any serious steps looking to the confiscation of this species of property. To me — whatever false accusation may have been brought against me to the contrary notwithstanding — it has ever appeared a cruel and unjust thing to do, and thus I have always taught. However, it seems to me — as to Cardinal Gibbons evidently — a waste of breath to refute the errors of Henry George. They are not a living issue. It is, however, worth our while diligently to read a book like " Progress and Poverty," and to gather from it the useful lessons which it undoubtedly teaches. With this I leave the land question for the present and pass over to other natural monopolies.

CHAPTER XVIII.

NATURAL MONOPOLIES AND COMPETITION.

EVIDENCE of the increasing indignation with which monopolies are viewed by the public accumulates daily. Mr. Rayner, who represents a Maryland constituency, has brought a bill into Congress for the suppression of trusts and other corporate combinations, while an investigation into this subject has actually been ordered. A similar bill has been brought forward in the legislature of New York, and in Illinois proceedings against the Chicago Gas Trust have been instituted. Can any question be more thoroughly alive than this? And is it not worth while to carefully consider the subject of monopolies in all its ramifications, in order that we may know how to deal with it practically? The truth is that we have come to a critical period in our economic development, and a great opportunity is offered our various legislative bodies to do something of permanent benefit for the people. When a learned judge, well-known in Baltimore, heard some time ago that I intended to write a series of articles on corporations, he sent me this message: "Lay on and spare not." The time has come when legislators and congressmen may "lay on and spare not," and feel sure that the people will support them. I dislike to mention the name of Cardinal Gibbons again, because I wish to keep this series of articles as free from personalities as possible, but I cannot refrain from mention of his able paper on the Knights of Labor, which, it seems to me, is a document of historical importance, and that on this account : He said in that letter that the time had come in the world's history when the church should seek an alliance with the masses, and should abandon special efforts to conciliate the mighty in war, the powerful in trade, the great ones of this earth, because in the future the control of the destinies of the world rested with the people. It seems to me that there never was so auspicious a time for a great popular leader as now. Such an one cutting loose from the influence of corporate combinations and all special interests, could become a veritable Moses for the American people and win immortal fame. But who has, on the one hand, the moral character, coupled with the qualities of leadership, and, on the other, the strength of intellect requisite for a correct apprehension of our social, industrial, and political situation? It is too much to be feared that this opportunity will be allowed to slip by, and through failure to discriminate between various classes of monopolies and to treat each by itself, absolutely nothing of permanent utility will be accomplished. The grangers in our Western states gained complete control of several legislatures and endeavored to restrain corporations from domination in the future. But what did they accomplish? Something undoubtedly. Yet it may be questioned whether corporate domination was ever so marked in our West as it is to-day, and every one knows that a considerable portion of what was done has since been undone. It strikes me that the farmers have been worsted in the conflict. Now, what is the reason that they have been driven from their vantage-ground and routed? Simply because they did not understand the nature of the subjects with which they were dealing.

When we hear speeches on monopolies now, and read articles on combinations, one thought is found to be clearly brought forward, and only one. It is this : Competition is our salvation ; competition is the life of trade ; combinations prevent competition, consequently they are injurious and should be abolished. Stated in this general form, the proposition is not true. Competition is not always a good thing ; competition does not always lower prices ; on the contrary, it frequently raises prices ; competition is not always a possibility ; competition has produced marvellous results in those pursuits which are adapted to competition, and the unwarranted conclusion is drawn from this fact that competition everywhere and at all times is a good thing. The practical danger which confronts us is this : that in attempting to force the application of the principles of competition to those pursuits which are not adapted to competition we will miss our present opportunity and do more harm than good.

There are certain businesses which are in their very nature — by reason, I mean, of their own inherent qualities — monopolies. These we call natural monopolies, and any endeavor to regulate natural and artificial monopolies by the same law is predestined to failure in the future, as it always has failed in the past. Had, indeed, the problem of natural monopolies been solved in the past, there would be few artificial monopolies, and these could be managed without difficulty. Natural monopolies are the basis of all monopolies of modern times.

The fact that certain businesses are natural monopolies has been so amply shown both by actual experience and by an elaboration of economic principles that I can scarcely regard it as anything else than an evidence of ignorance for any one to deny it ; yet our habits of thought are so governed by principles of competition that it is difficult to make this clear to those not accustomed to economic discussions. I beg my readers, therefore, to be patient while I attempt to explain very carefully, and at as much length as this series of papers will warrant, the doctrine of natural monopolies.

It will be most convenient to begin by an enumeration of those businesses which are natural monopolies. They are gas supply, street-car service, highways and streets, electric lighting, all railways, canals, bridges, lighthouses, ferries, docks, harbors, natural navigations, postal service, telegraphs and telephones. This, doubtless, does not include all natural monopolies, but with the exception of land, which will not be discussed, it embraces all the more important natural monopolies existing at the present time. It is claimed that the regulation of these natural monopolies must be different from the regulation of commerce, agriculture, and manufactures, because the underlying principles of these pursuits are peculiar. Now, it must not be supposed that competition is never felt by those who are interested in natural monopolies. On the contrary, they at times feel the keenest kind of competition. A pursuit is a natural monopoly when it is excluded from the steady, constant pressure of competition. When natural monopolies are engaged in industrial contests, these contests can after all scarcely be called competition, and popular instinct feels this, for it finds involuntary expression in language. We speak of struggles between natural monopolies as war. " A war has broken out between the gas companies," or between the trunk line railways, people say, and it is war in its characteristics. It is destructive, and has, like war, a termination of hostilities in view. Competition, on the other hand, never terminates. It is not a fierce and destructive onslaught, but a steady pressure which tends to stimulate enterprise and to bring about fair dealing. Compare a firm like Ham-

ilton Easter & Co. with the Consolidated Gas Company.
The one is subject to assaults from time to time which
always terminate, and must as surely terminate as to-morrow's sun must rise, while it can scarcely enter into the
range of human probabilities that the other can ever terminate.   It is hoped that the difference is clear.   If it is clear,
the reader will at once perceive the fallacies of those who
claim that government should no more send telegrams than
grind wheat into flour or convert the flour into bread.   This
is a favorite argument with monopolists, and is thus stated
in a recent editorial in a journal published in a neighboring
city : " There is no more reason why the government should
operate the telegraph than run the flour mills — less, in
fact, for everybody uses flour, while it is doubtful if even
three per cent. of the people use the telegraph."   It would
be hard to pack more errors into one short sentence.   The
one pursuit is a natural monopoly, the other not, and what
holds with one is not applicable to the other.   Secondly,
charges for the use of a natural monopoly are part of the
expenses of business, and, like indirect taxes, are shifted to
the consumer and felt by everybody.

While certain pursuits are liable to be injured by war,
they are not and cannot be subject to the steady pressure of
competition.   These pursuits are natural monopolies.   We
will be helped to understand why they are natural monopolies if some of their peculiarities are described, and I will
quote from a recent careful writer, and then pass on to a
further consideration of certain puzzling phenomena connected with natural monopolies : —

" 1. What they supply is necessary.

" 2. They occupy peculiarly favored spots or lines of land.

" 3. The article or convenience they supply is used at the

place where, and in connection with, the plant or machinery by which it is supplied.

" 4. This article or convenience can in general be largely, if not indefinitely, increased without proportionate increase in plant and capital.

" 5. Certainty and harmonious arrangement, which can only be obtained by unity, are paramount considerations."

CHAPTER XIX.

NATURAL MONOPOLIES FURTHER ELUCIDATED.

THE qualities of natural monopolies enumerated in the previous article are sufficient to show one versed in the principles of industrial society why those pursuits to which these qualities pertain must be monopolies. They can hardly be regarded as entirely satisfactory to one to whom economic discussions are not familiar. It is said that Agassiz could draw a picture of an animal if he but saw a single bone which had once been part of its frame, because natural laws which he had grasped showed him that the peculiarities of the bone which he saw necessarily determined the structure of the animal which he did not see. It is not enough, however, for us not versed in natural science to see a bone ; we want a complete drawing of the animal. It is similar with regard to economic institutions, only that there is this important difference : political economy is not so far advanced as natural science, and the political economist has not so marked an advantage in his specialty over the ordinary man.

The reason why some pursuits are monopolies may be stated in a somewhat different way. Why do men enter business? To make money. This is the dominant motive, and this keeps the world going. I do not mean that men are not animated by other motives, nor would I have it thought that even all commercial transactions can be explained by the pursuit of gain. I simply state that this motive is sufficient for our present purposes, and that ordinarily, if a man in business is permanently — not temporarily, but steadily, year after year — losing money, it is a sign that his activity is wasteful, involving a loss to the community as well as to himself. Having fixed the fact in mind that the dominant motive in business is gain, it follows naturally that those business methods which yield most gain are bound to prevail and to drive from the field of competition less profitable business methods. We have in these two simple facts an explanation of natural monopolies. Businesses of the kind mentioned can be most advantageously pursued under the form of monopoly. The services or things which they supply can be thus produced not merely for a smaller expenditure of labor or capital, but for a far smaller expenditure. There is, consequently, always an increase in gain for those men interested in natural monopolies who can bring about a combination ; and this increase in gain is a constant, never-ceasing attraction, tending to bring rivals together. It is a steady force, like the attraction of gravitation, and it will act in spite of all legislative enactment. It transcends in power any state legislature and even the federal Congress. But I go further than this. From the standpoint of political economy, which desires a cheap and abundant production of goods and services, the monopolistic method of production for those pursuits which are natural monopolies is not merely something inevitable — it is something desirable ; for attempts at competition waste the national resources and tend to bring about commercial crises and stagnation in business. We want monopoly in gas supply, water supply, and the like ; the only question is, what kind of a monopoly ?

Perhaps the tendency to monopoly will be made clearer by an illustration. Let us suppose two gas companies are competing, and each has a capital of $1,000,000. The total capital engaged in the gas business is $2,000,000. If the two consolidate, the amount of capital already invested will not be materially lessened, but expenses will be reduced. Instead of two central offices there will be but one, and the duplication of mains will be avoided for the future. Fewer collectors will be needed, fewer men to distribute bills, fewer men to put in meters, and the increased output of gas will not be attended with a proportionate increase of cost. If it costs a certain sum to manufacture ten million cubic feet of gas, it will not cost twice as much to manufacture twenty millions. This article can " be largely, if not indefinitely, increased, without proportionate increase in plant and capital." There is, then, always a very considerable advantage in combination.

It may be asked, then, Why are there so many attempts at competition? The answer is very simple. The number of enterprises in gas supply which attempt legitimate competition is extremely small, and can only be made by those who do not understand the business. Most apparent attempts at competition are simply raids on a company which has a good business ; and the end in view is a division of the business and a participation in the spoils. A test is easy. When a new gas company is formed in the interest of the "dear people," in order to give them, as it is usually said, the benefits of competition, let the confident citizen take the managers at their word and ask them to make a contract to supply gas at the current low rate for a number of years, and he will find that they will refuse. Rates go down and a bitter struggle ensues ; but it is not competition. It is a fight for mastery. The only question at issue is, Under what terms shall we combine or in what manner shall territory be divided? This has no special reference to Baltimore, for our case is but one of thousands, although I believe it rarely takes so long to come to an agreement. Nevertheless here, as elsewhere, it is only a matter of time ; and should in the future a thousand new companies be established, the result would be combination, for natural laws bring it about, and no one can help it.[1] While we have the testimony of reason, we are not restricted to that, for we have the testimony of experience. It is probably within bounds to say that over three thousand, very likely ten thousand, attempts at competition in gas supply have been made in this and other countries ; and *the civilized world has yet to show the first instance of permanent, successful competition in gas supply.* And this natural monopoly is not different from others, but is selected for special consideration because it is more easily understood on account of the restricted scope of action of a single gas company. It must not be supposed that the amount of capital required for an undertaking is an essential factor in determining whether it shall be a natural monopoly or not, for this is variable, and it often happens that a business always subject to competition has a larger capital than one which has the field all to itself. A bank may, often does, have a larger capital than a gas company ; so may a dry-goods establishment. Professor Henry C. Adams, in his monograph on the " Relation of the State to Industrial Action," divides business into three classes, namely : (1) those of diminishing returns; (2) those of constant returns ; (3) those of increasing returns. An undertaking is a business of diminishing returns when after a certain point, soon reached, an additional investment of labor and capital is not attended with proportional returns. Agriculture is the best illustration. After a farmer

---

[1] Since I wrote the above a formal consolidation of the three Baltimore gas companies has taken place.

puts a certain amount of labor and capital on a field of corn, he says it does not pay to invest more. If corn ought to be hoed three times, it may be of some use to hoe it four times, but the additional return will not be large enough to make it pay. The fourth hoeing yields far less than the third, the fifth far less than the fourth, and so on. Similarly, after a farm of suitable size has been brought under cultivation by one farmer, he will find that to extend operations, buy more land, and put more labor and capital into agriculture will not pay. Consequently, for one man to attempt to get a monopoly in farming is an absurdity. It cannot be done. After a certain point has been reached, returns fall off, and a man operating on a smaller scale has an advantage. Commerce and manufactures are businesses of constant returns. After a business has attained a normal size, additional investments will be accompanied at best with constant returns, and the manager will have no advantage over others by reason of an excessive amount of capital. It is surprising how far a gifted business man in our days can profitably extend his business ; but every one reaches his limit, and, except in case of artificial barriers, like protective tariffs, merchants and manufacturers, like farmers, always feel the pressure of competition. Enterprises which fall under the third class are quite different. The larger the business, the greater the relative profit ; and so there is always an inducement for an enlargement of the field of operations.

But this is not all. When it is stated that a business becomes relatively more profitable in proportion as the amount of capital invested increases, it is already granted that large concerns have the power to crush small ones ; for if business is more profitable, it is because production is cheaper, and if the big man produces cheaper he will crush the little man.

The principles of competition are, then, totally inapplicable to natural monopolies. Competition is impossible, and attempted competition wastes capital and ultimately raises prices. The temporarily low prices during industrial wars are illusory. Let us come back to the convenient illustration of gas supply. A practical man demonstrated before an association of gas manufacturers recently that gas could be made and sold for a handsome profit at fifty cents a thousand. This demonstration was printed in a journal devoted to the gas interest, and I am not aware that among themselves gas men have denied it. Yet there are few American cities where it can profitably be made to-day by existing companies for less than twice that, and even one dollar a thousand is considered cheap gas. Why? Simply because destructive gas wars have wasted property, increased the fixed charges which gas companies must meet, and rolled up their capitalization out of all reason. No honest man who knows anything about the business will deny this. General John Newton said recently that gas in New York City could profitably be supplied for seventy-five cents a thousand, and the high price he attributed to the wastes of competition, as seen in the duplication of mains by rival gas companies. Further proof of this statement is seen in the fact that cities which supply their own gas and exclude competition can do so for less than a dollar. Hon. Joseph Chamberlain when in Baltimore told one of my colleagues that the city of Birmingham, England, purchased the gasworks at his instigation when he was mayor, and that the results were most fortunate. Another colleague of mine, who has lived in Manchester, tells me that he never paid over sixty-four cents a thousand, and yet this price yields a handsome profit and has enabled the city to carry forward improvements without burden to the tax-payers. Some towns in Scotland supply gas for less than fifty cents, and I have even heard of a twenty-five-cent rate, though for that I will not vouch.

The following is an official statement of the gas-works in Wheeling, West Virginia : City bought the works in 1871 for $100,000. They were free from debt in 1880. Present value $500,000. Returns in 1887 were $39,000, from which $6000 must be deducted for payment of city debt, and $21,000 for "repairs, etc.," leaving $12,000 net. Rates, $1.50, later $1.20, and now 90 cents.[1] The number of inhabitants is 35,000.

We ought to have gas for fifty cents in Baltimore. Now, cheap gas is a great help to manufacturers, and especially to those doing business on a small scale. Thus a correct policy in regard to this natural monopoly helps to keep competition alive by preventing all unnatural and artificial monopolies.

[1] Since reduced to seventy-five cents.

CHAPTER XX.

THE PROPER METHOD OF DEALING WITH GAS SUPPLY AND STREET RAILROADS.

SINCE I wrote the last chapter, a gentleman who has lived in Belfast, Ireland, for some time has had the kindness to send me a letter about the experience of the people of that city with the gas supply, and as it is merely typical, I will quote some extracts from the letter: "I have had some experience of the gas supply for the town of Belfast. About fifteen years ago the town council obtained powers to purchase the gas-works, etc., of the company then supplying the town. The purchase-money was borrowed from the government. At the time the council took over the works the gas company were charging something like five shillings ($1.20) per 1000 feet. Under the management of the gas committee, the interest on the purchase-money and the requirements of the sinking fund for the payment of the debt have not only been met, but the committee have been able to make gradual reductions in the price to customers. The price, I believe, is now two shillings and nine pence (66 cents) per 1000 feet, and the profits would justify a greater reduction, but I understand the committee is strengthening its position and continually improving plant and machinery. When it is considered that Belfast has to import all its coal from England and Scotland, it can readily be seen that gas should be supplied at a very small figure in towns conveniently situated to coal mines. Two years ago the Belfast gas committee held an exhibition of gas stoves and gas-heating appliances, etc., and the exhibition has induced many to use the gas for motive power and cooking, etc. . . . Under the English 'Towns Improvement Act,' town commissioners can obtain compulsory powers to purchase gas companies, etc., if considered for the benefit of the public. It would be a great blessing if such powers were conferred upon town authorities in this country."

The American consul at Leeds tells me that the people of that city are well supplied with gas at forty-four cents a thousand.

There are several things which may be done in view of the fact that the gas supply is a natural monopoly, and one thing which clearly should not be done. It should never be attempted to introduce or compel competition between rival companies, for the result is only evil. Not one particle of good can accrue to the public by attempted competition. Streets are torn up and pavements are never properly relaid. This injures the health of citizens, for nothing is better calculated to promote malaria, — as many of us in Baltimore know to our sorrow, — and it wastes our property. If it is urged that money is spent, I reply that such a plea for competition proceeds either from ignorance or demagogism. What is spent is wasted, and if not so spent, it would have been employed in some other enterprise, very likely a legitimate enterprise which would have really benefited the people.

One of the things which may be done is to recognize the fact that an existing company has a monopoly, and to make it a legal monopoly in return for concessions. This was done in a Southern city recently. It was proposed to allow a rival company the privilege of laying pipes in the streets, and supplying the citizens with gas, and the members of the

municipal council were at first carried away with the idea of
competition, and to what extremes men go in the direction
of a popular illusion is shown by the statement of one
member, that competition in itself was a good thing, even if
it accomplished nothing. A gifted young lawyer, however,
who had read James on Gas Supply, went before the council,
and, with every member against him at the start, was able to
convince them of the folly of rival companies. The result
was that the existing company agreed to limit its price at
once, and in a certain contingency to lower it in the future.
The proper method for the city authorities to follow in the
case of gas supply, provided it does not furnish gas itself, is
very simple. The franchise should be sold at public auction,
widely advertised, for fifteen years, when it should expire, the
city reserving the right of purchase of the works at the expiration of the period for an appraised valuation. It should
be made clear that plant and other property of the corporation should be purchased only at their value at the time,
" having regard to their condition and their suitability to the
purpose of the undertaking, but without any addition for
compulsory purchase, good-will, or future profits."

This method, or, in fact, any method of private ownership,
leads to entanglement of public and private interests, which
is demoralizing, for nothing promotes corruption like com-
plexity in administration, while nothing is more wholesome
than simplicity in administration. It is desirable to separate
by as sharp a line as possible public and private undertakings, and this end can best be accomplished by ownership
of gas-works by municipalities. It is on this account that I
recommend in my report as tax commissioner that the
Maryland legislature refuse hereafter to grant any charter
to any private corporation to supply gas or water within the
borders of our state. A constitutional amendment prevent-

ing the legislature from granting any such charter would be desirable.　Nothing could be more calculated to prevent corruption and purify government, for nothing has so corrupted and debased our political life as private corporations in control of natural monopolies.　We have got so used to municipal corruption that it seems to us as something inevitable, but such is not the case.　I have lived for years in cities in which the breath of suspicion never touched the municipal government, where corruption and methods of avoiding it were not at all the questions of the day; and when the Hon. Joseph Chamberlain addressed the students of Johns Hopkins University, he claimed for municipal administration in England that it was above reproach.　It is idle for us to say "we must wait until we become morally better."　I believe we are as moral a people to-day as the English or the Germans.　Our terrible corruption in cities dates from the rise of private corporations in control of natural monopolies, and when we abolish them we do away with the chief cause of corruption.

"But we must take natural monopolies out of politics." It never has been done, and it is an impossible thing to do — absolutely impossible.　No gas-works, no water-works, no street-car lines, no steam railways, are so thoroughly in politics as those in the United States.　Who is so innocent as to think our great railway corporations "out of politics"? Any one so simple would have done well to spend a few weeks in the past winter in Washington or Annapolis and keep his eyes and ears open.　When I was in Berlin some years ago I made a report on Prussian railroads, under the direction of the American minister, Hon. Andrew D. White, for the Department of State at Washington.　Every facility was afforded me for my investigation, and my inquiry into the political effect of state ownership, which obtains in Germany, was most careful. Since that time I have followed the development of the Prussian policy with some care, and it cannot be charged that I have been influenced by the government view, for my favorite German newspaper — the only one which I take — is bitterly hostile to the existing government. I make bold to say that to-day our American railroads are incomparably more "in politics" than the German railroads. Not only this; those German railroads which have been bought by the state, I believe, are less "in politics" than they were when they were private property. Why this must be so will be considered hereafter. But the reader must not jump at the conclusion that I am going to advocate complete public ownership and management of all natural monopolies at the present time in the United States. I am going to do nothing of the kind. However, I unhesitatingly advocate such ownership and management for gas-works, and I challenge any one to instance a single American city — or, for that matter, any city, wheresoever situated — which has gone over to public ownership and which regrets it; which, indeed, has not found that a corrupt political influence was thereby removed and political life purified. The most unfortunate city in the world with its public gas-works has been Philadelphia; but when it was proposed to sell the gas-works, and when a ring had "fixed" the council, as well as many of the newspapers, there was such an outbreak of popular indignation, with hints of the penitentiary, that the council was terrified into doing its duty.

Street railroads are one of the most important natural monopolies, and a tendency for public ownership and management is beginning to become manifest. In the United States, however, there is but one public street railroad, and that is the one which is operated in connection with the Brooklyn bridge. Although it is said to be the best managed street railroad in the country, I am not prepared to advocate public ownership in Baltimore at present. What we want is the New Orleans system, and that is what I have recommended in my report on taxation. It is sale of franchise, with reserved right to purchase all the property, that is, land, buildings, horses, cars — in short, all the plant — at an appraised valuation at the expiration of a short period, say fifteen years. In this, as in every case of natural monopoly, it should be made perfectly clear that no compensation ought to be granted for compulsory purchase, good-will, or expectation of future profits. This yields a large revenue to the city and leaves the people free at the expiration of each period to adopt any system of street railroad service which they see fit. It works very well in New Orleans, where in 1886 nearly one-eighth of all municipal expenditures was defrayed by the sale of a single franchise for twenty-five years — the maximum period for which one should ever be granted.

When the first franchise was granted in Baltimore, in 1859, the mayor of the city appears to have been a man of rare integrity, for through him the right to acquire the most important street railroads at the expiration of each period of fifteen years, was reserved to the city, and in 1889 the city again comes into possession of a most valuable privilege. A franchise which now yields nine per cent. of gross revenues could be sold probably for twenty-five per cent. In New York City a franchise has been sold for forty per cent. of gross revenues, and in Buffalo, New York, half the size of Baltimore, thirty per cent. was offered for one.

What I should like to see, however, is the introduction of another system, which is hinted at in one of our acts of incorporation ; namely, reduction of fares. There is not a shadow of a doubt that passengers could be carried in Baltimore for three cents — more than is charged in Berlin, where the companies must keep the streets paved from curb to curb, must provide each passenger with a seat, must, in laying tracks, have some respect for the rights of owners of vehicles, and do a thousand and one things which an American corporation does not dream of, to say nothing about that fact that in 1911 their entire property reverts to the city without compensation. The report of the tax commission — and in this respect there was unanimity of opinion, for the other members agreed to my report — speaks of rendering proper methods of dealing with natural monopolies compulsory upon legislatures and municipalities. The people must do this, for their representatives in our days of "government by special interests" love corporations better than they do the people.[1]   It was for a long time supposed that the people had no rights which anybody was bound to respect, and you could even find professing Christians — men who claim that they love their neighbors as themselves — bartering away for a mess of pottage the rights of the public, women and children, and even unborn generations. Were Christ on earth, I expect He would call them liars and hypocrites. However, imprisonment of New York City aldermen in Sing Sing, and the conviction of Jacob Sharp, even if it proved a fiasco in the end, has helped to clarify somewhat the ideas of men with regard to the rights of the public. WHAT IS NOW NEEDED IS IN EVERY CITY A PUBLIC PROPERTY DEFENCE LEAGUE TO WATCH THE INTERESTS OF THE PUBLIC, AND TO HUNT DOWN AND SEND TO THE PENITENTIARY THOSE WHO FORGET THAT PUBLIC OFFICE IS A PUBLIC TRUST.

[1] A gentleman who suggested to certain office-holders in the Baltimore City Hall that the city should acquire the franchises which expire in 1889, was told that "We do not want to speculate off our own citizens." That is what they call protecting public property and public rights: "speculating off our own citizens." It is not difficult to imagine the causes of such strangely perverted moral views.

CHAPTER XXI.

WATER SUPPLY AND ELECTRIC LIGHTS.

THE next natural monopoly to be considered is water supply, and comparatively little need be said about this, for the principles which control it are precisely like those governing the gas supply, save that the reasons for public undertakings are still stronger. It is more easily managed, and the importance of general use of water in large quantities cannot be overestimated. One of our special blessings in Baltimore is our abundant supply, and it is questionable whether any special charge should be made for its use. Certain it is that the advantage of our public service over any private service must be measured by millions of dollars. It is true that on account of our water supply the number of municipal employés is larger than it would otherwise be, but he would be a bold man who would claim that our water supply has corrupted our politics a hundredth part as much as natural monopolies owned by private corporations. I have made special investigation of water supply in several towns, and I have yet to find one instance in which municipal self-help did not work better than the beneficent paternalism of private corporations. I have looked into the experience of a whole group of towns in New York state, and they all tell one story. I have before me as I write complete and trustworthy returns of two or three of these, procured with some labor by the exertions of friends. The experience of Randolph, in Cattaraugus County,

New York, tells the story for all. A private company wanted to put in water-works, and the lowest bid which they could be induced to make was $28,000, and that was under condition that the town should subscribe for stock. The charge for water was to be $10 for a household, with additional charges for extra faucets, closets, etc., in proportion Randolph finally built its own works for a total cost of $20,299.86, and with a charge of $4 for each household, instead of $10, is making a profit. Everybody is delighted with the experiment.[1] Gowanda, in the same county, has

[1] The following statement was sent me by a gentlemen living in Randolph : —

MEMORANDUM OF THE CONSTRUCTION AND OPERATION OF RANDOLPH (CATTARAUGUS COUNTY, NEW YORK), WATER-WORKS.

Dec. 19, 1885.	Cost of construction to date .	$19,997	75
June 9, 1886.	Building spring-houses and fen- cing reservoirs	29	86
Sept.-30, 1886.	Cost of two extensions . . .	272	25
	Total cost	$20,299	86
Jan. 1, 1888.	131 consumers paying a rental per annum of	$991	00
	The prices charged by water companies to villages in this section is $45 to $50 per hydrant. We have 17 hydrants at $45	765	00
		$1,756	00

Our bonded debt is $20,000, on which the interest is four per cent. per annum 800 00
The water-works are built on the gravity system. Have nearly five miles of pipe laid, and the total expenses of operating the first year were 75
Expenses of operating for 1887 . . . . . . 2 40
The village has a population of about 1200, and

had a similar experience, as have Fredonia and Dunkirk, in Chautauqua County, while the neighboring city of Jamestown tried the private corporation plan to its sorrow. The gentleman who sent me the account of the Randolph experiment writes me : " As to Jamestown, I have heard nothing but complaints." As I write, a gentleman who has entered my office tells me about the still more unfortunate experience of the people of Galesburg, Illinois, with private water-works. They have been so annoyed by failure of the company to fulfil its promises, and by perpetual litigation, that they would now gladly purchase the works, which have been idle for two years. Jamestown would gladly do the same, and it actually secured the passage of a bill through the legislature for the construction of gas-works, but it was vetoed on some constitutional pretext. Bradford, in Pennsylvania, not far from these towns in New York, the experience of which I have examined, tried private water-works, and, dissatisfied, finally bought out the private company, and is perfectly satisfied with the experiment of public water-works. The rates charged per year for one household by the company were $20 a year, by the city $8 a year. The works were owned by the company, for four years, and complaints were made of inadequate supply, of impurity of water, and high rates. An enthusiastic citizen of Bradford writes that since the purchase of works by the city, they

there will be a good many more consumers. Previous to constructing these water-works for the village a company was partly organized here to build on another plan, and they made a schedule of rates for household use at per annum 10 00

With extra faucets, closets, etc., in proportion, I enclose a schedule of water-rates from which please see we make ours per annum . . .   4 00

" have the best water of any city in the United States, and our fire companies and our fire protection cannot be beaten by any city of our size." It is interesting to notice that in Fredonia, New York, all the traditional arguments against public undertakings were brought forward. It was said that private enterprise was superior, that the public always made a fiasco with its undertakings, and the like, and opponents of the measure specially called attention to the Albany capitol, which has proved such an expensive undertaking for the state. This Albany capitol argument is always made to do duty on such occasions. Good sense, nevertheless, triumphed. The water-works were constructed within the original estimates, and they are successful in every respect. It would take a powerful microscope to discern that these works have introduced any corruption into village life. The plan of private companies is to get the towns to subscribe for a sufficient number of hydrants at a sufficient sum for each to pay nearly the entire interest on the total outlay, and all the other revenues are then clear profit. A gentleman who is attorney for one of the large companies engaged in supplying towns with water-works told me that his skill had been taxed in assisting them to pump water enough into their stock. It had been watered again and again, and it was still necessary to add to it to conceal the enormous profits.

When we take up electric lights, we shall find no reason to abandon the principle of local self-government and municipal self-help. No organization is doing so much to throw light on these questions as the American Economic Association, and no organization is more deserving of the hearty support of every patriotic American. One of its most useful publications is a monograph on municipal public works, from which I give a few facts. The part on electric lighting is contributed by Charles Moore, Esq., editor of the Detroit *Evening News* and is most interesting. Bay City, Michigan, put in a plant in October, 1886, and supplied lights for $42 each per year, whereas it had been paying a private company $100 per year.

"Lewiston, Maine, owns its plant," says Mr. Moore, "and by the use of water power has reduced the cost to 14 cents per lamp per night, or $51.10 per year. The plant for 100 arc lights cost $14,500; the cost of construction was $450 per running mile. The price paid under contract was from 55 to 65 cents for lights burning only till midnight. Now, at a cost of 14 cents each, the lights burn all night."

Madison, Indiana, also appears to have obtained good results from public works.

It may be asked, Why are these facts not generally known? One reason is that so many of our great newspapers are completely under the control of corporations, — for other cities are not so fortunate as we are in Baltimore, — and every instance of a failure of public works is heralded abroad to the four corners of the earth, while examples of success are not discussed. Who talks about our Baltimore City Hall, which was built for $200,000 less than the appropriation, or the fine public building put up in Indianapolis, Indiana, for less than the appropriation? These examples are not isolated. Careful inquiry will reveal an astonishing number. When, however, extravagance and comparative failure characterize a public enterprise, like the capitol at Albany, we never hear the last of it — as if private enterprise were not frequently a failure! The truth is, private enterprise generally, in its own sphere, — agriculture, commerce, manufactures, — goes far ahead of public enterprise; but in its own sphere public enterprise will in the long run go far ahead of private undertakings.

When we take up railroads we again turn from municipal problems to state and federal problems, and we enter upon a discussion which, while it is equally interesting, is more difficult of comprehension, for the operations of this natural monopoly are vast and far-reaching. Not only are the principles somewhat hard to understand, but the correct practice among us is not at once discernible, for it must be granted that federal ownership and management of railroads is a thing so far off that it does not enter into practical politics to-day. I will, however, try in my following chapter, to make a few principles clear, and to lay down certain practical rules which should govern us in our dealings with railroads.

CHAPTER XXII.

WAR AND CONSOLIDATION THE RESULT OF RAILROAD COMPETITION.

SOME years since I was passing a summer in a village in Western New York, Fredonia by name. The only railroad which the Fredonians could then use in going to Buffalo, about forty miles distant, was the Lake Shore and Michigan Southern, and the rates, three cents a mile, were felt to be excessive for so old and thickly settled a country. There was — as there still is — a provision in the charter of the old Lake Shore Road that fares should be reduced as soon as dividends reached a certain point, which, of course, they never have reached and never will reach. How the people like to be humbugged! But at this time a parallel railroad, the "Nickel Plate," from Buffalo to Chicago, was in process of construction, and the Fredonians were enthusiastic over the prospect of cheap tickets to Buffalo. I well remember the exclamation of a lady on the street-cars, "Now we are going to have cheap tickets to Buffalo!" and I can see as if it had happened but yesterday the attorney for the "Nickel Plate," to whom she was speaking, as he beamed assent from his benevolent countenance. Any one who knew anything about the economic principles controlling railroads, who had grasped even a few elementary facts about natural monopolies, could have told the people that they were doomed to disappointment in their hope of permanent relief from the competition of a parallel road;

but the illusion had taken such a strong hold on them that remonstrance was worse than useless. I felt tempted to call in question their predictions, but it is not pleasant to be called a crank or " mere theorist," so I held my peace and awaited developments. The road was built and has now become the property, to all intents and purposes, of the Lake Shore! Fares were never reduced. Single tickets to Buffalo are just what they have been for years, and round-trip tickets have — if my memory serves me correctly — been raised five cents. What earthly good has been accomplished by this parallel road? Doubtless speculators and construction companies put money in their pockets, but the people are poorer on account of the enormous waste of national resources. The fixed charges of the Lake Shore have been increased, its capital invested has been augmented, and a reduction, upon which the legislature could once have insisted, would probably now bankrupt the road.

Another bubble burst about the same time and in the same state. I refer to the West Shore Road, which parallels the New York Central and Hudson River Railway. What was not that going to accomplish! As a matter of fact a railroad war did break out, and passenger tickets fell to one-half the former rates for a short time. This was war, — not competition, — and the West Shore was beaten, badly beaten, and leased its lines for 499 years to the New York Central. Before this happened, however, passenger fares had been restored to their old rates, and a reduction, which would once have been practicable, is now out of the question.

It is estimated that the money wasted by these two single attempts at competition amounts to two hundred millions of dollars. Let the reader reflect for a moment on what this means. It will be admitted that, taking city and country together, comfortable homes can be constructed for an average of $1000 each. Two hundred thousand houses could be constructed for the sum wasted, and two hundred thousand houses means homes for one million people ! I suppose it is a very moderate estimate to place the amount wasted in the construction of useless railroads at a thousand millions, which, on the basis of our previous calculations, would construct homes for five millions of people. But this is probably altogether too small an estimate of even the direct waste resulting from the application of a faulty political economy to practical life. When the indirect losses are added, the result is something astounding, for the expense of a needless number of trains and of what would otherwise be an excessively large permanent force of employés must be added. Of course, nothing much better than guesswork is possible, but I believe that the total loss would be sufficient to provide a greater portion of the people of the United States with homes.

There is something almost pathetic in the amazement and disappointment of the general public when the Nickel Plate and West Shore were absorbed, and the same thing was seen in Baltimore last fall when the gas companies agreed to consolidate and when the Baltimore and Ohio telegraph lines were acquired by the Western Union. Attempts to prevent such consolidation had been made by legislation. A purchase of the West Shore would have been illegal, but a lease for 499 years was not ! The Baltimore and Ohio was required to give bonds in Philadelphia, to be forfeited in case of failure to compete. All this was as childish as the anger of the public on account of these various consolidations. Competition is foreign to the nature of natural monopolies, and all the laws of Congress and of state legislatures to force competition upon them will be as fruitless in the future as they have been in the past.   As well legislate that the water of all rivers shall flow up instead of down !   The anger of the public on account of these consolidations has always reminded me of the opposition of artisans and mechanics to the introduction of new machinery.   Resistance is fruitless, and the only sensible course is to recognize the inevitable and make the most of it ; and much can be made of it by the exercise of a little common sense.   Mr. Vanderbilt in acquiring the West Shore was as truly effecting an improvement in the processes of production as the one who introduces improved machinery in manufactures, for he made it thereby possible to perform certain services for the public with a smaller expenditure of labor and capital than would otherwise be possible.

There are certain phenomena connected with railroads in the United States which at first are likely to puzzle one who has just begun to doubt the efficacy of competition in the field of natural monopolies.   These are, for the most part, intimately associated with the fact that our railroad development is still incomplete, and the consequences of various policies are, therefore, not so clearly discernible as in an older country.   Probably England is the best country for an American to study who desires to see the legitimate effects of competition, for England started out with our theory of private competition, and under its influence two natural monopolies — the telegraph and the railroad — were fully developed.   I say developed, because little remains to be done in either direction.   A few minor extensions may be made, and a few branch roads constructed, but the general features are complete.   First, just one word about the telegraph policy of England.   England tried to force competition, and this was the result.   Her telegraph system cost her nearly as much as all the other telegraph systems of

Europe put together, for the estimated cost of the English telegraph is 272,000,000 of francs, and of all the other telegraphs of Europe put together only 285,000,000 of francs. Probably the best work on English railroads is that by Professor Gustave Cohn, and in this it is shown that the ultimate effects of competition in every case have been higher charges.

It is said that rates have fallen in the United States. This is true; but has the cause been competition? Competition has undoubtedly brought about a reduction in some cases sooner than it would otherwise have happened; but as the country developed and became thickly populated, it was natural for rates to fall. The principles which control monopoly charges are simple. A man who has a complete monopoly will fix prices at that point which will yield largest net returns, and up to a certain point he will steadily reduce charges, as he thereby increases business and gains a larger total net revenue. The most striking instance is given by the history of the post-office throughout the civilized world. A reduction of over fifty per cent. in charges has ultimately increased net revenues. Another illustration is given by the Standard Oil monopoly. Newspaper organs of monopoly tell us to admire the magnanimity of the Standard Oil people, who have reduced prices. This is a false statement. Prices have fallen in spite of their most strenuous efforts to keep them up, and this again illustrates the importance of political economy as a study for common schools. It is possible to say such absurd things in regard to the price of oil simply on account of the dense popular ignorance about those forces which make prices what they are. The production of oil has increased enormously, and those among my readers who are acquainted with the Standard Oil men will probably have heard them lament this. Now if they raised prices or maintained them, they would be obliged to keep their oil and waste it. They have always held back vast quantities of oil to maintain prices, and rumors reach us of a determined effort to diminish production; but, nevertheless, it has been necessary to lower prices time and time again to work off the quantity on hand. Prices must be lowered in order to increase demand for the commodity.

Apply this to railroads. They have enormous fixed charges which are entirely independent of the business they do, and the greater their business the more active use they make of their capital. In proportion as a road is not used to its utmost capacity, its capital is idle. Now, to help build up the country and supply themselves with business, it has been necessary for our railroads to reduce charges, otherwise they could not get the business which they needed. A portion of their business would simply not exist were it not for lower charges than those of earlier days. This tendency to lower prices stops in the case of private monopolies at precisely that point where increased business is not attended with increased net profits. One point to be observed is this : Legislatures have a control over rates, and could in many cases lower them materially, had not the wastes of competition raised expenses of the railroads. Second, it must be remembered that the number of even nominally competitive points is, and ever must remain, small. According to the chief of the bureau of statistics, there were, January 1, 1887, 33,694 railroad stations in the United States, and of these only 2778 were junction points, and many of these junction points, *i.e.* places having more than one road, were on railroads which had no terminus in common.

More important is the real competition of natural water routes, which sometimes exists, though there is a determined effort to crush it out.   Last summer, at Chautauqua, I witnessed a typical instance.   The Chautauqua Lake Rail-road bought every line of steamers on the lake.   Artificial waterways,— namely, canals,— are also important where the people of a state have had the good sense to retain and improve them.   This has happened in New York State, which now proposes to spend a million on the Erie Canal. This Erie Canal has helped to make New York the powerful Empire state she is, and its maintenance was due to the statesman, Horatio Seymour.

A few years ago New York was bound hand and foot like Maryland by a senseless, iron-clad constitution, which threatened to hand her over to the clutches of the corpo-rations ; but Horatio Seymour aroused the people, got the state constitution amended, and, abolishing tolls, made the Erie Canal a *free waterway*.   A further consideration of railroads will lead us back to the subject of federal finan-ciering, after we have touched upon several other important topics.

CHAPTER XXIII.

PUBLIC ROADS AND CANALS.

I SUPPOSE nothing is more thoroughly a problem of to-day with us in Maryland than the fate of the Chesapeake and Ohio Canal. The subject has been much discussed, but the discussion has not been of a nature to inspire the patriot with enthusiasm for the future of his country. There has been such an absence of any clearly defined purpose, of any manifestation of enlightened views in regard to the various means of communication and transportation and their relations to one another, such an utter lack of large and generous statesmanship, that one is reminded of the expression " peanut politics " rather than of the activity of those two political leaders, Horatio Seymour and the earlier and still greater De Witt Clinton, whose names stand out so prominently in the history of canals in the United States. There are a few points in regard to canals in general which should be carefully considered before action is taken.

It is commonly said that the day of canals is past. This is only a little less rational than to say that the day of the ordinary highways is past, because we have the steam railroad. Each means of communication has its own use, and the office of each is not to displace the others, but to supplement the others. It was a misfortune for us that we began to neglect our public roads when the era of rapid railroad construction began, and in this one respect at least it would have been a blessing for the United States had the age of railroads been somewhat delayed. A distinguished American, who has recently passed some time in Baltimore, said that our public roads in the United States were the poorest which existed in any civilized country, so far as he had observed, and he has travelled extensively. The loss which this entails upon the agricultural community and the community at large is enormous. It requires more horse power to pull a given load a given distance, and the waste resulting from the wear and tear of wagons and vehicles every year must amount to many millions of dollars. It was estimated some years ago that improved pavements in Berlin would save owners of horses on an average for each horse considerable over $25. There are over ten millions of horses in the United States ; and if to be quite within bounds we place the annual saving which would result from first-class roads throughout the country at $10 per horse, it would amount to over one hundred millions of dollars, which is interest on two billions. This is probably moderate, for in cities like Baltimore first-class streets in which only proper street-car rails were allowed would save easily $25 per horse ; and the farmers will bear me out, I am confident, when I say that in this part of the United States, at least, $15 per horse is a very low estimate for the annual saving which would result from excellent roads. The saving to vehicles and to harness must be added to the saving of horseflesh ; and when it is remembered that with good roads one horse would often suffice where two are now necessary, and always two where three are now required, it will be admitted that $20 a horse is not an extravagant estimate for the country. However, contenting ourselves with the low estimate of one hundred millions per annum, which is equal to interest on two billions of dollars, it will be seen how serious our loss in neglecting adequate provision for highways. The great French reformer, Turgot, who did so much for the province of which he was governor, elevating it from the condition of one of the poorest to one of the wealthiest provinces in France, turned his attention first of all to the ordinary public roads, and demonstrated by just such calculations the advantage of first-class highways. There can be no doubt that the excellent roads he constructed were one important cause of the prosperity of Limoges.

Now, as we have neglected public roads, so we are also overlooking the importance of canals, and the result is in many ways more serious, for we can go to work the moment we will and improve our roads, but the value of vast expenditures is forever lost by a false policy with respect to canals. England allowed her canals to fall into the hands of the railroad corporations, and it is now as live a question there to know how to get them "out of the clutches of the corporations" and restore them to their proper uses, as with us to know how to take certain great works "out of politics," all of which proves that there is no "royal road" to good administration, and least of all by reducing government to insignificance. However, it seems generally to be agreed in England that the conclusion that the era of canals had gone was over-hasty, and England proposes now to spend millions on canals.[1] France finds its canals still use-

---

[1] The following is a quotation from the English journal, *Engineering,* of December 30, 1887. It is taken from an article on the "Thames and Severn Canal":—

"As a nation we have sinned grievously in our neglect of canals, and we are reaping the punishment by finding ourselves under the heavy heel of the railway companies. Our friends on the Continent have been wiser than ourselves, and have never ceased to conserve their canals, continually increasing their extent and capacity, until now barges of comparatively large burden can penetrate hundreds of

ful, and they are able to carry large classes of freight for
two-thirds what it costs by rail. Germany, although the
various German states own the railroads, contemplates extensive improvements in canals. Why? Because what we
want in our national industrial life is to accomplish our ends
with the smallest expenditure of labor and capital, and this
purpose is attained by giving the canals a place in the various means of communication and transportation.

American states offer us valuable testimony from experience as well as these foreign countries. It is instructive
even now to go back to the construction of the Erie Canal
— finished in 1825 — and examine the circumstances under
which the undertaking was brought to a successful termination.

Politicians are of two classes — those who subserve special
interests, and thus renew day by day their life of deception,
fraud, and perjury, for in their oath of office they have
called Almighty God to witness that they will not do
that very thing — and those whose acts substantiate their
professions of devotion to general and public interests. It
is rather discouraging that under the influence of a high
protective tariff and corporations managing natural monopolies, politicians of the former class have gained such an
ascendency that all our various governments have become
so depraved that the term " government by special interests " is applicable to them. De Witt Clinton, however, was
a man who was always asking himself, What can I do to

miles into the country from the seaboard, and distribute imports at a
price very little above that at the port of entry.

"There are signs, however, that public opinion is awakening in this
country to the value of canals; but if it is to be of any avail, it must
lead to the inception of comprehensive schemes and must not end in a
system of patch work."

promote the general welfare? and he acquired a habit of looking at measures from that large and patriotic standpoint. Thus it was that he pushed through his canal project against great opposition. And what was the nature of this opposition? Such as always attends public improvements. It was a "visionary" scheme, as a public undertaking it could not succeed, and the like, and it was called "Clinton's Big Ditch." However, it was finished, and if our politicians could be induced to give some attention to De Witt Clinton's life and writings, it would be most fortunate. This Erie Canal has probably done more for New York State and City than any other one public enterprise, and to-day it is a powerful factor in determining freight rates all over the Union. It was in 1882 that the canal was imperilled by an iron-clad state constitution, and then it was that Horatio Seymour came to the rescue and brought about changes making it a free waterway. Against what senseless opposition did he not have to contend also? Perhaps not so much senseless opposition, however; for these very railroads which claim that the day of canals is past some way seemed to be very anxious to kill this useless institution, as they called it. The question naturally arises, If canals are of no use, why do railroads dread them and go to the expense of buying them and filling them up? Why not let them die a natural death?

But all the corporations in the world could not govern the people were it not for their own apathy, indifference, narrowness, selfishness, and apparent desire to be saddled, bridled, and ridden. Our fate rests with ourselves. There was an attempt to array the people of one part of the state against another. Especially did opposition manifest itself in those counties not adjacent to the canal, and the railroad organs suddenly displayed an unwonted affection for

the poor farmers who were to be taxed to support a canal
in which they had no interest.   Horatio Seymour demonstrated that the canal had so increased the taxable basis of
the state that the tax rate was lower than would otherwise
be possible.   All had thus gained, and no one lost a penny.
He also rebuked the petty spirit which could imagine that
the interests of all parts of the state were not harmonious.
" The spirit which prompts opposition to the amendment,"
said Seymour, " is best expressed by words which import
that if the counties which desire free canals, wish to have
them made so, let them pay the cost.   If this feeling is
made manifest, to what end will it lead?   It will," he said
in return, " if such counties wish to have their schools supported, ' let them pay the costs '; if they desire that their
members of the legislature or their judiciary should receive
their salaries, let them pay the costs !   This will throw upon
such counties a great sum of taxation, many times more in
amount than their share of making free canals.   I deplore
a result which would go so far to impair the honor and
interests of New York.   I should regret the defeat of the
amendment, because if it is adopted, it will lessen taxation
upon all sections and pursuits.   Canals are the routes most
needed by our farmers and mechanics.   Every dollar of tax
or tolls lifted off of their commerce adds to the value of
their products and lessens the charges they have to pay to
get them to market."

Hon. O. B. Potter, of New York, who is now interesting
himself in favor of the million-dollar appropriation for the
improvement of the Erie Canal, said in an argument before
the joint committee of the Senate and Assembly in February
2, 1886 : " However important and beneficial the railways,
now or hereafter, they will never supersede the necessity for
or the usefulness of these canals "; and speaking of projects

for canals in other states, he said: "There is not one of them that will not repay the state in which it is located, and of the wealth of which, when done, it forms a part, manifold."

With what truth it is said that canals can do nothing is seen in the fact that the canals alone brought to New York City last May, June, and July (to the 23d) over two millions more bushels of grain than the total amount received at Boston, Baltimore, and Philadelphia. Horatio Seymour, Jr., in a pamphlet entitled "The Canal Age," and dated March 23, 1886, undertakes to show that railroads cannot transport so cheaply as canals.[1]

A few facts must be borne in mind. One is, the day for canals owned by private corporations has passed, and that for two reasons. The first is that the gain of canals is of a public nature, rather than individual. There always have been public works which would not remunerate an individual, and yet are of the greatest advantage to the people at large. The streets of a city like Baltimore are an example. Should we try to derive a direct revenue from our streets, we would ruin the city, and grass would grow on Baltimore and Charles Streets. These undertakings, which are only indirectly remunerative, are often most profitable. The second

---

[1] In this same pamphlet Mr. Seymour says: "False and hurtful ideas exist that the people of this state have been taxed on account of the Erie Canal. This is not the case. Up to 1880 the canal had paid into the treasury of the state for tolls, etc., $118,142,837.81. Its cost had been to this date for construction and enlargement, $49,387,422.77. There had been spent for repairs and management, $26,857,575.45, leaving a balance paid into the treasury, without computing interest, $41,903,899.59. Although the canals are to-day supported by taxation, their maintenance is no loss to the state, as they pay back in direct revenue much more than they receive. . . . I know of no private enterprise that makes such a return."

is that private parties sell out to the railroads, and all agreements and contracts to do otherwise are not worth the paper on which they are written.

Should the Chesapeake and Ohio Canal be retained, all hope of direct profit ought to be abandoned. It has been suggested that the canal be extended to Baltimore. Whether this is wise or not, I do not know. It would require the opinion of those better acquainted with the cost of construction and with the advantages of cheap communication to Washington, and thence by canal to the coal regions, to decide. However, the advantage to the state in the canal can only be of an indirect nature in extending its business and in reducing the prices of commodities to consumers. It must be expected to keep it up at an annual outlay, as other public enterprises are maintained. This was what New York deliberately resolved to do. In a mass-meeting in Cooper Union, in New York City, it was said, "We have a new school of narrowness that wants to choke the canals because they do not earn enough to support themselves, but they earn enough to support or help support the millions of people that live in this state." It is noteworthy that Pennsylvanians regret their short-sighted policy in selling their canals. The Philadelphia *Record* said last year on this subject: "While other states were disposing of their public works and artificial waterways, New York retained possession of the Erie Canal. . . . Every wage-worker and small consumer, East and West, is a gainer by it. . . . The state of Pennsylvania transferred its public works to a railroad corporation thirty-eight years ago, and to-day nearly all the canals in the state are useless. The Pennsylvania Railroad applies to the legislature every session to abandon an additional section of the canal system, which it obtained under a pledge to maintain forever."

It is to be noticed further that it seems to be accepted that the more extensive a canal system is, the greater its relative advantages. A small strip of canal by itself may be worth little, but when part of a larger system it may be invaluable. Further, it is the opinion of those best qualified to speak, that no federal assistance for the Erie Canal is desired, because that would involve federal interference. "The Union for the Improvement of Canals in New York" is strongly opposed to federal aid.

Finally, nothing can be gained by a temporary and uncertain policy with reference to canals. It is proposed to give the Chesapeake and Ohio a trial for two years still! Can anything more futile be imagined? It cannot be utilized until people know what to expect. Who will build new boats and engage in canal business while this uncertainty lasts? The experience of Ohio is instructive. As soon as it was decided to retain the canals as the property of the state, business began to improve. The Ohio board of public works reported a gain of over $30,000 in the income from canals for 1886, and that was attributed to the hope that the canals were not to "be abandoned or allowed to fall into decay and disuse." The governor of Ohio says: "They constitute a valuable public property. The state should not dispose of any part of them."

The "two-year trial" scheme is predestined to failure, and the canal might as well be sold at once. If that is not already clear, it is to be hoped that the quotation from Horatio Seymour about the Erie Canal in 1882 will be sufficient. "This hostile and menacing attitude of our state toward canals and boatmen prevents the building of vessels and their use. It has lessened the receipts for tolls, for men will not engage in a business where they are liable to be ruined by an accident or by the designs of rich competitors. These will find it profitable to carry for losing rates for one year if they can destroy forever the boatmen or the canals which keep down their own rates for carrying the products of our own people. When they have destroyed their competition, they can ever after put up their own charges to suit their own interest."

CHAPTER XXIV.

THE FORCES PRODUCTIVE OF MUNICIPAL GREATNESS DISCUSSED WITH REFERENCE TO THE FUTURE OF BALTIMORE.

THE articles which have appeared in *The Sun* on openings in Baltimore for business men have very naturally attracted a good deal of attention and awakened a spirit of hopefulness and enterprise. Who can set any limit to the possible future developments of our favored city? President Gilman, in his address before the Johns Hopkins University on the 22d of last February, showed what had been done in a very short time to elevate Baltimore in all those things which go to make up a high civilization, and hinted at a possible future growth of the city in reminding the audience that London, with all its millions of people, was at the beginning of the century but a little larger than Baltimore at the present time. It has always been a favorite theory of mine that in Baltimore there are opportunities for the unfolding of a fuller and richer civilization than the New World has yet seen ; not only that, but that there are opportunities here which exist nowhere else. This opinion has not been carelessly formed, but is the result of careful reflection upon the nature of the various elements which are working together to promote the advancement of Baltimore. Baltimore is situated on the border line between North and South, and here are brought together the peculiar excellences of each section, and here they will blend together indistinguishably in our municipal life. The charm of Southern social life, the high social culture which distinguishes the South, will be supplemented by the indomitable push and energy of the hardy sons of New England. Music, painting, literature, and learning in all its various branches, are progressing favorably, while the economic basis of a high modern civilization is found in an expanding industrial life, as seen in our growing commerce and enlarging manufactures.

One thing to be borne in mind in reflections upon our future is that modern cities are to an unprecedented extent artificial products, the work of men's genius and energy. Formerly nature decided where a great city could grow up, and a high civilization was possible only on the seacoast or on the banks of great rivers. Now man has subjugated nature to such an extent that he is, comparatively speaking, independent of her whim and caprice. If natural waterways fail, he may construct artificial waterways, and even without the aid of navigation at all a city may spring up in the heart of a continent. Berlin, nearly the size of New York, is in the centre of a great open plain, on the continent of Europe, and may be regarded as a work of art. Only by canals can navigable rivers be reached, while the modern iron highway, the railroad, still more an artificial product, is a far more important element in developing Berlin, which has become an important railroad centre. It is the will of man which has made Berlin more important than the seaports Bremen and Hamburg.

Perhaps a better illustration can be found in two small cities in Western New York, — Dunkirk and Jamestown. Dunkirk is a port on Lake Erie, and is advantageously situated in a fruitful plain, extending along the shores of the lake. Jamestown, on the other hand, is on the top of the

Chautauqua hills, and its only navigable body of water is Chautauqua Lake, scarcely more than a great pond. The next most important place on the lake is Mayville, a village with perhaps ten or fifteen hundred inhabitants. Who would suppose that Jamestown would leave Dunkirk, its rival, and once its superior, far in the rear in the race for supremacy in Chautauqua County? Yet such has been the case, and Jamestown will probably soon be twice the size of Dunkirk. Now, more or less acquainted with both cities, I am unable to find any other explanation for this than the greater energy and enterprise of the people of Jamestown. Jamestown is, in other words, an artificial product. Two of the chief disadvantages of Jamestown which the people see — for they have tried to correct them, and have been defeated by constitutional quibbles — are their dependence on private gas and water companies, for in these respects they allowed things to take their own course, and did not keep in their own hands control of two of the essential elements of progress. Dunkirk, on the other hand, is blessed with excellent public water-works which may well be the envy of Jamestown, and in the future this may give her an advantage over her rival.

The application is sufficiently obvious. Nature has blessed us and done more for us than for some other great cities. These advantages are not to be despised, but they cannot be relied upon. It rests with us to say what the future shall be. If we, the people of Baltimore, *will* it, we can make Baltimore as big as London. Not only that; we can make Baltimore a happier, better, and more truly civilized city than London to-day with all its squalor and misery.

When the question is asked, How shall we outstrip our rivals in true greatness? it will be at once seen that all the previous papers in this series have a bearing on the answer.

It is now proposed to stop and apply some of the principles which have already been developed.

Those human forces which produce national or municipal greatness may be divided into two classes. The first are individual ; the second may be called social. The individual forces are obvious and have been so often elaborated in an age characterized by excessive individualism that it is not worth while to dwell long on them. The importance to each citizen and to the community of individual temperance, thrift, intelligence, and energy cannot be overestimated. Nothing can be done without individual excellence. A mistake is only made when it is supposed that individual superiority alone is sufficient. The individual by himself is powerless. Wealth is only possible in a community, and in this community no one lives for himself alone. Can art flourish where but one loves art ? On the contrary, the artist must be stimulated by a public which appreciates and encourages art, and, other things being equal, the more widely diffused the love and knowledge of art among the people, the higher the excellence which artists will attain. What hope is there for architecture among a people who prefer the cheap and gaudy to the eternal beauty of sublime and simple creations ? What hope for music among those who turn away from the great masters to applaud the rattling waltz of a fifth-class composer ? What hope for literature. where there are none to prefer George Eliot, Thackeray and Dickens to Ouida, Mrs. Braddon and Hugh Conway ? It is readily admitted by all who know what they are talking about that in all these pursuits the social atmosphere is of vital importance. It is likewise in business. What does the energy of a merchant amount to if there are none who have the means to purchase his commodities ? Can he develop a commerce by himself alone and unaided ? But how shall would-be customers provide themselves with means for large purchases without energy on their part? The energy of the merchant must then be supplemented by the energy of his fellows if he would develop any commerce. Thus is he dependent on others. "None of us liveth to himself."

Take a manufacturer, let us say, for example, of shoes. It will do him no good to produce shoes unless others have valuable things to give in exchange. The manufacturer desires a vast market, but this is impossible unless the masses are ambitious and industrious. They must have wants, and energy must accompany these wants. A laboring populace poor and indolent and contented with little will make few purchases, for they will not have valuable things to offer in exchange. Thus the manufacturer can only hope to thrive in a prosperous community. The larger the earnings of the artisan and mechanic, the more can he extend his business with advantage. But his dependence does not cease here. The quality of the labor which he employs is a chief factor in success. Labor of hand and brain is the most important element in production, and a highly qualified and moral population is an indispensable condition of permanent national and municipal prosperity. The more closely a community follows Christian principles and its members concern themselves with the welfare of others, the more generally will its prosperity be diffused and the more rapid will be its advance in wealth. "Am I my brother's keeper?" If in any nation at any time there is a general inclination to answer that question in the negative, that nation has already entered upon a course which leads to anarchy and barbarism.

There are, however, some more special and particular applications of these principles to the problems of municipal life. There are certain fundamental conditions of our future prosperity which no individual as such can supply, but which must be provided by us in our organic capacity as a city and as an important part of a commonwealth, or not at all.

CHAPTER XXV.

BAD TAXES BLIGHT A CITY'S GROWTH.

TAXES are levied to enable our state and city governments to perform their various important functions, and the burden which they impose upon us is by no means a light one. The total state and city tax rate for the residents of Baltimore is $1.78¾ on the $100 of property. This does not appear to be so high a rate of taxation as it really is. Taxes are paid out of income, and the important question is to know what ratio exists between taxation of property and its income. When we reduce our rate of $1.78¾ to a percentage on income, it will be found that it is often equivalent to an income tax varying from fifteen to forty per cent., a tax rate almost unknown in European countries.

Taxes are one of the chief elements in determining price in nearly all branches of business which are not monopolies, to which totally different principles apply. The proportion of expenditure which is caused by taxation is larger than is generally realized, even by business men, for they do not stop to reflect upon the effect of taxes on commodities, and other taxes, which are shifted from the shoulders of the one who originally pays them to the shoulders of somebody else. We have, then, in taxes one of those fundamental conditions of industrial life which are beyond the control of the individual as such.

Inconsiderate people who know nothing about the nature

of business talk as if it made little difference how taxes were laid. To them the problem appears very simple. There is so much money to be raised, and let us, say they, collect it indiscriminately in proportion to the actual selling value of all property. Inasmuch as there is just so much money and no more to be paid to the public treasury, it seems to them to make very little difference how it gets there, provided each one bears what is assumed to be his fair share. This is why our antiquated system of taxation is still maintained in Maryland.

We live in an age of sharp competition, — always excluding the growing number of monopolies, — and the addition of a small burden to the load already carried by a man engaged in this competitive struggle may bear him down completely, while the lessening of his load may enable him to go ahead and outstrip others. A small percentage on the expenses of business may make all the difference to the business community between prosperity and ruin. Now, nothing can be further from the truth than the statement that it makes no difference how the taxes are laid, since they must be laid some way. A man who acts upon that principle is like a man who should apply the principles and methods of blacksmithing to watchmaking. The machinery of taxation ought to be adjusted to the actual life of modern communities with the utmost delicacy by those who understand both business and the principles of taxation. This is another reason why active members of the community should give careful attention to economic and social problems. Their success in so far as it depends upon such a matter as taxation is conditional upon what others do, as well as upon what they themselves do, sometimes even more than upon what they themselves do ; and if I were called upon to name the most serious mistake of American business men, I should say it was the failure to give sufficient attention to the social forces which produce prosperity.

There are certain things which can neither leave us nor come to us. City lots will serve as an example. It is manifest that taxes upon city lots will not injure business. There is a certain amount of land accessible, neither more nor less, and no taxation will alter this circumstance. City lots in New York are not competing with city lots in Baltimore. More than this is true. If city lots are taxed on all that they are worth, — up to the last dollar of their selling value, as they should be by our law as it stands, — instead of discouraging enterprise it will encourage it ; for it will make it harder for speculators to withhold the land from those who wish to improve it.

Let us take shipping as an illustration of a business which may come to us or which may leave us. Elsewhere, shipping is either not taxed at all or is taxed only on earnings, and shipping conducted by foreigners is often positively subsidized. Shipping may either leave this port or other ports, and it will be determined by relative advantages. Can, then, anything more absurd be imagined than to tax a dwindling shipping at a high rate, as it was actually proposed to do in the last Maryland legislature? Will our shipping be improved if ships and other vessels are taxed on their full selling value? Can it be doubted that if a burden is laid upon shipping the business of our port will continue to decline? If so, who will derive the benefit from the attempt to apply a cast-iron system of taxation? Other tax-payers will lose, because they will derive no relief from an unsuccessful attempt to lay taxes, and they will be poorer on account of the loss of business which might have been theirs.

A large part of our manufacturing and mercantile business

is of a similar nature, and it can be completely prostrated by a bad policy of taxation on our part. Retail merchants and dealers in manufactured articles will not come to Baltimore if they can do much better elsewhere, and they will be able to do better elsewhere if the necessary expenses of business are heavier here than in other places. It is consequently to our interest to render these necessary expenses of active business as small as possible, for in that way prices will be lowered and business attracted. We render these expenses smaller when we lessen the burden of taxation on business. Who loses thereby? No one; because increased competition lowers prices, and all consumers get the advantage of cheaper prices. The problem is to extend the business of Baltimore; and an extension of business implies lower prices. This is sufficiently simple. As business extends, the demand for real estate increases, and real estate owners certainly do not lose. The difference between real estate and business, with respect to taxes, may be brought out by this statement, which seems paradoxical until one has reflected upon it: If all taxation should be removed to-day in Baltimore from real estate and placed on active business, particularly on commerce and manufactures, it would cause a sudden and unprecedented fall in real estate. Business would be crippled, and so many would leave Baltimore that owners of houses and lots would almost be glad to give them away. Should all taxes be removed from active business and placed on real estate, on the other hand, it is doubtful whether it would produce any permanent depreciation of real estate. The measure might indeed so improve business as to bring about higher prices for real estate, and increased activity in building. The experience of New York City goes to confirm this; for there business, although legally subject to taxation, is practically well-nigh exempt, and real estate nowhere sells for so high a price. It is to be noticed, further, that there is a deliberate, systematic attempt on the part of New York to draw business away from Baltimore by lower taxes. The mayor of New York practically refuses to try to enforce the laws as he finds them, — for there they have the same antiquated laws which we have here, — and urges their repeal on the ground that they are the outcome of impracticable theories and hamper business. He urges the repeal of all existing taxes on business, in order to swell the commerce of New York. It is such considerations as these which led a writer on taxation to frame a practical rule which he wished to " have cut into the stone of the Capitol (in large letters and have them gilded) in the Senate chamber, the hall of the House of Representatives, and in the governor's office." The rule reads as follows : "*Never tax anything that would be of value to your state, that could and would run away, or that could and would come to you.*"

While this rule may be too sweeping, it is worthy of careful consideration. The more one reflects upon the nature and the consequences of taxation, the more profoundly one is impressed with its far-reaching importance. Taxation may create monopolies, or it may prevent them ; it may diffuse wealth, or it may concentrate it ; it may promote liberty and equality of rights, or it may tend to the establishment of tyranny and despotism ; it may be used to bring about reforms in industrial society, or it may be so laid as to aggregate existing grievances and foster dissension and class-hate ; taxation may be so contrived by the skilful hand as to give free scope to every opportunity for the creation of wealth and the advancement of all true interests of the city, or it may be so shaped by ignoramuses as to place a dead weight on Baltimore in the race for municipal supremacy on the Atlantic coast.

The single business man, as an individual, is helpless in this matter. It rests with us, citizens of Baltimore and Maryland, to establish those social conditions which will allow every man the fullest and freest opportunity to do his best to make Baltimore what we wish Baltimore to become. Shall we wait until all our neighboring cities move in this matter, and lag behind with our abominable and barbarous system of business licenses and personal property taxes, or shall we be the first to strike out boldly in the establishment of a rational system of taxation, and thus have the advantage over others of a start in the race? It is a cheering sign that our business men have moved in this matter, and passed resolutions petitioning the legislature to submit a constitutional amendment to the people, making possible a new system of taxation. The move has been made none too soon, and it should be followed up by vigorous action.

CHAPTER XXVI.

A PLAN WHEREBY TAXES MAY BE REDUCED IN CITIES.

THE importance of a right placing of taxes has been considered. The amount of taxes raised is obviously an essential element in determining the future of a city. Our municipal taxes have become truly exorbitant. Much as we talk about them, few realize it. In my last chapter it was suggested that the burden might perhaps be better appreciated if our property tax was translated into a tax on the income which property yields. Comparative statistics help us also to understand how great the load of taxation in American cities is. Consider this fact, which I discovered a few years ago in comparing the budgets of New York and Berlin. The interest on the debt of New York was then nearly sufficient to defray all the expenses of Berlin, nearly as large a city, and one more disadvantageously situated with respect to sanitation and keeping the streets clean. Berlin is governed, it may be remarked, by those who make it their business to understand the principles of municipal administration; that is, so-called theorists. It is said to be the best governed city in the world, and so may not be a fair example; but this entire chapter could be filled with statistics to show how undue a burden we are sustaining in taxation in American cities.

It is the commonest thing in the world for worthy citizens to write to their daily papers exhorting the city fathers to

keep down expenses and reduce the tax rate, and the newspapers from time to time come out with head lines like this,
"Retrenchment a Necessity." Yet what good does it do?
Expenditures continue to swell in our cities relatively faster
than in our states or at Washington. While state expenditures double, municipal expenditures increase fourfold or
more. Ohio may serve as an illustration. The expenses
of the state increased about forty-six times in sixty years,
and the local expenses one hundred times. I have yet to
find one exception to this general rule that municipal expenditures increase faster than any other ; perhaps I should
say local expenditures, for I mean to include villages and
other political units as well as great cities.

It is well to say "reduce taxes," but it is said to no purpose unless it can be shown *how* taxes are to be reduced.
Let us clear the ground — not by theorizing, but by examin-
ing a few facts which can be established beyond controversy.

It is a general supposition that the increase in the burden
of taxation in our cities is due to corruption. This is doubtless a partial explanation, but very incomplete and imperfect. There are two European countries at least where
municipal administration is above reproach in respect to
integrity of officials, and these are England and Germany ;
whereas it may be said generally that in Europe municipal
corruption is hardly one of the problems of the day. Nevertheless, it is true that the expenditures of European cities
have increased in recent years with greater relative rapidity
than those of American cities. This has been satisfactorily
demonstrated by Dr. Simon N. Patten, of Illinois, in a monograph on the finances of American states and cities. This
must not be misunderstood. The statement is not that the
expenditures are as large as ours, but that the rate of in-

crease for ten or fifteen years at least has been more rapid. This also is different from saying that the rate of taxation has increased correspondingly, for there are many other possible sources of revenue than taxes. Dr. Patten has also shown some other interesting facts bearing on this problem. One is that democracy is not the cause of increased expenditures, as superficial observers so often suppose. European cities generally have at least some restrictions on the right of suffrage, yet their expenditures have increased more rapidly than our own. But there are American facts of still more striking character. It is said that universal suffrage gives a vote to those who have no economic interests at stake in the community, and that they consequently vote away other people's money with reckless prodigality. Dr. Patten has shown, however, that in small Northern towns, where the vast majority of voters are tax-payers, the tax rates have increased more rapidly than in the large cities ; further, he has given evidence to show that real estate speculators, by urging on untimely improvements, like sewers running into the country, — as recently happened in Buffalo, — have done more to raise taxes than the ignorant voter. The object of the real estate speculators is, of course, to keep a boom alive. Now, these are no fanciful theories ; they are hard facts. What do they show? They show at least this : The general public has not gone deep enough in its attempts to explain the growing burden of taxation.

The true causes for the growth of municipal expenditures are, after all, not difficult to discover. The functions of the local political unit have been increasing more rapidly than those of either state governments or our federal government. We hear a great deal about centralization. The truth is that, relatively speaking, we live in an age of decentralization. Our local political units are gaining in impor-

tance faster than our sovereign states or our sovereign federal government. I do not say that there is no tendency in
our central governments to extend their functions. I say
merely that relatively they do not hold their own in importance.

Sanitation and public schools are two great items in the
budgets of cities. Light and water are two more, and in all
these respects what satisfied us once is no longer tolerable.
Public parks cost hundreds of thousands and even millions
in cities. New York City, for example, proposes to spend
$1,000,000 a year to provide small parks in the most
crowded portions of the metropolis — a measure demanded
on sanitary no less than humanitarian grounds. Public
libraries are maintained by a growing number of cities,
and the expense of maintaining these is not insignificant. Boston spent over $160,000 on her public library in
a single year recently. Public baths are among the hundred
and one other items which might be mentioned. Go
through the whole list of things for which the modern city
spends money, and it will be found that many items are
quite new, while the expenditures for nearly all have increased enormously. We have now discovered the chief
cause of increased municipal expenditures. Extravagance
and dishonesty have, after all, been minor causes, and their
importance has been unduly magnified. Many an American
municipality is managed without fraud, and in only a few
great cities has the dishonesty been what the people have
imagined. It has been bad enough, it is true, and it is a
burning shame and disgrace to us that there has been
so much municipal corruption in America. Nevertheless,
that is not the chief cause of large expenditures of public
money.

It is further safe to say that we have not got to the end

of the era of increasing local expenditures. When one reflects upon certain current phenomena, one must be rather inclined to think at times that we have scarcely more than entered upon it. The public demands on the municipal administration grow steadily year by year. Better pavements, improved sewerage, more small parks, and manual training in schools are among the pressing needs of the hour, and a demand for other public expenditures is just beginning to be heard. Play grounds for children and opportunities of physical culture, that the rising generation may grow up strong and healthy, are among the things which people want. The housing of the poor is a matter over which English cities are extending their care, and who is wise enough to say that the common welfare may not yet compel American cities to move in this direction? It is needless to continue the enumeration. The growth of municipal expenditure is a part of the growth of civilization, and is likely to continue for an indefinite period. We cannot stop it without lagging behind in the march of progress. Whining and complaining do no good. To write articles containing nothing but the ceaseless refrain, "reduce taxes," is folly. Yes, we must reduce taxes ; but how?

There is a very simple way, and the American city which first enters upon it and keeps to it persistently and systematically is going to have a tremendous advantage over its competitors. *It is the full and complete utilization of all natural monopolies for the benefit of the public.* This is the way, and the only way, to reduce taxes. If our business men will turn their serious attention to this, and endeavor to force right action upon our municipal councillors and our legislators, they will see a most gratifying reduction in their tax bills, and will witness a new and unparalleled period of prosperity in Baltimore. It is, I believe, perfectly practicable to reduce the tax rate to one dollar on the hundred of property in our city, and that rate is quite enough.

The principle which should guide us is very simple, and will readily occur to those who have read the previous articles in this series. *It is to exact from every natural monopoly using public property full compensation.* What does full compensation mean? It means this: Making just as good terms for the public as a private man could make for himself. Let us imagine for the moment that a private man owned absolutely the streets of Baltimore. How would he manage the street-car business? He would give no favors to anybody. He would either operate the street cars himself or lease the privilege to the one who would give the most, and never under any circumstances — I take it for granted that the man is sane — would he give a perpetual lease. Short, terminable leases are the kind private men give, and thus keep complete control of their own property. Yet witness the carelessness and indifference of our business men and the general public about this matter. Every one of us has an interest, and the interest of a single family is very considerable, but no one seems to concern himself about his own share in the public property. Take the case of street-car fares. A certain public policy would ultimately lead to the establishment of three-cent fares, which would easily be worth fifty dollars a year to a family of five persons living a little distance from the centre of Baltimore. Forty dollars a year is interest on one thousand dollars. Now, if the head of an ordinary family heard that there was a chance for him to come into an inheritance of a thousand dollars, how eager would he be! How actively would he follow up all his legal claims! Yet he scarcely will turn on his heel to influence the legislature in the matter of some most astounding street-car bills now before that body. On the contrary, when you begin talking with him on this matter, he will make such petty and trivial objections to a sound policy — in successful operation elsewhere — that one is tempted to believe that three men out of four lose their common sense when they begin talking about public measures.[1]

Our merchants may be said to have a still greater interest in this matter. If fares are reduced, the surplus income of every man and woman in Baltimore will thereby be increased, and their sales will grow in amount. On the other hand, if

---

[1] It has been claimed that street cars cannot carry passengers for three cents in Baltimore. I do not say that they could and still pay nine per cent. of gross revenues to the city in addition to other taxes. I believe they could pay taxes and carry passengers for three cents. It would be necessary to consolidate all the roads, perhaps, and bring them under one management, and owners of the street railroads would be obliged to be content with fair returns on capital actually invested and could look for no returns on fictitious stock or needless issues of bonds. Washington street-car lines sell six tickets for twenty-five cents, — a trifle over four cents each, — and Congress has compelled each company to give free transfers from any one of its lines to any other. The dividends are said to be enormous, nevertheless. It must be remembered further that a reduction of fares would increase traffic enormously. The Philadelphia street-car lines reduced fares from six cents to five cents recently, and found their gross revenues increased the first year, while it is expected that the second year will show an increase of net revenues. The Richmond electric street-car line contemplates a reduction of fares to three cents purely from motives of self-interest. Moreover, the fact that street-car franchises have been sold for from thirty to forty per cent. of gross revenues proves that passengers can be carried in some cases for even less than three cents; for when forty per cent. of gross revenues is paid, only three cents out of five collected is left for the company, which, nevertheless, fails to receive the benefit of increased traffic from low fares. What I desire is to see franchises put up at auction under condition that fares shall be reduced to three cents.

franchises are sold at auction, taxes may be reduced, and thus they will gain. Who in our legislature suggests proper restrictions on franchises for natural monopolies? Is it not time for our business men to move in this matter? New York City has already moved, and will obtain increased revenues from franchises in the future, there is reason to believe, for under Mayor Hewitt a halt has been called in the prodigal waste of public resources, and his last message to the council of New York abounds in suggestions analogous to those in this article. Will Baltimore be the last to move? Will Baltimore business men delay action until opportunity to save what public property yet remains is lost?

The same principle holds good with regard to railroads operated by steam. Let them pay for every piece of public property its full value to the last cent. To exact less is to rob " the forgotten millions." North Street, public property, is occupied by a railroad. How much annual compensation does the city receive therefor? The use of a street in a great city ought to be worth many thousands of dollars a year in rent. If it were my property, I should demand for it what it was worth. Why should the city do less? Or is it not time to stop taking away the property of the many and giving it to the few?

Gas supply and electric lights are of the same nature, save that the city ought to make provision as soon as possible to acquire works of its own. Yet we hear a good deal of foolish talk about competition in electric lighting still! Experience will teach us better. But why wait until we have paid the dear tuition which experience charges, before we act? The correct method in such cases is simple enough. Existing companies should be bought out if they will sell at a reasonable price ; otherwise they should be brought to terms by a vigorous municipal competition. No legal monopoly should ever be granted a private corporation, for that is worth a great deal of money. As a legal monopoly can only be conferred by public authority, the public ought to derive the advantage therefrom, and what this advantage is, previous papers have shown. I will again only remind readers that Berlin now defrays eighteen per cent. of its expenditure from the profits on gas-works with gas at less than one dollar a thousand.

CHAPTER XXVII.

THE FUTURE OF BALTIMORE FURTHER DIS-
CUSSED.

A RECENT trip to New York City, and to Vassar College, near Poughkeepsie, gave me an opportunity to
observe certain phenomena of importance to a student of
municipal life, and also to examine with care the three
recent messages of Mayor Hewitt to the board of aldermen
of New York on the future of that city.

The manufacture of gas at Vassar College interested me.
The gas is of a superior quality, as good as it has ever been
my lot to burn. Less than twenty thousand feet are manufactured a day, and the coal must be carted two or three
miles from the Hudson River. I was told that it was worth
sixty cents a ton to cart the coal to the college. Yet even
on this small scale and under these disadvantageous circumstances, it costs the college only eighty cents a thousand to
manufacture its gas, while the people in the neighboring city
of Poughkeepsie pay $2.50 for an inferior quality of gas.
As gas is manufactured on a large scale in the city, which
comprises over twenty thousand inhabitants, and as coal is
more readily accessible, it can be seen that the people of
Poughkeepsie ought to have cheaper gas, whereas they pay
over three times as much as Vassar College.

Possibly mayors of American cities have in recent years
written abler messages than those of Mayor Hewitt, but it
has never been my good fortune to read one of them. The

vigorous defence of the public welfare and appreciation of the true nature of the needs of New York City revealed by these messages remind one of the patriotism of a man like De Witt Clinton. It seems to me that Mayor Hewitt ranks *facile princeps* among all mayors of American cities for the past twenty years or more.

An important question for all our states and cities is to know how to recover public rights which have been thoughtlessly allowed to pass into private hands, and to safeguard such public property as still exists after the reckless prodigality with which legislatures and municipal councils have squandered other people's money during the past generation. *The Sun* has already published editorials on constitutional changes which are needed to accomplish this desirable end, and the recommendations made in these editorials are in keeping with the teachings of political science. The chief of them is to provide by constitutional amendment that any corporation which seeks or accepts any new legislation thereby places itself under the reserved rights of the people to control all grants of privileges to corporations. Thus the effect of the unfortunate Dartmouth College decision is to a certain extent obviated, and artificial persons are rendered subject to the law more nearly like natural persons. The recommendations of Mayor Hewitt contain similar provisions for municipal franchises. He would make natural monopolies pay for every new privilege, and thus gather up the fragments of public property, that nothing further may be lost. The time appears to have come for a substitution of cable or electric traction for horses on street railways. This is desirable on many accounts, and is recommended by the mayor. But he adds the following remarks to his approval of the change : " Inasmuch as this change will be profitable, however, to the railroad companies, a portion of the saving should be secured to the city treasury. I recommend that a careful investigation be made as to the amount of this saving, in order that the necessary consent of the common council may be given upon conditions which shall be fair to both parties. The value of the franchise will depend, of course, largely upon the volume of the business, and therefore the same percentage of the receipts could hardly be exacted in every case. But the companies should compensate the public for the use of the streets upon an equitable basis of division, and the legislature should carefully guard the rights of the city and the interests of the tax-payers in any legislation authorizing the use of cable traction."

Suggestions in regard to rapid transit are made which are of value to us in Baltimore in shaping our future, and particularly in view of the proposition to utilize Jones's Falls for rapid transit. It is recommended by Mayor Hewitt that the city provide rapid transit, which it can do cheaper than private parties, for it can borrow money at three per cent., while private individuals must pay five. It is suggested that the rapid transit roads be leased for thirty-five years for five per cent. of their cost. The city would net two per cent., which in thirty-five years would redeem the principal, and thus the road would become public property without the expenditure of a cent in taxation. This is analogous to principles which have, without difficulty, been applied in other countries, and seems to be favored by men most competent to speak on this subject in New York, although some evidently think that the city should manage the entire enterprise without the intervention of a corporation. The success of the Brooklyn Bridge Street Car Line, operated by public authority, has been cited as a proof of the superiority of public management.

Public spirit should be cultivated by us in Baltimore if we would make our future what we would like it to be. Public spirit leads people to reflect on the public welfare, and to consider measures from the standpoint of the greatest good to the greatest number. A correct course of action is an inevitable result; public rights and public property are watched with jealous care, public enemies are exposed, and expensive errors in municipal measures are avoided. New York City now finds it necessary to go to an enormous expense in tearing down buildings in the crowded parts of the city to provide small parks as breathing places for the poor people. It would have been practicable to have reserved frequent open squares years ago, and it would not have cost the hundredth part of what it now does to construct these little parks. It was well known by those who thought about such matters that they would be needed, but there was not public spirit enough to induce action. Open squares are needed in Baltimore in various sections now destitute of them, and to acquire them to-day will involve a far smaller burden than to wait until population is denser in these sections. A little forethought and public spirit are the only requisites. New York now finds it advantageous to acquire water-front. This involves an enormous outlay. How much easier it would have been to reserve all the water-front at the beginning! Lack of public spirit led again to an expensive mistake.

There are various ways in which public spirit can be measured. The amount of public enterprise is a good test. The provinces of Quebec and Ontario, in Canada, may be profitably compared. The Canadians in Quebec have so little public spirit that it is impossible to maintain good roads by public authority; consequently highways are handed over to private corporations, who collect high tolls and thus obstruct business by what amounts to a system of indirect taxation. Public spirit is more active in Ontario, and there are few if any toll roads in that province. This difference in public spirit is a chief cause of difference in wealth. One of my earliest recollections — I can only just remember it — was a toll road in New York state, but for many years I have not seen one in New York or Massachusetts. One of the first conditions of prosperity is the freest exchange of services and commodities, and in a very wealthy community toll roads will hardly be found. This is but one illustration. Where public spirit is in a low condition public authority is unable to perform its proper functions, and they are with loss handed over to private individuals.

Huxley's article on "The Struggle for Existence" in the *Nineteenth Century* is valuable reading for those interested in the future of Baltimore. Huxley shows that highly qualified labor, both as respects physical development and training of hand and head, are to be the first conditions of success in the future struggle for national and municipal pre-eminence. On this ground he favors the restriction of child labor and generous provision for technical education. Huxley regards an ignorant person as a " burden upon, and, so far, an infringer of, the liberty of his fellows." So profoundly, indeed, is he impressed with the necessity for education as a condition of survival that he places a tax for education in the same category as "a war tax levied for purposes of defence." It was, in fact, when England saw her industrial supremacy threatened by the better educated German that she began to act vigorously in this matter, just as France, when she saw her military power overthrown by " the schoolmaster at Sedan," began to introduce universal and compulsory education. Would we in Baltimore hold our own with the cities like Boston, New York, Chicago, and St. Louis, doing so much more than we for education, we must bestir ourselves.

Similarly, Huxley shows that a temporary success gained by starvation wages and child labor is illusory because in lowering the efficiency of man, the chief factor in production, power to hold one's own in the struggle for existence is lost. "A population," says Huxley, "whose labor is insufficiently remunerated must become physically and morally unhealthy, and socially unstable, and though it may succeed for a while in industrial competition by reason of the cheapness of its produce, it must in the end fall, through hideous misery and degradation, to utter ruin."

Huxley emphasizes the fact that he speaks as a naturalist, and as such his pre-eminent ability will not be questioned. It is incomprehensible how a man can appreciate the advantages to a country of improved breeds of horses and cattle, and at the same time fail to see that a strong, vigorous, and intelligent population is a thousand times more important in the race for wealth.

What we want to do in Baltimore is to develop our strong points. A city is like an individual. Formerly every man did everything, — taught school, preached, practised medicine, made shoes, built houses, and I know not what else besides. Now the condition of success for states and cities, as well as men and women, is to find out their strong points, and to do some things better than anybody else.

It is often asked what makes Baltimore grow? Where do the people come from to occupy all these new houses? One reason for our growth is that Baltimore is a delightful city to live in, and also, comparatively speaking, a cheap one. People come here in vast numbers on these two accounts, for there is in modern society a large class of people who

are so situated that they can easily change their residences.[1]
A little inquiry will probably convince any one of the importance of these two facts.   These are strong points, and they
ought to be developed prudently but vigorously.   Public
improvements should go forward as fast as the municipal
finances will warrant; public property should be fully utilized for the benefit of the public ; cheap water, cheap light,
and cheap transportation should be provided.   The cheaper
these indispensable elements of life, the more will people be
attracted to Baltimore.   The indispensable conditions of life
are also elements in the cost of business, and to reduce
them gives us a superior advantage in the struggle for existence.

As to wages, the real question is not how much are wages
in money, but what will money wages buy?   Baltimore has
in this an advantage over a place like New York.   The Johns
Hopkins University, for example, has thus an advantage
over Columbia College in New York City.   Other things
being equal, Baltimore can, for the same salary, get a better
man than New York.   For my part, having lived in both
cities, I should prefer a salary of $2000 in Baltimore to one
of $4000 in New York.   The cheaper the cost of living, the
better the class of employés business men can get for a
given rate of wages.   This was why the manufacturers in
England worked so hard to get the duties off imported food
products forty years ago, and the cheaper cost of living
resulting therefrom made possible the industrial expansion of
England.

The educational advantages of Baltimore are a cause of
increased population, of considerable moment.   It is proba-

---

[1] Twenty new houses have recently been sold or rented on a square
near my home. Of the twenty families occupying them, seven have
come from abroad.

ble that the Johns Hopkins University alone will lead to an
expenditure of a million dollars a year by professors, students, and families who are by it brought to Baltimore, and
the present expenditures connected in the one way and
another with this institution are sufficient to support a small
town. The Hopkins Hospital will similarly help Baltimore,
as will the new Maryland College for Women. The Peabody
Institute, the Pratt Library, and even a private gallery, like
that of Mr. Walters, do their share to bring money and people to Baltimore, and thus to keep the city alive. Yet it
has actually been proposed to cripple all these institutions
— save the Pratt Library, which ranks as a public institution
— by taxation !

The severe storm which we experienced in March, in Baltimore, has again emphasized the importance of electrical
subways. The fact that there can never be any real competition in the matter of these subways is so self-evident
that no attempt has, so far as I know, been made to apply
the principles of competition to them. There is a choice
between two courses of action only ; namely, reliance upon a
private monopoly and a public undertaking. New York City
is trying a private monopoly, and valuable lessons may be
derived from the experience of that city. The private company was strongly resisted by the companies which it was
proposed to force to bury their wires, and finally the people
were startled one morning to see in their newspapers the
intelligence that Jay Gould, of the Western Union Telegraph
Company, against which the law authorizing the subways
was especially directed, had acquired a controlling interest
in the subway company. Something like this may always
be expected to happen. It is similar to what railroads have
always done with private competing canals. Again, it is
seen that one private company is not strong enough to co-

erce powerful electrical corporations of one kind and another, while a private monopoly encounters an obstacle in
the odium which always attaches to private monopolies.
Mayor Hewitt speaks of this system as " certainly very ob-
jectionable." It would be supposed that the experience of
New York would be sufficient to convince any one that it is
the function of a city to provide electrical subways. These
can readily be made to yield an income if constructed on
the plan outlined in the last article for rapid transit. Money
can be borrowed at three per cent. or a trifle over that, and
then a rental can be collected from the various electrical
companies which will yield more than the percentage paid
by the city on borrowed money. It would seem that very
moderate rentals ought to yield ten per cent. on the investment in a city like Baltimore, and this would soon pay off
the principal of the debt.[1]

It is important that cities as well as states should protect
person and property by public authority, and the prospect of
a possible departure from sound policy in this respect in
Maryland led me to use these words in one of my articles
for the Baltimore *Sun :* —

Reports of proceedings in the legislature at Annapolis
compel me to mention a matter which would naturally be
treated in a later paper. A bill has already passed the Senate providing for the employment of special policemen by
corporations and firms. It is very questionable to entrust
even to this extent functions of government to private
parties. It is a return to the anarchistic, disorganized
state of society, when the old barons had their retainers
and engaged in warfare to suit their special pleasure. It
was generally supposed that we had left this barbarism, but

---

[1] Paris derives a large annual rental from the gas company which
supplies Paris with gas for the use of the municipal subways.

there is an unfortunate tendency to return to it in the United States. It is well to notice some thoughtful remarks on occurrences of the year 1886, which appeared in two newspapers. The *Missouri Republican*, in its issue for January 1, 1887, says: "The past year will be forever memorable as the year in which private armies of mercenary soldiers began to be established in this country. . . . It has been fondly supposed that public law was strong enough to do right and maintain right between the citizens over whom the commonwealth has jurisdiction. That, it now seems, was an error. When a difference occurs between a great porkpacker and his employés, it is not to the state that either party has resort; and to check apprehended resistance the pork-packer finds it easier and perhaps cheaper to call out a regiment of hired soldiers who have been armed and trained for the service of the highest bidder." The New York *Nation*, in its issue for January 27, 1887, says: "It cannot be too soon or too well understood that, as an armed organization offering itself for hire for purposes of defence in various parts of the Union, Pinkerton's men are, we must all admit, the greatest disgrace that has befallen the United States. . . . Its appearance in any other civilized country would fill to-day every man in it with shame and astonishment." More may be said: It would be impossible elsewhere. It is not clear what is the intention of those who are behind this bill, but it would seem that it opens the door to all sorts of abuses. We in Maryland are quite capable of maintaining the peace without the assistance of imported cutthroats and assassins from the slums of other cities, and the least concession to public decency that can be demanded is the Ohio law, which forbids the employment of non-residents as special policemen or deputy sheriffs. In Ohio no one outside of the county may be sworn in as deputy, and in Baltimore no one not a resident of the city should be employed as a special policeman. This is the minimum concession. The proper way, it would seem, to regulate the matter would be to have all policeman appointed by public authorities, and allow, under certain circumstances, the employment of policemen by private parties willing to pay therefor. It is to be noticed that after sad experience other states are passing laws to forbid the employment of non-residents as deputy sheriffs or special policemen ; and by a little forethought in this matter we can prevent bloodshed and bitterness between classes such as we see elsewhere. It is to be hoped that working-men and all who have the welfare of our state and city at heart will bestir themselves in this matter before it is too late. This is one of those cases where employment of home labor is the only safe policy.

The bill to which reference was here made passed the legislature, but was fortunately defeated by the governor's veto.

Municipal problems must now be left, in order to devote the remaining papers in this series to other subjects.

CHAPTER XXVIII.

OUR FUTURE RAILROAD POLICY.

RAILROADS have already been discussed in one paper in this series, but certain aspects of the problems connected with railroads were then reserved for future consideration.

Probably among German statesmen of recent years no one has had a higher appreciation of America than Edward Lasker, and probably no one has entertained general views more in harmony with prevailing sentiment in this country. It will be remembered that Congress passed resolutions of sympathy on occasion of his death, which Bismarck was requested to transmit to the German Parliament, and that the great German statesman refused to comply with the request to assist in honoring his bitter political opponent. Lasker had relatives in America, and shortly before his death visited our country, and in various ways seems to have acquired some familiarity with our institutions. I met Lasker in 1880 in Berlin at a reception given by the American minister, and talked with him about the railroad problem, then nearing its solution in Prussia by the purchase of the private roads. Lasker had conducted a remarkable parliamentary investigation into the affairs of the private railroads in 1873, and exposed their moral rottenness so thoroughly that public opinion began to react in favor of state railroads. It was natural, then, that he should be found on the side of the government in the proposed acquisition of

the railroads, although on other occasions so bitter an opponent of the government. I was, however, specially struck
by his remark about American railroads. He said : " You
in America must sooner or later acquire your railroads and
place them under public management. It will come as a
necessity, for natural forces are at work which will compel
you to take this course." This would have been a less surprising statement from other members of the Parliament,
but coming from him, it deserves careful attention. Is it
true that forces are at work which will bring about public ownership and management of railroads in the United
States? Who can read the future? Certainly it seemed as
improbable ten years ago that a mayor of New York City
should advocate municipal ownership of a system of rapid
transit as it now does that a President of the United States
should ever cast his influence in favor of a federal railroad
system. It must be said, too, that the proper railroad system for Germany was still an open question ten years ago,
whereas now it is no longer a problem of the day. It is
settled, and the settlement is endorsed by an overwhelming
majority of the German people of all shades of political opinion. One of my professors while I was a student in the University of Halle questioned, in 1877, seriously, the expedi-
ency of state railroads, and brought against them precisely
those arguments which we hear to-day in America ; but actual experience has made him even an enthusiastic adherent
of the Prussian system, while another recent and competent
writer says the suitability of government for railroad management is no longer open to question, since it has been settled
by the test of actual experience.

These facts deserve careful consideration ; and while the
correct course for us in the United States is by no means
clear, it seems like a wise thing so to regulate our policy as

to enable us to give that shape to our railroad system in the future which will best answer the demands of the situation. Those who have read the previous articles on natural monopolies will at once be able to state what should be done at present. It is a very simple thing to limit charters and to provide for the acquisition of railroad property at their expiration at an appraised valuation. It forces no new railroad system upon a people, but simply leaves a country free in the future to determine upon a suitable policy without well-nigh insurmountable obstacles of vested interests. This is the old Jeffersonian principle. It leaves each generation free to manage its own affairs in its own way. We have been giving perpetual charters and grants, and have thus squandered the rights of those who are to come after us. He has read history to little purpose who cannot foresee trouble in perpetual grants. The Almighty has set a limit to human life, and evidently did not intend that the dead should by acts, which profess to be forever binding, rule the living by hampering them in their freedom of movement. Efforts to do so are not likely to be successful, but they are likely to produce endless harm. What has been gained by perpetual grants of charters? Nothing; while it is easy to see how many existing evils would have been obviated by limited charters. All French and Austrian charters for railroads expire before 1950, and no one yet has ever shown that this limitation has worked harm to the public, while it is certain that these two countries will then come into an enormous possession. France expects the railroads to pay the present vast public debt. Limitations of charters may prevent much stock-watering and issues of enormous quantities of bonds, but it has never been found to check enterprise. Suppose we had limited charters, and, as a consequence, the Vanderbilts and Goulds had been able to make only ten or twelve millions of

dollars from railroad enterprise instead of three or four hundred millions : would they not still have been willing to go on
with their railroading? How could they have done better?
The plea that such vast fortunes are necessary for railroad construction is disproved by the fact that excellent railroads have
been built without the assistance of men of enormous wealth.
The excellent railroad system of Würtemberg was constructed
under the supervision of a man who received some $3000 a
year for his services, and seems to have been quite contented.

Much that has been done cannot readily be undone, but
there is no reason why future charters should not be limited
and means provided for the acquisition of the railroads which
they authorize, should it be thought desirable. The Western Maryland Railroad desires to lease a part of the Chesapeake and Ohio Canal, and perhaps under the circumstances
nothing better could be done than to hand the part of the
canal in question over to this corporation ; but can any one
give any reason why the lease should read for ninety-nine
years, " renewable forever"? Is it not enough if we bind
three generations? Great teachers like Bluntschli and John
Stuart Mill said we had no right to bind more than one. If
it is provided that the state shall at the expiration of ninety-
nine years have power to acquire the property at an appraised valuation, all interests are satisfactorily protected.

One difficulty in the way of reforms of this character is
that a class of men among us have become accustomed to
bulldoze the public. So in many states railroads used to
threaten to go around towns unless they contributed for
their construction. It is largely through such means that
our local political units have contributed some two hundred
millions of dollars for the construction of private railroads.
This has been prevented by constitutional amendments to
many state constitutions, which forbid any public contribu-

tions to private corporations. This has not been found to prevent railroad building, but it has forced private parties to use private money, and then left them free to·select natural routes. If our federal constitution prevented any charter for any purpose whatsoever from being granted for over fifty years, and compelled the reservation of right to re-purchase, and of other rights in behalf of the general public, it would be a reform worth talking about. The English Parliament has gone even further than this with respect to certain classes of charters, rendering it impossible to grant them for over twenty-one years.

The federal government ought to embrace every opportunity to acquire railroad property, to be leased, perhaps, for the present. What propriety was there in the construction of the Pacific railroads at the public expense, and then turning them over to private parties? Would not the people have been better served if government had kept the right of property in the roads and leased them for a limited period, under stringent conditions, to the highest bidder?

The course for Congress to pursue at the present time in regard to these roads is sufficiently clear, and if pursued would be the first step towards reform. It is to foreclose the mortgages, acquire the property, and lease it for twenty years.[1] Should the federal government guard properly all public property and all public rights, it would find itself in the possession of very considerable annual revenues from

---

[1] Two things should be kept in view in leases of railroads: first, the lowest possible freight and passenger charges; second, the highest possible percentage of gross revenues for the public treasury. Our Baltimore experience is instructive. Although we charge nine per cent. of gross revenues for street-car franchises, and in addition tax all their stock and plant, it has never been found to prevent street-railroad construction.

other sources than forms of taxation, which are restrictions
on the free movements of commerce and industry.

A federal tax which is needed is one which will yield a
steady revenue, and a revenue which can be increased if
need be.   A tax on the gross revenues of all railroads, sleep-
ing car, express, telegraph companies, and the like, engaged
in interstate commerce, might not be an undesirable form of
taxation, and might remove the possibility of a recurrence
of past financial embarrassments.   There is the more reason
for this because these powerful corporations are now trying
to resist every effort to make them contribute their proper
share of state and municipal burdens, on the ground that
states cannot tax them, because in so doing it interferes
with interstate commerce.

CHAPTER XXIX.

THE INNOCENT SHAREHOLDER.

WE hear much in these days of the innocent purchaser of railroad shares and other property with which fraud has been connected. The innocent shareholder has been made to cover a multitude of sins in the discussions on the Pacific Railroad, in the United States Senate; and this same character figured largely in the arguments on the Jacob Sharp Broadway franchise before the Court of Appeals in New York state. It must be acknowledged that the innocent stockholder, especially in the person of the widow and orphan, has done excellent service in the past, and is likely to become more prominent in the future. The Court of Appeals rendered a decision in the Broadway street-car case which must strike the economist as a little startling, and which, I will venture to assert, will come to be recognized as bad law inside of twenty years.

The charter was revoked; but the franchise and all the rights of this corporation, after it had met with legal death, passed over to the directors of the railroad, to be used for the benefit of the various claimants; and of course, claims for all it was worth had been established at the earliest possible moment. The people got the law, the shell of the nut; but the thieves got the property, the meat of the nut. History will surely have something to say about this legal hair-splitting. Suppose the public has rights like private individuals, what must necessarily result therefrom? Those

who receive property stolen from the public must be treated
like any other innocent receivers of stolen goods. We may
feel very sorry for them, but we take the property away
nevertheless, and restore it to the rightful owner. But let
us consider the case of the innocent shareholder a little
more carefully. A recovery of public property might work
hardship in some cases; but is the innocent shareholder the
only person to be considered? By no means; the millions
comprised in the term "the general public" are again forgotten. A very few persons might have suffered if the property which Jacob Sharp stole had been restored to its rightful owners, the public; but over a million people suffer in
New York on account of this theft, and some of them are
widows, and orphans, and day-laborers. No one will for a
moment deny, provided he knows anything at all, about the
facts that passengers can be carried at a large profit on
Broadway, in New York City, for three cents each. The
franchise could have been sold for a small percentage of
gross receipts on condition that passengers should be carried for three cents. This would have been a slight relief to
the tax-payer and a very great one to all poor people. Many
a poor widow and orphan and thousands of workingmen
trudge the streets of New York wearily for miles to-day who
might ride if fares were three cents. Every day of the year
sorrow and hardship are inflicted upon thousands of innocent and worthy people because they were forgotten, while
a few other innocent people, receivers of stolen goods, were
remembered. I submit that this is an iniquity. Those who
had money enough to buy shares and bonds were not the
most helpless class in the community. It is easy enough
for one who thinks the rights of the many equal to the rights
of the few to say what ought to be done. It is to defend
public property just as private property is defended. This

is the way to root out the anarchists, and the only way to make a permanent impression on them. Not an abolition of property rights is wanted, but an extension of property rights, and vigorous measures to defend the rights of the property of the many as well as of the few. Property is sacred; and when all property, that of the public as well as of the individual, that which resides in one's own person, one's strength — the labor power and the health, bodily vigor, and mind of the workingman — are properly guarded, attacks on private property need never be dreaded. So long as public thieves can crawl behind the innocent stockholder and place the widow and orphan between themselves and public wrath, public property has no adequate defence, and can have none, because those who get it at once begin to dispose of it. If, however, we as a people begin to show a higher appreciation of our own rights and treat our enemies with less gentle consideration, people will hesitate about purchasing property fraudulently acquired; and this will produce a wholesome habit on the part of purchasers of stocks and bonds of making inquiry about methods whereby alleged rights were secured. The proper method for protecting really innocent purchasers of stocks and bonds is easy enough. It is to provide civil as well as criminal remedies against the thieves. It is not difficult to give those who suffer at the hands of a man like Jacob Sharp ample civil remedies whereby they can recover damages. It is a thing which has already been done in other places, and for which precedent in somewhat similar cases can probably be found in the legislation of every American state. I think the English law of corporations already provides ample remedies for a case like that of Jacob Sharp, and I am very sure that the German law — the latest and most admirable law for private corporations — is all that could be desired in this respect. As for the rest, people will soon become disgusted with the " widow and orphan " plea, for it is made to do duty so often by scoundrels. It has been said we should not pay off the public debt of the United States because the widow and orphan might suffer ; and a good deal of pathos has been evolved on their account. Henry C. Adams, however, takes up the public debt and analyzes it in his work " Public Debts." He shows that out of $664,000,000 of registered bonds, $410,000,000 are held in sums of $50,000 and over, and he expresses the not unnatural conclusion, " It seems a little ludicrous to urge the maintenance of a federal debt as a measure of charity to dependent persons." Over 73,000 persons held registered bonds, but of these about 1500 held two-thirds of the total amount. It is not enough for corporations to come before the public with statements of the number of holders of stock and their wide distribution. We want to know more than that. We want an analysis of the wealth of the corporation in question ; and if the information is to be of value, we must be told just what percentage of stock is owned in small amounts, what in moderate quantities, and what percentage in large blocks. Should one of our states or our federal government begin from this time forth a vigorous defence of public property and public rights, a few persons of undoubted innocence and integrity would suffer at first ; but only at first, for people would soon be more circumspect than heretofore in purchases of stocks and bonds ; and as for the few real sufferers, we could well afford to indemnify them out of the public purse. As this would be bad policy on many accounts, it would be better to raise money needed for this purpose by private and voluntary offerings. When it happens that members of the dependent classes, like widows and orphans, are injured by a recovery of public property which has been stolen, I am willing to put my name down on a subscription list for their relief for a generous sum, and to use all the influence I have in inducing others to do likewise.

CHAPTER . XXX.

THE DEPENDENCE OF ARTIFICIAL MONOPOLIES ON NATURAL MONOPOLIES.

THE man of one idea is in some respects a useful man, for he sees a portion of the truth, and the intensity of his conviction in regard to its importance leads him to become an apostle on its behalf. Tariff reformers who find in protectionism an explanation of all the evils with which America is inflicted are doubtless blind to the real significance of innumerable classes of phenomena, but they are often on this account the more ardent in the propagation of the truth which they do see. Doubtless fanatics are needed to help on in the world's work. Nevertheless, one-sided advocacy of true principles has its disadvantages, for an exposure of the exaggerations into which men are thereby drawn leads many to overlook the kernel of truth about which so much error has gathered ; or, to use a different figure, those who perceive the vast amount of chaff which incloses the wheat are too often inclined to reject the chaff and the wheat alike rather than to take the trouble to separate the two.

Much nonsense is written about the tariff and monopoly, and the Chicago Gas Trust has even been connected with protectionism, with which in reality it has about as much connection as the rainfall of Baltimore with the length of the river Nile. It seems to me desirable for us to form clear notions about the actual workings of a protective tariff, and the consequences which in reality may be attributed to it.

I think that we will thus, on the whole, contribute vastly more to true and permanent progress than by a blind advocacy of we know not what.

It has been attempted in previous articles to show that certain pursuits are in their own inherent nature monopolies. These have been enumerated and described. They have become of vast importance during the past fifty years, but, nevertheless, they include only the minor part of our industrial life. The great majority of men are engaged in pursuits which are not natural monopolies; and if these men contrive to make of them business monopolies, it shows at once that something is wrong. Commerce, agriculture, mining, and manufactures are only in rare and exceptional cases natural monopolies. Yet we see a great many monopolies which may be placed in one of these classes. They are all artificial monopolies, and consequently are evils which should be suppressed. They violate the fundamental principles of our existing social and economic order, and are, as has been already stated, socialistic and revolutionary.

There are two causes of artificial monopolies. The first is legislation in behalf of men engaged in a pursuit not a natural monopoly. The second is the connection of a pursuit not a natural monopoly with one which is a natural monopoly, so that the two become, to a certain extent, one. I lay it down as a general proposition that artificial monopolies are businesses which have become monopolies only by an alliance with a business which is a natural monopoly. What legislation, as seen in a protective tariff, does, is simply to aid this alliance, to render it easier to form it, and to make it more impregnable when formed. He who thinks that tariff reform alone would remove monopolies and trusts, has not grasped the ABC of political economy. I ask the readers of the *Sun* to remember this. I believe that politi-

cal economy is sufficiently advanced to enable me to predict this with almost as great certainty as an astronomer
can predict a coming eclipse, and I am willing to take upon
myself whatever risks to my reputation as a scientific man
are involved in this prediction.   A reform in the field of
natural monopolies must accompany tariff reform in order
to uproot artificial monopolies.

The transfer of baggage from houses and hotels to railroad stations, and from railroad stations to houses and
hotels, is not a natural monopoly, but it is a business which
in every one of our great cities has become a partial monopoly.   How did the business become an artificial monopoly?   How has competition been well-nigh crushed?   Because in each great city one or two companies form alliances
with railroad companies and obtain exclusive privileges on
the trains and in the stations, the railroad companies obtain-
ing some *quid pro quo* — the railroad companies or some of
their officials, for I think it is not so often the stockholder
who receives the benefit as various officials who are let in
on the ground floor.   Thus it was that in 1879 the Erie
Railroad was found covered with barnacles ; but on the
whole there has been an improvement in this respect in
recent years.   But this is merely said " by the way."

As railroads are natural monopolies, those dependent
upon them are often made monopolies by their action.

The Standard Oil Company serves as another illustration.
It obtained a monopoly through an alliance with the railroads of the country, and this gave it special freight rates
which no one else could secure.   The report of the special
committee appointed to investigate the railroads in New
York in 1879 showed that the Standard Oil Company had
received in rebates ten millions of dollars in eighteen
months.   It was impossible for competitors to stand up

against such frightful odds. Quite recently a railroad in Ohio was found to have given the Standard Oil Company an advantage of three hundred and fifty per cent. over Mr. George Rice, of Macksburg and Marietta, their chief competitor in that part of Ohio.[1]   It was this alliance with a nat-

---

[1] This is not quite accurate. The arrangement was that, on oil shipped from Macksburg to Marietta, Mr. Rice should pay thirty-five cents a barrel, and the Standard Oil Company ten cents, but that of the thirty-five cents collected from Mr. Rice, twenty-five should be turned over to the Standard Oil Company. The railroad was the Cleveland and Marietta, then in the hands of a receiver, who was removed by Judge Baxter, of the United States Circuit Court. The following account, condensed from reports which appeared at the time, gives the details of the case : —

THE CIRCUIT COURT OF THE UNITED STATES,

Southern District of Ohio, Eastern Division.

PARKER HANDY AND JOHN PATEN, TRUSTEES, *vs.* THE CLEVELAND AND MARIETTA RAILROAD COMPANY ET AL.

This suit was commenced in the Common Pleas Court of Washington County, Ohio, January 12, 1885, to foreclose a mortgage upon the road and other property of the defendant, the Cleveland and Marietta Railroad Company, in which Phineas Pease was appointed receiver. . . In March, it was transferred to this Court. Everything progressed satisfactorily until October, 1885, when, upon complaint made of unjust discrimination by the receiver, an investigation was had, resulting in the development of the following facts : —

The Standard Oil Company owned or controlled certain pipe lines through and by means of which it collected and piped the oil procured by it in the vicinity of Macksburg, a station on the said road, to be carried thence by rail, either to Cleveland or Marietta. It thus controlled a large amount of freight which the receiver was, very naturally, solicitous of securing. But the conditions proposed were so unusual and unjust, and oppressive to rival shippers, that the receiver, after reluctantly acquiescing in the company's demand, sought to fortify himself by the advice of an attorney, and to this end wrote the following communication : —

ural monopoly, and this alone, which enabled the Standard Oil Company to secure a monopoly. The competitors of this concern have not retired before its superior business ability, but before its cheaper freight rates. It is by pursu-

CAMBRIDGE, OHIO, Feb. 25, 1885.

Edward S. Rapallo, Esq., General Counsel for Receiver, 32 Nassau Street, New York:

DEAR SIR: This will introduce Mr. J. E. Terry, Assistant General Freight Agent of this road, whom I send to New York to counsel with you in regard to verbal arrangements made with the Standard Oil Company for transporting the oil product along the line of our road to Marietta. Upon my taking possession of this road, the question came up as to whether I would agree to carry the Standard Company's oil to Marietta for ten cents per barrel in lieu of their laying a pipe-line and piping their oil. I of course assented to this, as the matter had been fully talked over with the W. & L. E. Company before my taking possession of the road, and I wanted all the revenue that could be had in this trade.

Mr. O'Day, Manager of the Standard Oil Company met the General Freight Agent of the W. & L. E. Railroad, and our Mr. Terry, at Toledo, about February 12, and made an agreement (verbal) to carry their oil at ten cents per barrel. But Mr. O'Day compelled Mr. Terry to make a thirty-five cent rate on all other oil going to Marietta, and that we should make the rebate of twenty-five cents per barrel on all oil shipped by other parties, and that the rebate should be paid over to them (the Standard Oil Company), thus giving us ten cents per barrel for all oil shipped to Marietta, and the rebate of twenty-five cents per barrel going to the Standard Oil Company, making that company save twenty-five dollars per day clear money on Mr. George Rice's oil alone.

In order to save the oil trade along our line, and especially save the Standard Oil trade, which would amount to seven times as much as Mr. Rice's, Mr. Terry verbally agreed to the arrangement, which, upon his report to me, I reluctantly acquiesced in, feeling that I could not afford to lose the shipment of seven hundred barrels of oil per day from the Standard Oil Company.

But when Mr. Terry issued instructions that on and after February 23, the rate on oil would be thirty-five cents per barrel to Marietta, Mr. George Rice, who has a refinery in Marietta, very naturally called on me yesterday, and notified me that he would not submit to the advance because his business would not justify it, and that the move was made by the Standard Oil Company to crush him out. [Too true.]

ing a shrewd policy in this respect that Mr. Rice has been able to maintain an existence as an oil refiner. Wherever freight rates are too much against him he retires from the field and seeks another market where he can contend on an

Mr. Rice said: " I am willing to continue the 17½ cent rate, which I have been paying from December to this date."

Now, the question naturally presents itself to my mind, if Mr. George Rice should see fit to prosecute the case on the ground of unjust discrimination, would the receiver be held, as the manager of this property, for violation of law? While I am determined to use all honorable means to secure traffic for the company, I am not willing to do an illegal act (if this can be called illegal) and lay this company liable for damages. Mr. Terry is able to explain all minor questions relative to this matter.

Hoping for your careful consideration of this matter and an early reply,

I remain, sir, truly yours,

P. PEASE,

Receiver and General Manager.

REPLY OF MR. RAPALLO.

32 NASSAU STREET, NEW YORK, March 2, 1885.

General Phineas Pease, Receiver Cleveland & Marietta Railroad Co.:

DEAR SIR: My opinion is asked as to the legality of your making such an arrangement with the Standard Oil Company as set forth below:

The facts, as I understand them, are as follows: The Standard Oil Company proposes to ship, or control the shipping of a large amount of oil over your road, say a quantity sufficient to yield you $3000 freight per month. That company also owns the pipes through which oil is conveyed from the wells owned by individuals to your railroad, except those pipes leading from the wells of Mr. George Rice, which pipes are his own. This company has, or can acquire, facilities for storing all its oil until such time as it can lay pipes to Marietta, and thus deprive your company of the carriage of its oil.

The amount of oil shipped by Mr. Rice is comparatively small, say a quantity sufficient to yield $300 per month for freight.

The Standard Oil Company threatens to store, and afterwards pipe all oil under its control, unless you make the following arrangement, viz.: You shall make a uniform rate of thirty-five cents per barrel for all persons excepting the Standard Oil Company; you shall charge them ten cents per

equal footing. The competitors of the Standard Oil Company have never complained of the superior skill or superior
business ability of the Standard Oil men, but of the favoritism which has been shown them by the railroads; and

barrel for oil, and also pay them twenty-five cents per barrel out of the
thirty-five cents collected from other shippers.

It may render the subject less difficult of consideration to determine,
first, those acts which you cannot with propriety do as Receiver.

You are by the decree vested with all the powers of receiver according to
the rules and practice of the court, are directed to continue the operations of
the railroad, and can safely make disbursements from such moneys as come
into your hands for such purposes only as the decree directs, viz.: wages,
interest, taxes, rents, freights, mileage on rolling stock, traffic balances, and
certain debts for supplies. In my opinion this would not protect you in
collecting freight from one shipper and paying it over to another. All
moneys received therefor, from any person for freight over your road, must
pass into your hands and there remain to be disbursed by proper authority.
After an examination of your statutes, however, I find no prohibition
against your allowing a discount, or charging a rate less than the schedule
rate to a shipper on account of the large amount shipped by him.

As you are acting, therefore, in the interest of the company, and endeav-
oring to increase its legitimate earnings as much as possible, I find nothing
in the statutes to prevent your making a discrimination, especially where
the circumstances are such that a large shipper declines to give your road
his freight unless you allow him to ship at less than the schedule rates.
Therefore, there is no legal objection to the making of an arrangement,
which in practical effect may be the same as that proposed, provided the
objections pointed out above are obviated.

You may, with propriety, allow the Standard Oil Company to charge
twenty-five cents per barrel for all oil transported through their pipes to your
road, and I understand from Mr. Terry that it is practicable to so arrange
the details that the company can, in effect, collect this direct, without its
passing through your hands. You may agree to carry all such oil of the
Standard Oil Company, or of others, delivered to your road through their
pipes, at ten cents per barrel. You may also charge all other shippers thirty-
five cents per barrel freight, even though they deliver oil to your road
through their own pipes, and this I gather from your letter and from Mr.
Terry would include Mr. Rice.

You are at liberty, also, to arrange for the payment of a freight by the
Standard Oil Company calculated upon the following basis, viz.: Such
company to be charged an amount equal to ten cents per barrel, less an

how close the alliance is can be seen in freight classifications
and changes therein in order to secure special favors for
the monopoly, and by hook and crook to make competitors an impossibility.

amount equivalent to twenty-five cents per barrel for all oil shipped by Rice,
the agreement between you and the company thus being that the charge to
be paid by them is a certain sum ascertained by such a calculation.

If it is impracticable so to arrange the business that the Standard Oil
Company shall in effect collect the twenty-five cents per barrel from those
persons using the company's pipes from the wells to the railroad without
its passing into your hands, you may properly, also, deduct from the price
to be paid by the company an amount equal to twenty-five cents per barrel
upon the oil shipped by such persons, provided your accounts, bills, vouch-
ers, etc., are consistent with the real arrangement actually made, you will
incur no personal responsibility by carrying out such an arrangement as
I suggest.

It is possible that by a proper application to the court, some person may
prevent you in future from permitting any discrimination. Even if Mr.
Rice should compel you subsequently to refund to him the excess charged
over the Standard Oil Company, the result would not be a loss to your road,
taking into consideration the receipts from the Standard Oil Company, if I
understand correctly the figures. There is no theory, however, in my
opinion, under the decisions of the Courts, relating to this subject, upon
which, for that purpose, an action could be successfully maintained in this
instance. Yours truly,

EDWARD S. RAPALLO.

The *Leader*, of Marietta, of November 24, 1885, says: Judge Baxter
characterized Rapallo's letter " as being the most insolent paper he ever
heard presented to a Court. . . . It is very clear that these enormous
discriminations have been disastrous to the business interests of our
city, for the difference in rate against all our independent refiners is so
great as to about equal their full profit on oil refined, and so their business has been nearly destroyed, except that of Mr. Rice, who was
driven to save himself by the construction of a pipe-line of his own.

" While this is so, the road has not been benefited by the action of
the receiver, for the Macksburg pipe-line carries its own oil to Parkers-
burg; the road has thus been deprived of the freight, and our city
of the successful refining business it should have."

The curious will find the story well told under the title of "A Commercial Crime," in Hudson's "Railways and the Republic."

The production of coal furnishes another illustration. This ought not to be a monopoly, but as to anthracite coal it has become such by its connection with railroad companies. A group of men interested in mines control the roads, and are thus able to dictate to other operators and rule them with a rod of iron, which renders the trades-union tyranny, of which we hear so much, insignificant in comparison. Men living in Maryland know full well that they are not at liberty to pay their men what they will, to mine coal where they will, and in quantities which suit their own convenience. They must do what they are told to do, or suffer financial ruin. A pursuit not a natural monopoly has become an artificial monopoly through an alliance with a business on which it depended, and which is in its own nature a monopoly. It is on this account that the constitution of Pennsylvania renders it illegal for a railroad to engage in any other lines of business than those connected with transportation. It is an entirely correct policy to demand that the railroads shall be held rigidly to their own proper functions, and that they shall serve all alike in order to avoid artificial monopolies. This was also the purpose of the interstate commerce law. The aim is correct, but there is no reason to think that the purpose of the Pennsylvania constitution or the interstate commerce law will be accomplished by present methods. The state constitutional provision and the federal law are of value as establishing a principle, but that alone is their chief significance.

There may be rare and exceptional cases in which the

tariff alone will enable men to secure a monopoly, but the approved method is to get control of the home market by alliances with natural monopolies, and then to keep foreign competition out by a high-tariff wall. The two go hand in hand.

CHAPTER XXXI.

GOVERNMENT BY SPECIAL INTERESTS.

GOVERNMENT is created to promote the general welfare, and when it is used to advance special interests which are not at the same time general interests, it is perverted from its original purpose. Our federal, state, and local governments are now controlled by men who hold their offices in trust for powerful private parties, and they view public measures, not from the standpoint of the general public, but from the standpoint of those in whose employ they are. This has been previously mentioned in this series of articles and need not be enlarged upon, for it is sufficiently obvious to those who "have eyes to see." One proof of this is the way in which legislative favors are exchanged. A. promises to support B.'s bill if B., in turn, will vote for some measure which interests A. This occurs daily, and would of course be an impossibility if A. and B. both voted simply for measures which they regarded as designed to benefit the public. Another evidence of the influence of private interests is seen in the question so often asked by legislators of the powerful when they visit the legislative halls, "Well, what can I do for you to-day?" The power held as a trust for the people is in return for some bribe, direct or indirect, placed at the disposal of a private person. The lobbies which exist everywhere are a further proof. These are maintained to instruct legislators in regard to private interests and to make it worth while for them to help forward some scheme for plundering the people. Again and again have citizens found it an absolute impossibility to secure any attention for measures designed simply to benefit the general public. Legislatures and city councils will not even take time to give them superficial attention. Consequently the practical man does not go in a straightforward manner to any one of our legislative bodies, and say: "I have devised plans for public improvements which will be of great benefit to our city, and I desire to explain them to you." On the contrary, he goes to some one who has influence and brings his plans forward in this indirect manner. It took a scandal like the Jacob Sharp case to force a bill through the New York legislature, rendering the sale of street-car franchises compulsory; and when in the legislature it was suggested that charters be limited as to length of time as in Louisiana, the influence of boodle was too strong. I say this because I hold that there was no lack of knowledge as to correct methods of dealing with the problem. It is simply impossible to find any grounds for unlimited street-car franchises, and had public interests been decisive, the franchises would have been limited in time. We have the fact of government by special interests known to all men. Now what is the cause?

The more carefully I examine the facts of the case, and the more I reflect upon the nature of the problem, the more inclined I feel to agree with those who find a chief cause in the protective tariff. The moment a tax is placed on imported goods, that moment those engaged in its production at home have an interest in the control of legislation to suit their private ends. It is unavoidable. The temptation to do wrong is absolutely inseparable from protectionism. Those who are protected form an association and keep agents at Washington, whose business it is on the one hand to raise the tariff, on the other to prevent a reduction in the tax on imported commodities. Special private interests are thus created by legislation, and these make free use of money. Assessments are levied on producers of taxed commodities to support a lobby at Washington, and in certain branches of productions manufacturers have come to look upon these assessments as a mere matter of course. The money goes to Washington, and no account is ever rendered of the mode in which it is expended. Legislators get in the habit of looking for remuneration of some kind for the performance of their legislative functions, and the most unscrupulous use office for what it will bring. There are two ways in which money can be made by legislators. They can receive money for their aid in getting through bills in which private parties are interested, and they can bring forward unjust bills designed to injure private parties purposely to be bought off. Proper bills, designed to guard the public interests, are also frequently brought forward, and then a shrewd legislator can obtain credit with the public for his service at the same time that he receives boodle for secretly killing his own bill. There is every reason to believe that such things happen at Albany, but of course not in connection with the tariff. The corruption of state legislatures and municipal councils is the work of those in possession of natural monopolies. The natural monopolies must be controlled, because it has been demonstrated by actual experience that it is impossible to turn over transportation, light, water, and the like to private corporations without regulation. Now the moment regulation begins, a diversity of interest between the public and private parties is created, and a wide door is opened for corruption.

It is easier to see this in a small town. Let us, therefore, again take the case of water-works in two places already mentioned. Fredonia, New York, has public works. No corporation exists to corrupt the village trustees; no powerful private interests adverse to those of the general public exist. The only source of corruption is the civil service, and the appointment of one or two officials has never been found to be appreciably demoralizing. Let us leave Fredonia and go to Jamestown, in New York, where a private water company exists. This company has from the start been engaged in litigation with the city. Now can any one fail to see how this at once introduces a corrupt and debasing influence in municipal politics? What has taken place in Jamestown I will not attempt to say; but the usual course is for the private corporation first to get control of the press, or a portion of it, then to send men to the council to decide all disputed questions between the corporation and the city in favor of the former, also to effect a repeal of any reserved public rights. The corporations have a tremendous advantage because they are utterly unscrupulous. Parties are to them merely tools. " In Republican districts I am a Republican, in Democratic districts I am a Democrat," is the assertion of a notorious railroad president. I might name a Western city in which there is reason to believe that the street-car corporations elect every municipal councillor, whether a Democrat or Republican, because in all the wards they control both parties. When I used to live in New York City I was in a position to know that nothing was so effectual in securing employment on the street-car lines as "a political pull," and there is reason to suppose that the same condition of things exists to-day. The street-car conductors and drivers were practically in the employ of politicians, and were a worse cause of demoralization than the same number of municipal employés, as there was not the same opportunity for exposure and improvement in methods of appointments.

Both causes of corruption and government by special interests are something inseparable from present policy. What should be done with respect to natural monopolies has already been explained at sufficient length. It may be well to add a word about tariff reform.

Let us first examine all the different sorts of protective tariffs which can be defended on rational grounds, thus summing up and completing what has gone before on this topic. A protective tariff is not a good thing in itself. It prevents some people from doing what they would like, and thus restricts their liberty. It also causes these people a pecuniary loss, at least for the immediate future ; either they pay the tax, or the tax is so high that they do not pay it, but purchase other commodities at a higher price than that demanded for tne foreign commodity. Both cases alike require a sacrifice of financial resources. An inferior article may perhaps be purchased at the same price, but this course also entails loss. If neither a foreign nor a domestic commodity is purchased, a sacrifice is still required, because we must suppose that the commodity would subserve some purpose. Whichever alternative we take, we find that, for the time being at least, protective tariffs interfere with liberty and cause sacrifice. They must then justify themselves. They stand on the defensive.

The first kind of a protective tariff, which can be defended in certain places and at certain times, is what we may term an *Educational Tariff*. The protection of infant industries would fall under this head. The case of infant industries has already been discussed with reference to the United States. If there ever was a time when protective tariffs were justifiable in the United States on account of the infancy of our industries, that time has long passed. The practical difficulty connected with the protection of infant industries has already been mentioned. It requires a great deal of wisdom to know how to apply such a tariff, and it requires a remarkable degree of integrity — one, it is safe to say, never yet found in an American Congress — to lessen the protection gradually and finally to withdraw it altogether. Protective tariffs have a terrible hold on a country when once established. Educational tariffs would include tariffs to protect some lines of industries to which a country might be peculiarly adapted, but for the pursuit of which it might require a certain amount of industrial education. Japan may serve as an example. It is conceivable that when such a country first enters upon international trade, the industrially backward condition of its people who are at the same time by nature gifted, and are progressively inclined, may place it at a peculiar disadvantage in pursuits in which it may reasonably hope shortly to excel. A temporary disadvantage may thus, it is conceivable, rest on such a country with respect to those pursuits for which it will shortly possess relatively the greatest facilities. It takes time to accumulate capital, to break with old customs, to become familiar with modern methods, and to adopt them as part of the new economic life. The temporary sacrifice of a protective tariff would then be counterbalanced by permanent gain in the future.

The only kind of a protective tariff advocated by Frederick List, already mentioned as perhaps the ablest of the protectionists, is an educational protective tariff. I am not prepared to say that great as are the difficulties of such a tariff, I would never advocate it under any circumstances. It may be mentioned incidentally that the art of government has progressed rapidly during the past fifty years, that it is still progressing rapidly, and that people through governmental agency are daily performing successfully things which the older theorists pronounced impossible. However, any one who says that an educational tariff is now needed in the United States simply talks nonsense. It may be doubted if it ever was needed. If the manufacturers needed any assistance to tide over the difficulties of 1816, it could have been given them in other ways described in previous chapters. Large capital accumulations exist in this country. Marvellous and almost unequalled natural facilities for wealth creation are here found, and the American people are alert, active, intelligent, gifted withal with wonderful inventive genius. It is not with respect to industrial education certainly that we are in a backward condition.

The second kind of a rational protective tariff may be called a *Social Tariff.* This is a tariff laid to help the laboring classes for social reasons. The general public is interested in the condition of the laboring classes, and it is altogether desirable that wages should be high ; that hours should be shortened ; that dwellings should be improved ; that the reckless waste of life in our industries should be diminished by employers' liability acts and factory laws for sanitary inspection of workshops, for the fencing in of dangerous machinery, for prohibition of child labor, for restriction of the employment of women, and the like. The happier, the more intelligent, the more prosperous, the more moral the laboring classes, the better, and every measure which improves their environment deserves commendation. But does the welfare of the laboring classes require us to establish a protective tariff ? It has already been mentioned that high-priced labor is the cheapest labor, and those countries where laborers work the fewest hours and receive the highest wages are most dreaded in international competition. It has been said that German manufacturers require some temporary protection on account of social changes there going forward. Expensive schemes are there being inaugurated which look to the compulsory insurance of all artisans and mechanics to provide for accident, disability, and nearly all disasters which overtake working people. Part of the cost must be defrayed by the employers. Granting all the premises, it is conceivable that there may be justification for a limited and moderate protection. Professor Lexis of Breslau, a careful and scholarly writer, speaks of a tariff of thirty per cent. as the extreme limit of desirable protection.[1] But whatever may be the situation of German manufacturers, there is no ground for advocating a social protective tariff in the United States. Our labor is so efficient and our resources are so boundless that employers can still pay current wages and derive larger average profits from their capital than European competitors.

International factory legislation has been suggested as preferable to a social protective tariff. It is proposed that the great nations of the world come to some common agreement respecting the hours of daily toil, or the normal working day; also employers' liability, safeguards against accidents, child labor, the labor of women, the education of the masses, workingmen's insurance, and such matters, so that no nation shall be placed at a disadvantage on account of what it does for the laboring classes. Switzerland has, indeed, made propositions looking to international factory legislation to other governments, but these have not met with a warm reception. As between the two, there can be no doubt that international agreement respecting factory

[1] See his monograph on Handel in the 2d edition of Schönberg's " Handbuch der Politischen Oekonomie," Tübingen, 1886.

legislation is preferable to a social protective tariff. But it will be very difficult to bring about such agreement.

The third kind of a rational protective tariff we may call a *Military Defence Tariff*. If a tariff is required to insure the production of things absolutely necessary to the safety of a country in time of war, and of which it may possibly be deprived by its enemies, it goes without saying that the tariff is rational. The manufacture of powder in Switzerland is, perhaps, an example. It is conceivable — though not probable — that Switzerland might, under certain contingencies, be deprived of the opportunity to obtain powder from foreign nations. If there is even a remote possibility that the supply of arms and ammunition could be cut off, a country might do well to protect the manufacture of these articles by a protective tariff. It will, however, generally, if not always, be more profitable to support government establishments for the production of such things, and so to contrive them that it be possible to increase largely their product at a moment's notice.

There never can be any propriety in a military defence protective tariff in the United States. First, it is difficult to see what thing necessary in war would not in our country be produced without a tariff; second, it is inconceivable that a country whose boundaries are twenty-five thousand miles long should be shut off from all intercourse with foreign nations. It is quite proper and answers all purposes that government should maintain a few navy yards and establishments for the manufacture of things needed in war, and that in ship construction, outside of its own establishments, it should make contracts with home producers.

A fourth kind of protective tariff we may call a *Relief Tariff*. It is conceivable that on account of the general welfare it may be well to tax the community to bolster up an important special interest, or to prolong a transition period from one sort of industrial life to another, and to mitigate the distress incident to such a period. The only example which occurs to me is that of the land-owning and agricultural classes of Germany. These are the backbone of the country, and their economic ruin would involve radical changes in the political and social character of the nation. The competition of American farmers has produced great distress, among the agriculturists and rural land-owners of Germany. They labor under mortgages and heavy fixed charges, and it is a long and painful operation for them to adjust themselves to a much lower range of prices for agricultural products. Educated and intelligent Germans say that their peculiar condition justifies a moderate protective tariff. Yet there can be no doubt that the taxes thereby imposed upon the community have produced distress, and tend to retard the development of manufactures by increasing the price of food, and consequently raising wages. A relief tariff will produce more distress than it cures unless it is applied with discretion and moderation.

The fifth kind of a rational protective tariff we may, for lack of a better term, call an *Historical Continuity Tariff.* The present depends on the past. We cannot neglect historical conditions without harm. Sudden and radical changes ruin important industrial factors. A tariff of a hundred years' duration in the United States cannot be left out of consideration, even if it has given an unnatural and injurious direction in some important instances to capital and labor. A sudden change of policy—an introduction to-morrow, for example, of free trade in the United States — might increase imports largely and cause a temporary outflow of a part of our supply of precious metals. This might bring about a readjustment of prices and lower prices in the United States.

Now while high or low prices in themselves may be a matter of little importance, it is of vast importance whether prices rise or fall.   Lower prices would bring about an increase in value of all bonds, mortgages, and fixed obligations ; consequently would increase public burdens resting on the community, and private burdens resting on all debtors and on all others having fixed payments.   This would be most disastrous in its consequences.

Free trade would open up to us many foreign markets, and in the end there is reason to believe would increase our supply of money as well as of other commodities.   It would in the end add to our wealth in every respect.   But too sudden transitions are dangerous.

These are, I conceive, the only kinds of rational protective tariffs, and only the last is applicable to the United States.   It is to be noticed that they are all temporary in character, and I think no protectionist writer of first-rate ability has ever contemplated protectionism as a permanent policy.

Retaliatory Tariffs have been frequently mentioned.   Their aim is to force countries to lower or remove commercial restrictions by retaliatory duties.   Nothing seems ever to have been gained by such measures.   Retaliation is more likely to lead to retaliation in turn by increasing instead of removing restrictions.   Retaliatory tariffs are not called for in the United States.   The aim of retaliatory tariffs is free trade and not protection.   Retaliatory tariffs are measures whereby it is hoped that free trade may become reciprocal, and can be consistently advocated only by those who accept the proposition that free trade is a good thing.   The English " fair traders " advocate retaliatory tariffs in order to force other countries to adopt the principles of free trade.   It seems clear, however, that the fair trade movement — if it should ever lead to practical results, of which there is no prospect — would injure England, and attain no results whatever in the desired direction. The adoption of fair trade by Eng-land would certainly strengthen the protectionists in the United States. Even the fair-trade agitation has done that.

Tax-Equalizing Tariffs are tariffs laid on goods to coun-terbalance excise or internal revenue taxes, and as they do not change relations between home and foreign producers, are not really protective at all.

Did free trade already exist, there is reason to believe that it would be a good thing for the country. We have supe-rior advantages over other countries, and the strongest is not the one to suffer in competition. Farmers and workingmen are the last ones to gain by protection, and I have no doubt that both would gain were trade as free between Europe and America as between our states. However, the fact of the tariff exists, and the fact is of vast importance. Our indus-tries have grown up under it for over seventy years, and have become more or less adjusted to an artificial state of things. Good faith requires that we should in dealing with manufacturers bear this fact in mind, and move carefully in readjusting trade relations. This is not saying that we should do nothing, but simply that rash, hasty movement should be avoided. No one has received any pledge that tariff laws would not be changed, yet it seems only fair that those who have relied upon a traditional policy should have a little time in which to adjust themselves to a new state of things. While it is true that the fears entertained in many quarters in regard to the effects of even radical tariff reform are greatly exaggerated, there can be no doubt that immedi-ate free trade would ruin a good many manufacturers. Now our industrial life has become an organism, and you cannot injure one member without injuring the entire body. This is well established. Industrial shocks are propagated. An injury to manufacturers may involve banks, these in turn the farmers, and so on indefinitely. Industrial organism is extremely sensitive, and displacements of labor and capital are attended with a great deal of pain.

Farmers have nothing whatever to hope from protection, and as a step towards tariff reform free raw materials will be likely to benefit the general public and to produce no industrial shock. Free raw material should be accompanied by correspondingly lower duties, or even by duties a little more than proportionately lower. Whenever any article is placed on the free list, it is a clear gain, and one temptation to government by special interests is removed. A steady, persistent effort should be made to tax as few things as possible, as thus interference with trade and temptation to corruption will be reduced. A fruitful source of fraud and injustice as between various ports is caused by difficulties attending valuations. It is desirable to simplify administration by substituting in every practicable case specific for ad valorem duties.

PART II.

.

THE NEEDS OF THE CITY.

INTRODUCTORY NOTE.

THIS address was delivered at the General Christian Conference, held under the auspices and direction of the Evangelical Alliance of the United States, at Boston, Dec. 4, 1889. Another address was announced by the secretary of the Alliance, Rev. Josiah Strong, D.D., and a discussion was also advertised. On this account I attempted to present one line of thought chiefly, leaving other aspects of the question for other speakers. Had this address been intended to stand by itself, it might have been necessary to enlarge on individual work, considered in itself and in its relation to public work. I speak of the importance of the work of the Earl of Shaftesbury as a legislator : years of hard private work on his part, and on the part of many others, were required, to make his legislative reforms a possibility. While legislation often lags behind its possibilities, it is likewise true that it sometimes is in advance of public sentiment, and that it consequently is ineffective.

There is plenty of work to do ; and no one need feel discouraged because he cannot enter a state legislature, or Congress. Every good influence exerted on any human being helps to render all other good work more successful. Yet in certain classes of the community, — and those, the most influential, — the truths which I tried to impress on my audience need emphasis at the present time. When all qualifications are made, it remains true that no power for good equals that of good government. I was reading an account of the work of the Salvation Army, in saving fallen women, in the slums of cities, when the thought occurred to me, Here is, after all, highly beneficial work of a purely private and individual character; but reading further in Mrs. Booth's book, " Beneath Two Flags," I came to these words in regard to the " Rescue Homes " for fallen women: " Of the thirteen homes, in different foreign lands, those in Australia are the most prosperous. This can be attributed largely to the appreciative government support they receive. The Victorian government had even made a grant to the Melbourne Home."

The addresses delivered at the General Christian Conference are all to be published for the Evangelical Alliance, by the Baker & Taylor Company; and my thanks are due to the Alliance for permission to print the paper in this place.

RICHARD T. ELY.

THE NEEDS OF THE CITY.

————◆————

WORKING in East London there are two devoted
city missionaries, — Rev. Samuel A. Barnett, and his
wife, Mrs. Henrietta O. Barnett. Mr. Barnett is rector of
St. Jude's Church; and he and his wife have been faithfully
toiling among the masses, for their material, moral, intellectual, and spiritual uplifting, for fifteen years. During this
time they have gained a vast fund of information respecting
the needs of the city and the appropriate means for satisfy-
ing these needs ; and a part of this fund of information they

---

LITERATURE.

Practicable Socialism, by SAMUEL A. and HENRIETTA O BARNETT.
London: Longmans, Green, & Co.; New York, 1 East 16th
Street. 1888.

FREMANTLE'S *The World as the Subject of Redemption.* Bampton
Lectures, 1883. New York: E. & J. B. Young & Co., Cooper
Union, Fourth Avenue. 1885.

ALBERT SHAW'S *Municipal Government in England*, published as part
of the " Notes " issued in connection with the Johns Hopkins University Studies in *History and Political Science.* Baltimore, 1888
Also his forthcoming *Century* article on Glasgow. Also his forthcoming book on *European Municipal Government.*

BRACE'S *Dangerous Classes in New York.* New York: Wynkoop &
Hallenbeck, 113 Fulton Street, New York. 1872. Recommended,
with a protest against his attitude towards labor organization ; also
against his idea that emigration to the country can be regarded as a
permanent and sufficient remedy for any class of urban evils.

LOOMIS' *Modern Cities.* New York: Baker and Taylor Co., 740 Broadway, New York. 1887.

have rendered accessible to the general public, in their excellent little work, " Practical Socialism." I shall quote at once several passages from this book ; and these will serve as the central thoughts about which I shall group my brief remarks.

" The social reformer must go alongside the Christian missionary, if he be not himself the Christian missionary." — Page 195.

" The one satisfactory method of social reform is that which tends to make more common the good things which wealth has gained for the few. The nationalization of luxury must be the object of social reform." — Page 65.

" The conversion of sinners, — at any rate, while the sinners are sought chiefly among the poor, — the emigration of children, the spread of thrift and temperance among the work people, will still leave families occupying single rooms, and the sons of men the joyless slaves of work, — a state of society for which no defence can be made." — Page 65.

" Societies which absorb much wealth, and which relieve their subscribers of their responsibility, are failing ; it remains only to adopt the principle of the education act, of the poor law, and of other socialistic legislation, and call on society to do what societies fail to do. There is much which may be urged in favor of such a course. It is only society — or, to use the title by which society expresses itself in towns, it is only town councils (*i.e.* city councils) — which can cover all the ground, and see that each locality gets equal treatment. It is by common action that a healthy spirit becomes common ; and the tone of public opinion may be more healthy when the town council engages in good doing than when good doing is the monopoly of individuals or of societies. *If nations have been ennobled by wars undertaken against an enemy, towns may be ennobled by work undertaken against the evils of poverty.*" — Page 66.

"Some way must be found which, without pauperizing, without affecting the spirit of energy and independence, shall give to the inhabitants of our great towns the surroundings which will increase joy and develop life." — Page 67.

"The first practical work is to rouse the town councils to the sense of their powers; to make them feel that their reason of being is not political, but social; that their duty is not to protect the pockets of the rich, but to save the people. The care of the people is the care of the community, and not of any philanthropic section." — Page 72.

"The people, not politics, must be our cry," says Mr. Barnett.

"As a rule, it may be laid down that the voluntary work is most effective when it is in connection with official work." — Page 73.

I have finished my quotations, and I have no apology to make for their length. They are worthy of the most careful study.

WHAT ARE THE NEEDS OF THE CITY?

1. First of all, I would mention this need, — a profound revival of religion; not in any narrow or technical sense, but, in the broadest, largest, fullest sense, a great religious awakening which shall shake things, going down into the depths of men's lives and modifying their character. The city needs religion, and without religion the salvation of the city is impossible.

All successful workers among the masses say we need religion, and yet this is — almost invariably, I think — accompanied by a protest. I join this protest. You remember words which I have read to you from the book, "Practicable Socialism": "The conversion of sinners — at

any rate, while the sinners are sought chiefly among the poor
—will still leave families occupying single rooms, and the sons
of men the joyless slaves of work, — a state of society for
which no defence can be made." I ask your attention, also,
to these words, taken from Mr. Brace's " Dangerous Classes
of New York " : " In religious communities, such as the
English and American, there is too great a confidence in
technical religious means. The mistake we refer to is a too
great use of, or confidence in, the old technical methods,
such as distributing tracts, and holding prayer-meetings, and
scattering Bibles. The neglected and ruffian classes . . .
are in no way affected directly by such influences as these."
You all know Mr. Brace, the head and heart of that magnificent movement in New York represented by the Children's Aid Society, and you all know how religious his
work is.

You will get a hint of what is wanted in my first quotation
from Mr. Barnett, " The social reformer must go alongside
the Christian missionary, if he be not himself the Christian
missionary."

You may read of a remarkable religious awakening in the
fifteenth and sixteenth centuries, under the influence of which
great leaders were unable to separate religion and politics.
It is this kind of a religious awakening which our modern
city needs.

What must be the direction of this religious reform? It
must infuse a religious spirit into every department of political life, and, with Canon Fremantle, recognize the nation
itself as the truest development of the Church, and " the
attempt to establish the political and social relations on a
religious basis " as " the most divine work given to man." [1]

---

[1] "The World as the Subject of Redemption," page 208.

2. This leads me to remark that the second great need of the city — which is the first need re-stated from a different point of view — is a renaissance of nationalism, or, if you will, to narrow it down to our present theme, *municipalism*. Government is the God-given agency through which we must work. To many, I am aware, this is not a welcome word ; but it is a true word. We may twist and turn as long as we please, but we are bound to come back to a recognition of this truth. Societies have failed. Societies, particularly as organized in city councils or city governments, — to adopt what is, with us, the more comprehensive designation, — must recognize the work we want done as the concern of the community, and must themselves do it. The most successful work, says Barnett, after his long striving, is done by the Education Act, the Poor Law, and other socialistic legislation. That that is the most successful work is also illustrated by the life and career of the seventh Earl of Shaftesbury, who carried through Parliament legislation which has benefited millions of Englishmen. If simply by touching a person you could confer a distinct benefit on the person touched, it would take you twenty years to benefit as many people as have been benefited by legislation chiefly due to this great philanthropist. Also the experience of Elberfeld, Berlin, and other German towns so celebrated for the administration of charity, confirms what is here said. Their success is due to private co-operation with official work. " If nations have been ennobled by wars undertaken against an enemy, towns may be ennobled by work undertaken against the evils of poverty."

Societies have failed, and will fail. They cannot, acting simply as societies, do the work. Their resources are inadequate, the territory they can cover is too small, and their power is insufficient. The Evangelical Alliance, simply as such, can never do the work. The Evangelical Alliance, like other societies, must put itself behind municipal government, and recognize the reform and elevation of municipal government as one of the chief features of its work. It must strive to establish among us true cities of God. There is plenty of room for the individual, and for individual activity. Not all the work can be done by government, although without government very little can be accomplished. But in addition to strictly private work, there is room for any amount of individual work in stimulating official work and in co-operation with official work.

We must recognize this ; and the sooner we recognize it, the better. This doctrine was long resisted in the matter of popular education, but now its recognition in this department of life is universal. In all the world's history we have never had anything like universal education, save when and where government has furnished it. How long and arduously have people with us (and more arduously and still longer in England) tried with private means to educate the people, and how ineffectually ! But when your Horace Mann comes forward, and convinces the people that "voluntary work is most effective when it is in connection with official work," then, indeed, the people's cause moves forward. We need to-day in our cities new men to arise and to preach this doctrine with the apostolic zeal of Horace Mann. Not more private schools are needed, but the better maintenance of such as exist, and otherwise the use of private means to stimulate public endeavor. This is, I am happy to say, being done to some extent. As I understand it, this is what the trustees of the Peabody and Slater Funds are most wisely trying to do.

It takes a great effort, and persistent, unflagging zeal, to keep alive a few industrial schools like those which Mr.

Brace has established in New York. He has my admiration, for his great work; but I cannot help asking the question, If a little more energy had been used in stimulating public authorities and co-operating with them, would not greater things have been accomplished? Shameful, incredibly disgraceful, as it may be to the authorities of New York City, fourteen thousand children in that city were this fall turned from the doors of the public schools because there was not room for them. Now, with two hundred children to a school, it would take seventy private schools to educate these children; whereas the energy and zeal necessary to support ten such schools, expended in enlightening the public and stimulating the conscience of the municipal authorities, would have rendered this criminal record an impossibility.

Mr. Jacob A. Riis has written an article on the tenement house population of New York, which appeared in *Scribner's Magazine* for December, 1889. It is called, "How the Other Half Lives," and is a noteworthy article. One passage in it shows the ineffectiveness of private work dissociated from official work or inadequately supported by legislation and administration. It is as follows: "The ten-cent lodging houses more than counterbalance the good done by the free reading room, lectures, and all other agencies of reform. Such lodging houses have caused more destitution, more beggary and crime, than any other agency I know of." Mr. Riis quotes this from one of the justices on the Police Court bench. Now, these lodging houses can never in the world be abolished by private effort. Insufficient as it has been, public authority, I believe, has already done more to improve the dwellings of the poor than all private agencies combined. But we want a co-operation of both. "The first practical work is to rouse the town councils to the sense of their powers; to make them feel that their duty is not to protect the pockets of the rich [by reducing taxes and turning children away from public schools, as in New York], but to save the people." And "the care of the people is the care of the community, and not of any philanthropic section."

Time is short, and things, even at the risk of misunderstanding, must be passed over briefly.

We need, then, two things, — religion and nationalism. Put these together, and we have religious nationalism. But is this not Christian socialism? Yes, it is, in a certain sense ; and I rejoice in the growth here in Boston, I may say frankly, of nationalism and Christian socialism. It is not that I accept all the principles of those who support these movements. I must, with equal frankness, say that I can only go part way with them ; for I think they go too far. I do think, however, — and I do not hesitate to say that I think, — that to-day they are the leaven which is needed in American society ; and as I fear nothing from those doctrines of theirs which strike me as extreme, I rejoice in their activity. Christian socialism — if you will take it in my conservative sense — is what I think we need ; that is, religion coupled with true nationalism.

An objection may be raised here, on account of the poor character of our government of cities. Of course our governments are poor. Why should they not be? We have done everything to make them so. We have been taught to turn away from government for the accomplishment of business purposes and for social improvement. We have been trying to reduce government to a contemptible insignificance, and, in many cases, have succeeded in reducing it to contemptible impotence. Lest men should do some wrong thing, we have made it impossible for them to do any good thing. We have succeeded in turning the energy and talent of the community, for the most part, away from public life, and diverted the great bulk of talent and energy into private life. We have reaped the legitimate fruits that might have been expected — one is tempted to say, which have been deserved.

Government never, in the world's history, has been made good government by the application of the maxim, " That is the best government that governs least." It never will be made good by reducing it to insignificance. It is, as a matter of fact, the opposite policy which has made good government, whenever and wherever good government has existed.

You have read about the cathedral-building, four, five, and six hundred years ago. How could our ancestors in those times, in some respects so rude, accomplish such matchless marvels in cathedral-building? Simply by putting their souls into the work. Similarly, when we put some portion of our intellectual and spiritual resources into the duties of government, recognizing the nation as church, we shall have good government.

We are considering the needs of the city. But this means an increasing proportion of the population; and on the whole, I think we may rejoice that it does mean an ever-increasing proportion of the population. The statistics of the increasing urban population throughout the civilized world have often been presented. We all know that one hundred years ago a thirtieth of the population of our country lived in cities, that now one-fourth lives in cities, and that presently half of our population will be urban. This movement is inevitable. It is not due, as some think, in any considerable degree to the inclinations and desires of the people, but it is due to an economic force which is well-nigh as irresistible as the movements of the tide. Let us cherish no Utopian schemes of turning people back to the rural districts. Every new good road, every new canal, every new railway, every new invention, every economic improvement, — in short, nearly all industrial progress, — centralizes the population in cities. It is, on the whole, good, because man finds his welfare in association with his fellows : by nature, as Aristotle says, he is a social being ; and city life makes a higher degree of association possible. This means progress of all kinds, if we are but equal to the increasing strains city life puts upon our civilization.

But what do we want for this increasing urban population ? Let us again come back to this question. Barnett states our problem in these words : "Some way must be found which, without pauperizing, without affecting the spirit of energy and independence, shall give to the inhabitants of our great towns the surroundings which will increase joy and develop life."

Some one may here interpose this objection, " I thought we were talking about religious reform ? " So we are. But do you notice these words, " Increase joy and develop life " ? What is all sin but lack of life ? Do you remember the words of Christ, — how he said he came to bring us life ; how, in one place, he said he came that we might have life, and have it more abundantly ; and how he constantly spoke of his highest, all-inclusive gift as " life eternal " ? Yes, we are speaking about religious reform, and all reform must become religious reform. You remember these words of an Italian statesman, " Every political question is becoming a social question, and every social question a religious question." Tract distribution and revivals, in the narrow sense, are not enough : environment must be changed. All social and statistical science teaches this ; and every rational man practically acknowledges it in his own conduct, especially when his own family is concerned. It is only in theoretical disputation that any one will deny it. Read Mr. Brace's book, and see its tremendous importance; see how a change of environment saved all except four out of two thousand children and young persons, the vast majority of whom were, in their old environment, inevitably doomed to perdition. Listen carefully to these words, written by Mr. Brace himself: "Few girls can grow up to maturity in such dens as exist in the first, sixth, eleventh, and seventeenth wards and be virtuous; few boys can have such places as homes, and not be thieves and vagabonds. In such places typhus and cholera will always be rife, and the death rate will reach its most terrible maximum. While the poorest population dwell in these cellars and crowded attics, neither Sunday-schools nor churches nor charities can accomplish a thorough reform." Read the results of the investigations of the ablest statisticians about regularly recurring crime and wrongdoing, and ask yourself, How can all this be changed except through changed environment? This changed environment must precede or accompany — or, at any rate, closely follow — exhortation and other individual treatment.

We are told that the nationalization of luxury is required; let us say again, if you will, the municipalization of luxury. Luxury is here used in a good sense, as equivalent of means of abundance of life, like libraries, museums, and art galleries.

Let us go into details regarding the needs of the city; and here, on account of the time-limit, I must confine myself to remarks which will be but a little more than the enumeration of items. You may place in connection with each item, "Church Work." If I say education, then I point out work for the church, and consequently for the Evangelical Alliance, — a work in bringing about the best education, and infusing into it the right spirit.

ENUMERATION OF THINGS NEEDED BY THE CITY.

1. Let me first mention the means of education, which should be liberally provided, and which should, for the most part, be gratuitously offered. I do not speak simply of schools of the lower grades, but of schools of all grades, and of much besides schools. I would thus broaden the way to success, and utilize all talent in the community. With these schools I would establish a sifting process, so that only the more gifted should advance to higher grades. Such a scheme has already been working in New York state for some time. There are state scholarships, entitling the recipients to free tuition in Cornell University, and one of them is offered for competition, in each assembly district, each year. There are thus over five hundred all told. It may be that the ideal thing is a public educational system, comprising all grades of school up to, and inclusive of, the university. That I will not discuss. It seems, however, that in a state like Massachusetts, the proper course is, by means of such scholarships, to connect the public schools with your academies, colleges, and universities, institutions like Amherst College, Clark and Harvard Universities, which are private foundations. I think a beginning has already been made in the Massachusetts Institute of Technology. But public education does not begin early enough for the needs of the city. The majority of children in cities are under bad home influences, and free kindergartens should be a part of the school system. It is all very well to talk about the work of the family, but what about the majority of children in large cities, for whom no wholesome family life exists? I have sometimes feared that my good friend Dr. Dike favored reactionary elements, in not taking into account sufficiently the actual situation. Industrial training ought to be made

important everywhere, and I note with satisfaction the progress it is making in Boston. Mr. Brace speaks of industrial schools as the best agency for reforming the worst class of children in cities; and the experience of the Elmira Reformatory in New York shows that a majority, even of young convicted criminals, can be reformed by it, when coupled with good discipline. We find that many criminals and paupers are uneducated, and untrained in any trade. The apprenticeship system is antiquated, and city dwellings furnish no opportunity for girls to learn womanly occupations. Preparation for life must, for all, come from the school; for the many, it is the only place whence it can come.

But our educational system should not cease to provide for people when they leave school. Education ought to end only with life. This brings me to mention such educational facilities as free libraries, free reading rooms, within convenient distance of every part of the city — perhaps, in many cases, attached to schoolhouses, and open after school hours.

University-extension lectures ought to be provided; and Mr. Dewey, of New York, has been working on some large plans for extension lectures to be connected with the public schools of New York state, and to be conducted under the auspices of the Board of Regents. Private undertakings like Chautauqua could well supplement whatever public authority does.

Schoolhouses should be better utilized as gathering places for clubs, debating societies, and all bodies of men who would give guarantee of proper behavior. Open in the evening, they would help to counteract the baleful influences of the saloon.[1]

Art galleries and museums — which may multiply the value

---

[1] See Barnett, pages 70 and 71.

of pictures and other enjoyable articles a hundredfold, by rendering them accessible to all — may be mentioned under this general head ; and in my opinion they ought all to be open on Sunday. I do not believe in leaving a free field to the devil every seventh day.

It goes without the saying that religious education is an important part of all education and that the church should become more active than ever, and become to a greater extent than at present, a real people's church. Church buildings also are not as fully utilized as they might be.

2. As a second item and one closely connected, I mention play-grounds, parade grounds, play-rooms and gymnasiums. I would include universal military drill for boys and young men.

Experienced educators will tell you what a remarkable agency physical drill is for the cultivation of good morals ; half of the wrong-doings of young rascals in cities is due to the fact that they have no innocent outlet for their animal spirits.

3. The third item is free public baths and public wash-houses, like those which in Glasgow have proved so successful.[1]

4. The fourth item is public gardens and parks and good open-air music.

5. Very important in all large cities is an improvement of artisans'' dwellings, and the housing of the poor generally. All those who work among the poor speak about the great obstacle to reform and improvement found in rent. Mr. Barnett speaks of it as absorbing a large proportion of the earnings of artisans, namely, the fourth of a regular income (pages 68 and 70), and Mr. Brace (page 223) speaks of it

[1] See Shaw's " Municipal Socialism " in *Juridical Review*, January, 1889.

repeatedly. A lady working in connection with the Charity organization of Baltimore spoke of it thus a few days since in conversation : " Rent, oh that is the dreadful thing ! the rent of the poor just goes on increasing all the time. So do their appetites, but these have to wait while the rent has to be paid!"

I cannot speak of the many things which can be done and which are being done to improve the housing of the poorer urban classes. One of the most promising reforms, it seems to me, is to obey the law and assess all unimproved city land up to its full value, the very last dollar of its value, and then exempt all new dwellings from taxation for a period of five years. A somewhat similar plan appears to have produced excellent results in Vienna. Of course, this alone is not sufficient.

6. My sixth item is complete municipalization of markets and slaughter houses, rendering food inspection easier and more thorough.

7. The seventh item is organized medical relief, rendering medical attendance and medicines accessible to the poor without a sacrifice of self-respect and independence. Interesting details may be read in Barnett's book. — I think the Johns Hopkins Hospital in Baltimore is likely to contribute something to the solution of this problem.

8. Poor relief ought to be better organized, almshouses should be workhouses and workhouses should be industrial schools. We may consider in this connection an extension of public and private pensions, and I was glad recently to notice remarks on this subject by President Eliot of Harvard University. Any one may witness in Germany the beneficial effects of an extensive pension system. It is a great economy of resources, as smaller salaries are sufficient under a pension system ; it diminishes poverty and pauperism, and thus relieves the public treasuries. It prevents anxiety, and checks

the greed begotten of uncertainty. An extension of the principle of insurance is desirable for similar reasons.

9. The ninth item is improved sanitary legislation and administration. Great strides have already been made in this direction, but probably the urban death-rate among children of the poor, under five years of age, could still be reduced one-half.[1]

10. The next item is a better regulation of the liquor traffic where its suppression is impossible. I think something better than high license is practicable, and I have worked out a system, which I have called modified prohibition, and I must be allowed on account of lack of time to refer you to my treatment of this subject in my book: " Taxation in American States and Cities." I would include local option in wards and full payment for every privilege to sell intoxicating beverages. To limit the number of saloons, as in Boston, Pittsburgh and elsewhere, and then to give licenses for a fixed sum, is a crying injustice to all who are refused licenses. Such licenses should be sold at auction.

But temperance reform ought to include positive measures, as well as negative, and how effective positive measures are, Mr. Brace's book amply demonstrates. The use of town halls and schoolrooms for political and other gatherings in England, has proved a good temperance measure. Do not simply drive out the saloon ; replace it.

11. Municipal savings banks. Such institutions have produced most gratifying results in many German cities. Deposits should be invested in city bonds, and other good securities. The investment in city bonds would tend to give depositors a realizing sense of what they have at stake in municipal government.

---

[1] See Barnett, pages 68–70.

12. Ownership and management by the city of natural monopolies of a local character, like electric lights, gas works, street-car lines, docks, etc. Read Dr. Shaw on the excellent results accomplished elsewhere, notably in Glasgow, by this policy.

I will not enumerate further items in this connection. I have already said that the individual force and energy of citizens should be used to inaugurate and carry out these reforms. I would utilize in a higher degree than heretofore the help of women. Police matrons have done something for one class of our urban population in several American cities, and in Glasgow lady health inspectors have proved an efficient adjunct to the health department. Lady members of school boards have done good service in several cities.

We should also have private associations of women to insist on the enforcement of law. Something has been done in New York by " The Ladies' Health Protective Association," which aims to secure enforcement of sanitary legislation and to insist on a proper street-cleaning service. We ought also to have in every city ladies' public educational associations, to stimulate the educational authorities and to see that the last letter of the law is obeyed ; in New York, for instance, see that schoolhouses are provided for all children and that the compulsory educational law is enforced.

We should also have business men's associations, clergymen's associations, and the like, all to help to make the life of public servants who neglect their duty a burden to them.

RESOURCES FOR THESE REFORMS.

Whence shall come the resources for these reforms? I have already given the answer. A moderate and conserva-

tive nationalism will provide resources. ·It is simply necessary to utilize public resources. Comptroller Myers of New
York recently said that he could pay all the expenses of the
city government from dock rents, miscellaneous receipts,
and the annual value of street-car and other similar franchises. Berlin pays over fifteen per cent. of its expenses
from the profits of gas works; Richmond, Va., when I last
looked at the report, about seven per cent. We have also
electric lighting as a source of revenue. Then we have
plans, which I have elsewhere described, for securing a portion of the increment in value of city real estate for the public, and that without depriving any one of his property rights.
Inheritances, and particularly collateral inheritances, may be
taxed, and intestate collateral inheritances might be even
abolished. Resources for every needed reform can be found
in abundance whenever any honest search is made for them.
We have yet no adequate idea of the public resources of a
great city.

As I began with quotations from Mr. Barnett, so I will
close with a quotation from one of his essays. It is this:
" I can conceive a great change in the condition of the people, worked out in our own generation without any revolution
or break with the past. With wages at their present rate,
I can yet imagine the houses made strong and healthy,
education and public baths made free, and the possibility of
investing in land made easy. I can imagine that, without
increase of their private wealth, the poor might have in libraries, music halls, and flower gardens, that on which wealth
is spent. I can imagine the youth of the nation made strong
by means of fresh air and the doctor's care, the aged made
restful by means of honorable pensions. I can imagine the
church as the people's church, its buildings, the halls where
they are taught by their chosen leaders, the meeting places

where they learn the secret of union and brotherly love, the houses of prayer, where, in the presence of the Best, they lift themselves into the higher life of duty and devotion to right. All this I can imagine because it is practicable."

NATURAL MONOPOLIES AND LOCAL TAXATION.

NATURAL MONOPOLIES AND LOCAL TAXATION.

AN ADDRESS DELIVERED BEFORE THE BOSTON MERCHANTS'
ASSOCIATION, JAN. 8, 1889.

*Gentlemen of the Boston Merchants' Association and their
Friends :* .

THE general subject for consideration this evening has
been announced as "Combinations and Competition,"
and a large subject it is. The subject itself savors of monopoly; for it is often said of a monopolist, "He wants the
earth." I think that is what the Boston Merchants' Association wants ! Surely, industrially speaking, "combinations
and competition include the whole earth" ; and after we have
finished this evening, no economic or social topic will be left
for discussion at a banquet to be held elsewhere, or at any
future banquet to be held in Boston ! Such remorseless
monopolists are we ! We have, so far as political economy
is concerned, grasped the entire earth, perhaps the entire
universe ! Speaking seriously, the topic assigned to me,
"Natural Monopolies and Local Taxation," although only
one aspect of our subject, is so large that I must necessarily
leave much unsaid which is essential to a full comprehension
of the position I take on these matters ; and I wish you to
regard my address rather as suggestive than exhaustive. I
give you an outline sketch, and I beg you to trust that if
filled in, it would be satisfactorily done. I shall try to speak
plainly, and so as to avoid any reasonable ground for misunderstanding—except for those malignant natures who want

to misunderstand, and I am very sure that none such are present this evening.

One word more by way of introduction. I say I shall speak plainly. There may be those here who would lose by reform in municipal life. Every reform hurts large numbers, and among them many good people. But what are we to do? To stand still and do nothing is impossible. As a political economist it is my duty to find out what will bene-fit the people as a whole ; to " hew to the line, let the chips fall where they may."

I notice everybody seems willing to discuss fairly every abuse except that particular one on which he fattens at the expense of the public. Thus the president of an electric lighting company does not want to hear municipal public works discussed, but is quite willing to listen to disquisitions on the iniquity of protective tariffs. I have a concrete in-stance in mind. The protected manufacturer is willing to be shown that public electric lights and gas works are better than private enterprise, but would rather not hear too much about free trade. Now, the truth is that the only way to do is, in every instance, to look aside from private interests and to endeavor to ascertain what is for the public good, assured that in this way we shall all, in the long run, fare best. This is what I seek to do ; and I try not to spare myself. In fact, as a member of the Maryland Tax Commission, I have made recommendations in regard to taxation in Baltimore and Maryland which would treble my own taxes. I say frankly I am one of those not paying their fair share of taxes. So electric lights and gas works must be considered from the standpoint of public welfare : we have no right to tax the many for the sake of the few.

I appear before you as an advocate of monopoly in certain quarters of the industrial field ; as one, then, who rejoices in the progress which, in these quarters, monopoly is making, and as one who would gladly see this progress accelerated. But I oppose private monopolies. What I favor is the management of certain monopolies by public authorities, and in the interests of the public.

Monopolies are the field for public activity: competitive pursuits are the field for private activity.

It is thus that I draw the line; and it is, as I hold, clearly and sharply drawn. It is curious to notice the rapid springs which some economists are making in these days of combinations. Some of them, indeed, are performing somersaults in a manner worthy of professional acrobats. Among economists I find myself surrounded by socialists; and the most thorough-going socialists were but yesterday extreme individualists, who told us that the free play of natural forces as seen in universal competition was beneficent. The length to which people went in favor of competition, at all times and in all places, is illustrated by the attitude of some members of the municipal council of Augusta, Ga., a few years ago. The question arose whether a charter should be granted to a new gas company; and when it was urged that it would bring about no reduction in prices, and accomplish no useful purpose, they still wanted to give the charter, simply for the ardor with which they loved the principle of competition. Fortunately, however, they were convinced that attempted competition would do positive harm, and wiser counsels prevailed. I say I find myself surrounded by socialists when I am among economists. By that I mean I find myself among those who approve of all combinations and trusts; and it is, of course, only necessary for combinations to go forward, to bring us to pure socialism. Every socialist knows this, and rejoices in trusts. Take up Laurence Gronlund's " Danton in the French Revolution," and you will find this idea clearly brought out. Take up the last number of the *New Haven Workmen's Advocate*, and you will find combinations spoken of as an encouraging sign of the times. These are words from an editorial : "Centralization (*i.e.* in business) is more and more recognized as necessary for order and economy. Progress in this." One of the ablest political economists in the country told me, a few days since, that, in conversation with a socialist, this socialist said : "Every time I hear of a new trust, I feel like throwing up my hat and shouting 'hurrah !'" And the political economist added : "If I were a socialist, I would say to our industrial leaders, 'Keep right on, gentlemen. You are realizing for me my dreams. It is now only necessary for me to fold my hands.'" Socialism means a universal trust. Centralize all business in a trust, and then it is only necessary to put a representative of the people in control to have socialism, pure and simple. Now, all this I oppose ; therefore I see myself becoming in public opinion — so far as public opinion deigns to take any notice of me — more conservative with every day, although I have not changed. A few years ago I was regarded as a radical — of course I always claimed that I was a conservative ; but I fear that if this change in my fellow-economists continues, in a few years more I shall be called an old fogy.

There can be no doubt, gentlemen, that people have been staggered by the industrial phenomena of the past few years, and many do not know what to think about the fundamental principles of our social order. This was illustrated, in a manner both amusing and — I think I may say — pathetic, in Baltimore a couple of years since. It was a great blow to our people to see the Baltimore and Ohio Telegraph swallowed up by the Western Union. Its officers had been protesting vigorously, year in and year out, in season and out of season, that such a thing would never happen. But the

Baltimoreans had scarcely recovered from that shock when they received another blow, in the consolidation of the gas companies, which likewise had assured us that they never would do that wicked thing — assured us most solemnly. And among those who gave us these assurances were solid business men and most respectable church members. There are two causes for the confusion of thought and perplexity of the public mind.

1. Most people have looked upon the form of society which we see all about us as something natural and unchangeable. Now, the truth is, that our social and industrial order is but of yesterday, and those things most familiar to us were entirely unknown to our forefathers a hundred years ago. I could give hundreds of illustrations. Free labor over our entire country, the free sale and purchase of land, — that did not exist everywhere, even in Massachusetts, two hundred years ago, and in many other parts of the world it is not a century old, — the banking business, — one hundred years ago there were but three banks in the country, — free competition as a fundamental principle : all these are new. So also telegraphs, telephones, railroads, streetcar lines, great manufacturing corporations, etc., etc. Even great public debts, and taxation itself as we know it, are scarce two hundred years old. I do not mean that taxes did not exist in earlier ages ; but they were, in important particulars, different from modern taxation. It is not, therefore, incorrect to speak of modern taxation as a new thing. A stationary condition of society is something the world has never seen. The law is, either progress or decline — never a stationary condition. We make a mistake in supposing our present industrial forms final.

2. We have failed to discriminate between different kinds of industries. It has been recognized that competition is in

many places a good thing and has accomplished marvels. The conclusion is drawn that it must everywhere and at all times be a good thing. But this is a great mistake. It is not everywhere possible, and an attempt to apply it in quarters where it is not possible results only in disaster. We observe these phenomena : *While competition is increasing in intensity in some parts of the economic field it is decreasing steadily in others; and as the pressure of competition steadily increases, an ever-increasing number withdraw themselves from its influence.*

Competition is a good thing where it is possible, but there are certain pursuits which are monopolies in their own nature. They are liable to injury by industrial war, but they are not controlled by competition. Let me explain what I mean. Industrial war is one thing, industrial competition is another. Industrial war is a fierce assault of one enterprise on another. Industrial competition is a steady pressure, compelling those under its influence to render valuable service for valuable returns. Industrial war seeks to destroy an enemy and always has in view a cessation of hostilities on some terms. Consequently for a time services are rendered at a loss. Struggles between natural monopolies are warlike.

The time is too short to allow me to describe natural monopolies and to show why certain pursuits must be monopolies. That I have done elsewhere. I will simply enumerate the more important natural monopolies — gas supply, water supply and electric lighting, street railroads of all kinds, steam railroads, telegraphs, telephones, all public roads, the express business. These businesses never can be conducted except as monopolies, and any phenomena which appear like competition are temporary and illusory. The gas business serves well as an illustration. I suppose competition has been tried over a thousand times, very likely two thousand times, and it never has yet been permanent, and it can be demonstrated, almost mathematically, that it never can be permanent. It is easy to explain a thing after it happened, but it is often said to be the test of the correctness of a scientific theory to predict that a thing will happen. Now, during the gas war in Baltimore, while we were receiving gas for fifty cents a thousand, I told my classes repeatedly that it could not last many years, and that all the agreements of the companies not to consolidate, of whatever nature they might be, like all laws and constitutions forbidding consolidation, were not worth the paper on which they were written. In the same way, on strictly scientific principles, when nobody in Baltimore believed it, I predicted the consolidation of the Baltimore and Ohio Telegraph and the Western Union, and even ventured to print my prediction. I was willing to stake my reputation as a political economist on its accuracy. Well, you all know what happened.

So now I am ready to predict that in most places we shall witness a consolidation of private electric lighting and gas companies in a few years. Indeed, this has already begun. Certain monopolies are local in their nature, — *e.g.* street cars, electric lights, gas supply, water supply, — and for these I favor the principle of municipal self-help, as opposed to the perpetual interference with private corporations which render these services.

There are two principles, one of which must be violated in these matters. One is the "keep-out" principle; the other is the "let-alone" principle. The keep-out principle means that government should not perform industrial functions. The let-alone principle means that government should let private parties manage their own business in their own way. Now I believe in this let-alone principle. Its violation brings about an intermingling of private and public interests which is most demoralizing, and which is to-day the chief cause of corruption in public life. The keep-out principle can be violated with greater safety. I say then that cities should pursue a policy looking to the ultimate ownership and management of all local monopolies. In other words, for these pursuits I favor the principle of co-operation, for that is what governmental industrial enterprises mean. The people act together and accomplish certain results. Let us call this form of activity co-operative self-help. Of course you all know that all government enterprise is frequently condemned as paternalism, but those who designate it thus have failed to grasp the fundamental idea of modern democracy and have never become true Americans. We see lingering on in the minds of these timid people European traditions. When the Czar of Russia is graciously pleased to construct a railroad for his people, you may call that beneficent paternalism ; but when the people of an American town meet together and resolve that rather than be dependent on a private corporation for light, they will, in their organic capacity, construct their own electric lighting or gas works, this is a noble form of co-operative self-help. The arguments on the subject of natural monopolies bring this out clearly. Those who favor private undertakings do so because they accuse the people of incompetence. I have in mind the introduction of water works in a certain village where the enterprise was most successfully inaugurated, and where it has been admirably managed ever since by the village authorities. It was opposed by some citizens on the ground that the people collectively were too dishonest and inefficient in managing their own affairs. The arguments, when analyzed, all insulted the character of the citizens of this village. Now that the water works have been introduced by the village for a good deal less than any private corporation would have charged, and now that the annual charges for use of water are only about forty per cent. as much as private corporations usually charge under similar circumstances, I call this a triumph of the principle of municipal self-help.

The system of public ownership of natural monopolies relies on self-help. It gives continuous opportunity for self-help, and calls out energy and self-reliance. If publicly owned water works or gas works are not well managed, an opportunity exists for citizens to correct mismanagement by working together for a better and purer administration. If the works are private property, self-help is out of the question, and apathy and indifference are the results which can be observed readily in our cities. Under the system of private ownership, the only help is childish complaints and humble supplication to corporations, as when the farmers of a Maryland county, where toll roads owned by private corporations are found, paraded through the country with banners inscribed: "No improvements, no tolls," and the like. Complaints are ineffectual, and toll roads privately owned are poor — far poorer than your publicly owned roads in New England.[1] By the way, in the South toll roads prevail, and in the North free public roads. Has any one ever observed that the poor southern roads have developed energy and self-reliance in the South, or that your far better public roads have weakened the New England character? On the contrary, your roads are a proof of your capacity for self-help.

HOW THIS IS CONNECTED WITH TAXATION.

This is most intimately connected with local taxation. One of two methods may be pursued. 1. These monopo-

---

[1] I am told that the toll roads of Kentucky are good, but as might naturally be expected, this fact renders the public administration of

lies may be worked for a profit, and by profit taxes may be reduced; or, 2. Charges may be reduced, and increased general prosperity will furnish a more plentiful source of taxes and thus allow a reduction of the tax rate. Enormous waste is thereby obviated. Baltimore again furnishes an illustration with which I must content myself, although I could give a thousand. I suppose we have had six or seven attempts at competition in gas supply. Our streets are full of gas mains. Now all these different plants must be paid for, and every time a consolidation takes place fixed charges and capital stock have both been increased. The result is that it does not now appear to be a very profitable business for our private company to supply gas at $1.25 a thousand, the rate fixed by the legislature, although it can be made and sold at a profit for 37 cents. I say it can be done, because it is done in the city of Philadelphia, parties supplying the city with gas at that figure.[1]

IT WORKS WELL IN EXPERIENCE.

Some of you may whisper to yourselves " theory." But I do not confine myself to theory. Natural monopolies owned and controlled by cities always work well, and you may search the world over for an exception. This is one of the few rules without exception. You may mention Philadelphia's gas works to me as a proof to the contrary, but Philadelphia

roads in that commonwealth weak and ineffective. People have learned to rely on private corporations instead of doing things for themselves.

[1] Philadelphia owns its own gas works, but the demand for gas increasing rapidly, the city contracted with a private corporation to furnish a certain amount of gas, delivered in the city receivers, for 37 cents a thousand; of course it costs considerably more to deliver it to consumers, but there is reason to believe that the private corporation

I regard as a proof of the excellence of the practice I commend. Where municipal gas works have been worse managed than anywhere else, the citizens have fared better than we have in Baltimore or than the citizens in New York under private works, and it is the best citizens of Philadelphia who insisted that the gas works should remain city property when the gas trust expired a few years ago. In other words, the worst instance of municipal works has proved better than ordinary private works, and probably less demoralizing politically.

Other instances of gas works owned and operated successfully by the city are Richmond, Va., Alexandria, Va., and Wheeling, West Virginia, where the city is supplying gas at 90 cents a thousand and making profits which go to reduce taxes. The experience with electric light is still more striking. Bay City, Mich., Lewiston, Me., Madison, Ind., and Dunkirk, N.Y., are supplying electric lights of 2000 candle-power each, I believe, for about 13 cents a night, whereas cities are paying private corporations from 40 cents to 65 cents. Sixty-five cents is, I believe, your rate in Boston; just five times as much. I wrote some time since to the mayor of Dunkirk, N.Y., to find out how they were succeeding with this experiment, — not that I had any doubt as to the matter, for I hold that cities are always more successful in supplying themselves with electric lights or gas than in hiring this service of private corporations, and that their success is due to economic laws closely resembling laws of nature. Here is the letter of the mayor, which is accompanied with a detailed statement of cost : —

makes a large profit on its contract. This is water gas. . The coal gas manufactured by the city itself cost somewhat less than $1 a thousand, delivered to consumers. The city charges $1.50, and the balance is profit. The cost to the city is too high, but it has been reduced over twenty-five per cent. within a few years, and the management is rapidly improving. Much could be written on this topic were not space too limited.

"MAYOR'S OFFICE,
DUNKIRK, N.Y., Dec. 1, 1888.

"*Professor R. T. Ely:*

" The cost of each arc light per night running all night and every night is 13½ cents.   Enclosed I send you a detailed statement of same.   The capacity of the arc light is 2000 candle power and they are fifty-five in number.   The system is the Western Electric of Chicago, and we claim we are having better results than they are having at Erie or Buffalo.[1]   We are greatly pleased with our system.   Our plant complete cost $11,025.31.   This includes two Rice engines of fifty horse-power each, two dynamos of thirty-five arc lights each, and all the necessary apparatus.   The length of the line is about eleven miles.   In order to make sufficient room for the plant in the water-works building, an addition was made at an expense of $1630.50, making the total cost of plant and building $13,338.71.   You are aware our city owns and operates its water plant, and the great saving comes from the city's owning and operating both plants.   No extra labor is required but a lineman, for whose services we pay $45 per month.   The same engineers, fireman, and superintendent operate both plants, and the same boiler power is used.   I saw the superintendent this morning after the receipt of your letter, and he assures me the cost per night can be reduced below 13½ cents.[2]   If I can be of further service to you, please write me.   Very truly yours,

.** WILLIAM BOOKSTAVER,**
Mayor."

The superintendent's report gives the details.

Private parties cannot render the service so cheaply, as I know from a friend engaged in the business.   There are many reasons why cities can render this service more cheaply, into which I cannot enter at this moment.   I hear it said here in Boston that a reason urged for paying the outrageous

---

[1] Where a private corporation operating the same system receives 45 cents.

[2] I saw the mayor in August, 1889, and he told me that the cost had then been reduced to ten cents.   Naturally he was enthusiastic over the results.

price which you do, viz. 65 cents per arc light per night, is the large territorial extent of your city. This is not valid. If your city covers a larger area than a city like Dunkirk, N.Y., or Lewiston, Me., the number of lights increases in proportion, and the cost per light ought not to be greater. On the contrary, it ought to be smaller, because a business like electric lighting is much more efficiently and cheaply managed on a large scale than on a small scale. The same men can manage a large plant as well as a small one, and there is a considerable saving in salaries. But again we have experience to fall back upon. The city of Chicago, Ill., has introduced a plant and furnishes electric lights along the river front. There has been some extra expense on account of burial of wires, — and, by the way, there never is any diffi-culty in burying electric wires owned and operated by gov-ernment, either here or elsewhere, — but the cost per arc light of 2000 candle-power is reported as about 15 cents a night, lights burning all night, and this includes the interest on the investment. The city is greatly pleased, and it is proposed to extend the plant during the present year. In addition to the cities named, I have found electric lighting plants owned and operated by the following cities, viz.: Painesville, Portsmouth, and Xenia, Ohio; Champaign, Aurora, Paris, and Decatur, Ill.; Easton, Pa.; Ypsilanti and Grand Ledge, Mich.; Huntington and Michigan City, Ind.; Topeka, Kas.; Little Rock, Ark.; Lyons, Iowa; Han-nibal, Mo. The mayor of Easton, Hon. Charles F. Chidsey, writes me: "The light gives our people great satisfaction," and this is like the testimony of people everywhere where the city owns and operates an electric lighting plant.[1]

[1] Since that time several cities have voted to introduce municipal ownership of an electric lighting plant, and the subject is being investi-gated in several others.

It can scarcely be too much to say that where it has been tried municipal ownership and management of electric lights are enthusiastically praised. I have made inquiries in every city which I knew owned and operated an electric lighting plant, and I have not received one reply unfavorable to the system. In five cities, viz. Bay City, Mich., Painesville, Ohio, Huntington, Ind., Lewiston, Me., and Aurora, Ill., the average cost per light per night under the private system was 45.1 cents, whereas under the public system it is only 13.9 cents.[1]

This extension of the sphere of government I do not regard as something to be regretted. On the contrary, I welcome it. It will, by its variety, make our entire social life richer and fuller. I regard these proposals as the strongest bulwark against socialism. It will bring about a reformation of our political life. *The door to civil service reform is industrial reform.* We all agree that municipal public life is not what it should be, even if its badness is often exaggerated. But what are the causes?

The usual explanations fail to go below the surface. Universal suffrage is alleged to be the cause, and it is said that the poor vote away the property of the rich. The facts do

---

[1] The following note is supplied by Mr. Robert J. Finley, one of my graduate students : —

The movement for municipal ownership and operation of electric lighting plant thus far has been confined principally to the smaller cities, although the larger cities, as Chicago, are beginning to recognize that the element of size is not a bar to their entrance upon the same course. Reports from twenty-five cities which own and operate their own electric lighting plants show that in each individual case the plan has worked satisfactorily. The mayor of Little Rock, Ark., writes : "Our light is eminently successful and manifestly popular. Our citizens would never consent to do without it, though it was established amid the formidable opposition of the gas company and its numerous and powerful friends." This extract gives a fair presentation of the satis-

not tally with the theory. I have looked into this matter with care, and I think I have had some facilities for so doing. I know of no American city which is not controlled by wealth. The truth is this: *unscrupulous wealth uses vicious poverty as a tool;* not that all wealth is unscrupulous, nor all poverty vicious. One city, which I will not mention by name, serves as an illustration. In the council recently there were two street-car presidents and ten liquor-dealers. Of course I do not mean by this that all street-car presidents are bad men. Let us see.

We have our choice between direct management of natural monopolies and delegated management with control, and the common law requires at least regulation. Now when you attempt to control a man who renders public service

faction with which municipal electric lights are regarded by those cities which have undertaken for themselves the operation of these works. Definite information received from twenty of these cities regarding the net cost of light per night for each arc light, is presented here : —

Aurora, Ill............15.3 cents.	Little Rock, Ark......13. cents.
Bangor, Me..........13. "	Lewiston, Me........14. "
Bay City, Mich.......16. "	Lyons, Iowa......... 8.2 "
Champaign, Ill. ......12.3 "	Madison, Ind........ 16. "
Chicago, Ill..........15. "	Michigan City, Ind....12. "
Decatur, Ill..........13.7 "	Painesville, Ohio.....10.6 "
Dunkirk, N.Y........13.5 "	Paris, Ill............10.4 "
Easton, Pa..........27.3 "	Portsmouth, Ohio....10. "
Grand Ledge, Mich... 1.8 "	Topeka, Kas.........20. "
Huntington, Ind......13.7 "	Ypsilanti, Mich.......11.2 "

Average cost per night.........................13.4 cents.

It is seen that, of these twenty cities, seven are able to furnish their own electric light at a cost of 12 cents or under for each arc light of 2000 candle-power per night, eleven at a cost of between 12 and 16 cents per night, and two at a cost of above 16 cents. The low net cost in Lyons, Iowa, and in Grand Ledge, Mich., is due to the fact

you create antagonism and diversity of interests.   Those
who supply these services attempt to escape control or to
shape the regulation of their industries for private ends.
Sometimes, on the other hand, unscrupulous politicians
attempt to abuse the power of control and regulation, to
oppress corporations so as to be bought off.   An instance
that these cities own and operate commercial wires, from which they
derive a profit.

The full significance of these statistics is revealed when a comparison is made between the cost of the same light under private and
municipal control.   Fortunately, a comparison can be made, as five
of these cities, previous to assuming control of their own works, were
supplied with light by private companies.   The cost of each arc light
per night under both systems of control is given here in tabular form : —

	Private.	City.
Bay City, Mich...................	27.5 cents.	16. cents.
Painesville, Ohio.................	19.7 "	10.6 "
Huntington, Ind..................	39. "	13.7 "
Lewiston, Me.....................	50. "	14. "
Aurora, Ill......................	89.5 "	15.3 "
Average per night............	45.1 cents.	13.9 cents.

To make these statistics accurate, it should be stated that in Lewiston, under private control, the lights burned only half the night.
It is seen from these figures that in five cities the minimum saving
which follows the change from private to public ownership and management of electric lighting plants was nearly one-half, and the maximum saving nearly five-sixths, of the former charge.

Nor is the cost per light in these instances of private control cited,
exceptional.   Returns from seventy-five cities which are supplied with
light by private corporations gives 42 cents as the average cost per
light, or only 3 cents less than the average cost under private control for the five cities mentioned.   The commonly accepted belief that
municipalities cannot operate their own electric lighting plants and
other works of a similar nature so economically as can private enterprise is shown by these examples to have no foundation whatever in
practice.

like this occurred in Maryland, and a politician received, I am told, $10,000 a year not to take a certain course.[1] Thus in one way or another are corporations of a monopolistic nature forced into politics. This is the real source of political corruption. This is the real explanation of an unscrupulous lobby, which steals bills from Senate files and buys directly and indirectly legislators and sometimes buys judges, but oftener controls their appointment. When the management of natural monopolies is direct, we have, on the other hand, a harmony of public and private interests, an awakened public spirit, an intensified municipal self-consciousness, if I may use the expression. A field is thus furnished for talent in the service of the city, and our colleges and universities are full of young men eager for honorable public service. If they are given only a little encouragement they will prepare themselves thoroughly. I have noticed these effects from public works. I have noticed the disastrous effects described from private works. Compare Jamestown, N.Y., with Fredonia, N.Y., the former with private water works, the latter with public works; or Lockport, N.Y., with Dunkirk, N.Y., the former with private electric lighting works, and the latter with public electric lighting works; and you will observe those phenomena which I have described. You will find in Lockport, N.Y., the rich and influential people resisting the mayor's attempt at reform because they derive a profit from things as they are; and this, I will venture to say, is the cause of indifference of many influential people to proposed political reforms. This is what I find when I study politics in the concrete. I have in mind a good friend of mine in Baltimore who is in the electric lighting busi-

[1] I have been told, on good authority, that a single political assessment on one gas company in New York City during the Tweed régime, was $100,000! Was that company in or out of politics?

ness. This friend is a most excellent gentleman, a good Christian, who tries to do his duty, but is it not asking too much of human nature to expect him to take an active interest in the reformation of municipal politics? If we had the right kind of a city government, we certainly would not pay fifty cents a night for each electric light.

The mayor of Bay City, Mich., writes me that the rich and influential people were in numerous instances arrayed against the reform which has proved so beneficial. Their interests as stockholders were arrayed against their interests as citizens. A member of the municipal council of Paris, Ill., as quoted by Mr. Whipple in his pamphlet on " Municipal Lighting," uses these words : " Many reasons *pro* and *con* were advanced before our plant was purchased. First, that it would have a tendency to purify city politics, as these light companies are generally composed of sharp, shrewd men. Their stock is distributed where it will do the most good in making city contracts, sometimes aldermen, and even mayors being interested.[1] It was observed also the company took a special interest in city elections. Men who never seemed to care who was made legislator, congressman, governor, or president, would shell out their money, go into the wards and voting precincts, and spend their time and money to elect a man who had no credit or standing in the community he lived in. It was a common thing for councilmen to burn free gas, sprinkle his street and lawn with free water, or such that the city was paying for. There was a constant issue of this kind. Politics cut no figure. The question was : 'Are you for the light company?' "

[1] It was found that when electric lighting was introduced in Northampton, Mass., "All the city government from the mayor down were holders of stock in the electric lighting company."

There is scarcely a prominent politician of the corrupt "spoils" system in the land, who is not opposed to ownership and management of natural monopolies by nation, state, or city. The shrewd ones among them see that by rendering government of real vital concern to all, and of concern which all could perceive, it would necessarily break up the spoils system. It would show the ordinary artisans and mechanics that politics mean something more than quarrels about the distribution of offices.

Notice, once more, that I propose that *industrial reform should begin at home.* I want to see strong, pure, local governments developed among us, and they cannot be pure unless they are strong. *Industrial power means, and always must mean, political power,* and the impotence of our cities is one cause of their badness. They are pitted against unequal adversaries. When we have good local self-government, I believe we shall be able to cope with questions of state and federal politics.

Notice another advantage of the plan I have advocated. I do not commit the entire nation at once to any line of policy; all that I ask is that it shall be given a fair trial. One city, one village at a time can try it; and I simply want a sufficient number of experiments to give us a fair trial. If the plan does not work well, it can be easily given up. The most suspicious thing about the attitude of opponents of the plan is their dread of any actual experiments. They are afraid of experience.

The temptations of the practice of the principles of delegated agency in electric lights, etc., are simply irresistible. If men were angels, it might be satisfactory, not otherwise. Public works will always be in politics, and that is the reason why gas companies and electric lighting companies so often have politicians for presidents, and when not for presidents, for attorneys. They must understand how to manage politicians. I could give you any number of instances. The manager of the electric lighting company in Baltimore is also president of a strong political club in the city, and the president of our strongest street-car company is an ex-governor. Recently, when an electric motor company wanted an attorney, they employed a very shrewd politician, who is a friend of mine. The city solicitor of Baltimore is also attorney for a great railroad company. It is always thus, and I have given the correct explanation. Public works will always be in politics. The only question is whether it shall be open and above board, or concealed. Philadelphia furnishes a good illustration. The street cars are owned and managed by city politicians, and are actively in politics. The gas works are in politics, but they are manageable because they are public. The former are unmanageable, and far more dangerous.

Again, the principle of delegated agency is bad, because the agent becomes more powerful than the principal. Corporations are stronger than our states and cities. There is not a city in the Union strong enough to compel the burial of electric wires, or the laying of properly grooved street car rails, or the running of a sufficient number of street cars to accommodate the public with seats at all hours ; not a city or state in this Union strong enough to protect the citizens against crossings of railroads at grade ; and in the study of taxation I have yet to find a state or city which in taxation can deal satisfactorily with this class of corporations.

I have calculated that by the application of correct principles in the treatment of natural monopolies, we could have reduced taxes in Baltimore one-third, I suppose in New York two-thirds, probably in Boston at least one-half.

This would enable us to carry out many reforms which

insufficient funds render impracticable at present. Your mayor tells us that he wants $2,000,000 more than he has. I do not doubt for a moment that this sum could be advantageously expended by Boston during the coming year. Why then squander money by the hundred thousand in gifts to electric lighting companies? Why tax the poor to swell their already enormous profits? I see that the neighboring city of Cambridge, Mass., is too poor to do things which need doing, yet it seems to be able to afford to throw money away by the thousand, in making contracts with the electric lighting company, paying $180 a year for each arc light, whereas it could supply itself for one-third that sum. It is the old story, — niggardly appropriations for the public library, lavish appropriations to private corporations. That is what makes American municipal government so expensive.

I will read you an extract from a paper by a careful observer, travelling in England, who has attempted to get at the secret of their good municipal governments. I refer to Dr. Albert Shaw, of the *Minneapolis Tribune*. The article takes the form of an interview : —

"THE MONOPOLIES OF SERVICE.

" ' I suppose Glasgow owns its gas and water?'

" ' Certainly ; and so ought every municipality. All the monopolies of service, such as gas, water, trams, and the like, should belong to the community, and experience has shown that they can be administered with quite as much freedom from assumption as when they were left in the hands of private adventurers. The great difficulty of municipal finance hitherto has been that it has relied far too much upon rates, and a rate is always an unpopular means of raising money. If, on the other hand, the community kept the monopolies of service in its own hands, it would be able in many cases ultimately to raise a magnificent revenue without laying on a rate at all.'

" ' Then, on the whole, Mr. Shaw, you are satisfied with our municipal institutions? '

·' ' More than satisfied — I am delighted; and I think the experience of Glasgow is full of lessons for our new communities that are springing up all over the United States.'

" ' What lessons do you deduce from it? '

" ' First, simplify your administration; secondly, trust the people; thirdly, give the municipality plenty to do, so as to bring the best men to the work; fourthly, keep all the monopolies of service in the hands of the municipality, regard the supply of gas and water and the letting of the use of the streets to tramway companies as very promising sources of revenue; and lastly, use the authority and the influence of the municipality in order to secure for the poorest advantages in the shape of cheap trams, healthy and clean lodging, baths, washhouses, hospitals, reading-rooms, etc., to such extent, at least, as in a given case private enterprise shows itself inadequate to do what the welfare of the community requires should be done. I say this with no ardent bias toward socialism, and with due regard for the financial aspects of these questions.' " [1]

But time fails me, and I must stop abruptly, without showing how natural monopolies are connected with trusts. I hold that in so far as they are dangerous, trusts and combinations are largely the fruit of our system of private ownership of natural monopolies, but I cannot elaborate the idea.

What I want, in conclusion, is to separate sharply the sphere of private industry from the sphere of public industry, and I hold that in so doing I am keeping close to old Anglo-Saxon and American traditions. I contend for free

---

[1] It has been urged against municipal ownership of gas works and other similar works that only few people use gas, electricity, etc. It is said that every one uses water; therefore a municipality may properly furnish water. This argument is so shallow that it ought scarcely to be necessary to reply to it. We cannot separate in this way the interests

and individual development, for individual initiative and responsibility accompanying beneficent collective activity; I contend for this, on the one hand, against proletarian socialists; on the other, against aristocratic socialists. I contend for old American traditions of self-help in matters of government as elsewhere, for self-direction and self-determination, and against paternalism and oppression, whether proceeding from government, as in other ages, or, as in our own times, from private corporations.

of social classes. Whatever will confer a benefit on all consumers of gas, electricity, and like services, will benefit the entire community. A good turnpike may benefit a man who never travels on it more than some people who walk over it every day. Such a case is easily conceivable. Moreover, everybody pays for gas, electric lights, telephone and telegraph services and the like, because the charges for them are a part of the cost of doing business, and we all pay our share, even those of us who live in rural districts, in the prices of articles which we purchase.

THE TELEGRAPH MONOPOLY.

THE TELEGRAPH MONOPOLY.

REPRINTED FROM THE NORTH AMERICAN REVIEW OF JULY, 1889, BY PERMISSION.

THERE was something ludicrous in the surprise and consternation expressed by the general public when it became known that the Western Union Telegraph Company had acquired the lines of the Baltimore and Ohio. It was manifestly a hard, and at the time it seemed almost a shattering, blow to those who worship the idol of "private competition" as a sufficient power to save us from all industrial evils. Yet nothing was more groundless than the expectation that the temporary competition between these two powerful rivals could have any other termination than that which we have witnessed, for the telegraph business is, in its very nature, a monopoly. Experience and reason alike teach that combination between rival telegraph lines can be predicted almost with the certainty of a coming eclipse. Fifty years ago a clear-headed merchant-prince of England uttered this famous dictum : "Where combination is possible, competition is impossible."

Two years ago Professor Henry C. Adams demonstrated, in his monograph, "The Relation of the State to Industrial Action," the impossibility of competition in a business like the telegraph service, and in July, 1887, at Chautauqua, when the telegraph officials were protesting that there was no thought in their minds of combination, I used these words in a public address, basing what I said, not upon any special knowledge of the affairs of the two great companies, but on scientific principles : —

"One telegraph company can send telegrams all over the country cheaper than two ; hence the absorption of all companies, save the Baltimore and Ohio, by the Western Union.[1] It is so in the nature of things that I do not see how the Baltimore and Ohio can permanently resist the economic gravitation which draws it to its rival."

As it is of the first importance, in a discussion of the telegraph question, to grasp the fact that monopoly is inevitable, it is well to give a little space to an interrogation of past experience and of reason. First, it must be noticed that, while telegraph lines extend over the entire globe and while this industry is forty years old, the world has yet to see one single example of permanent successful competition. Over thirty companies were chartered in England, but it was never possible to secure more than temporary competition, and the attempt to secure competition was finally abandoned as impracticable and unsatisfactory. There were over fifty companies in the United States in 1851, but the most important consolidated in the same year, and combination has ever since been the end of attempted competition.

Of course, there must be some grounds in the nature of things for this, and these are, in fact, sufficiently evident on reflection. Telegraph companies always consolidate because one company can do all the business much more cheaply than two or more : consequently all derive a profit from combination. The struggle or warfare which precedes this is merely to determine the terms on which the two will unite. Strictly speaking, it is not competition at all, for competition

---

[1] I left out of consideration, as not worthy of special notice, certain minor attempts at competition.

is not a war of extinction, but a constant, permanent pressure. Why do not all the great dry-goods houses in New York combine? Why did not the late A. T. Stewart consolidate his business with that of Lord & Taylor and of Arnold & Constable? Because it was not to their manifest advantage; but it is always in the interest of natural monopolies to unite.

Mr. Farrar, in his work, "The State in its Relation to Trade," gives the following characteristics of natural monopolies, which will help to render this clearer : —

"*First* — What they supply is necessary.

"*Second* — They occupy peculiarly favored spots or lines of land.

"*Third* — The article or convenience they supply is used at the place where and in connection with the plant or machinery by which it is supplied,

"*Fourth* — This article or convenience can, in general, be largely, if not indefinitely, increased without proportionate increase in plant and capital.

"*Fifth* — Certainty and harmonious arrangement, which can only be attained by unity, are paramount considerations."

We see, then, that there is a certain class of pursuits for which there is no escape from monopoly. Without attempting an enumeration of them, I will remark that gas and water works are local monopolies, and are for a municipality what telegraphs are for a nation; and the good people of Baltimore had scarcely recovered from the shock which the absorption of the Baltimore and Ohio Telegraph caused them before they were again startled by the consolidation of their two gas companies and an increase of 200 per cent in price. Had they understood the fundamental principles of industrial science, they would not have allowed their streets to be torn up time and time again in their fruitless attempts to grasp such a Utopia as competition in the gas supply.

We consequently see that we have a choice between two alternatives, and there is no middle ground between them. These are (*a*) private monopoly and (*b*) public monopoly ; and the desirability of each will be considered in the order named.

Private monopolies are contrary alike to the spirit of English law and American institutions, and must be pronounced odious. There is no place for them among a liberty-loving people, and the attempt to reconcile us to them is as difficult as to fit a square pin into a round hole. One thing has been decided beyond all doubt : private monopolies cannot be left unregulated and uncontrolled. The attempt to do that has been definitely abandoned in the United States ; but it cannot be said that regulation and control have worked satisfactorily. Regulation and control mean interference of government in private affairs — a bad thing, complicating government and opening the flood-gates of corruption. Private monopolies are, at this moment, the cause of that perpetual interference of the government which we witness all about us, and are the most fruitful cause of corruption in public life ; incomparably more so than the government management and ownership of public business. To deny this seems to me simply a confession of profound ignorance of what is passing about us and among us daily. A bill is brought into the legislature to regulate the price of gas supplied by a private company, and this at once brings about a conflict between the public interest and a powerful private interest. It involves, in its very nature, a strong and often irresistible temptation to bribery and corruption, and that in two ways. On the one hand, monopolies attempt to prevent unjust legislation by abundant use of money, and, indirectly, by the bestowal of special favors and privileges, such as passes on railways,[1] opportunities to buy stock or presents of stock, freight rebates, telegraph franks given to members of Congress, and so forth. On the other hand, unscrupulous legislators bring in bills attacking corporations, purposely to be bought off, so that otherwise upright men are almost forced to use money improperly to protect themselves and those whom they represent. Between the two currents political life becomes demoralized, as is well known, and the chief cause is the private monopoly. Corruption inheres in its very nature, in its very essence. It is a bad thing and must remain such. Why dwell on this? Does not one of the most powerful, and in some respects one of the most admirable, corporations of the United States maintain, as a regular part of its business, a corruption bureau to manipulate and purchase legislatures? Do not street-car and gas companies perpetually interfere in politics? Is there not a prominent city in our West in which both Republican and Democratic members of the council are nominated by a private street-car company? Do not lobbies, supported by .corporations, steal bills from House and Senate files? After a bill regulating the price of gas had been stolen from the Senate files in Maryland, was it not necessary for Governor Jackson to go to the State House and watch a new bill pass with his own eyes and sign it then and there, lest it should be stolen?

The public monopoly is at any rate the lesser of the two evils. Doubtless that is not an ideal thing; doubtless we shall not for a long time find perfection. · What we want is simplification in public business, and this is promoted every

---

[1] Even newspaper editors receive free passes and are expected to render valuable services in editorial articles therefor.

time a private monopoly is abolished by the substitution of a public monopoly. How simple the post-office business ! How few opportunities, comparatively, it offers for fraud ! How complex, how intricate, how passing ordinary understanding, the relations between our governments and our railway corporations !

It is on account of these reasons that I desire government monopoly of the telegraph business, and I will at once state why it is desirable that a government should purchase existing lines rather than compete with other lines, in particular with the Western Union.

First, the competition by the government with existing lines would increase the expense of the telegraph service, and would thus occasion a loss which would be by no means counterbalanced by the fact that lines could be constructed more cheaply than purchased. The private companies would make a fight for business between great centres, and would take away some of the most profitable business, while they would leave all the poor business for the government lines. This would necessitate higher rates than would be requisite under a public monopoly. Why can government carry a letter three thousand miles for two cents? Because it has a monopoly. Again, any private company would certainly resort to corrupt measures either to ward off government competition or to moderate it. Can any one fail to see the hand of private express companies in many of our post-office laws and regulations? Why does our Federal Government send newspapers for publishers for a cent a pound and require sixteen cents a pound for merchandise? Why does it add to excessive charges for that business which competes with express companies, annoying and absurd regulations? Such things are unknown where powerful express companies do not exist.

Competition between government enterprise and private

enterprise has been tried in the railway business in Germany and elsewhere, but has not been satisfactory, and has generally been abandoned.

Some cry " paternalism " when government telegraphy is mentioned. This word " paternalism " has become a prize bogey with which to frighten the unthinking. The state is not something above us, doing something for us. It is one kind of co-operation. It shows greater self-reliance to provide a telegraph service for ourselves than to say at " we are so dishonest and inefficient in government methods that we dare not trust ourselves. Will not some rich men kindly provide us with a good telegraph system, and please give us cheap rates?" It has always seemed to me that those who call government enterprise " paternalism " have never become real Americans. It is beginning to be seen that such designation is unscientific. The English economist, Professor Sidgwick, of Cambridge, styles public enterprises, like the telegraph and municipal gas works, an extension of the principle of individualism, and not socialism at all.

It is, however, urged that public ownership of telegraphs is a step towards socialism. Why does not government bake bread for us as well as send telegrams? Questions like this are asked. Manifestly the two functions are not analogous. The one is a natural monopoly ; the other not. The tendency to absorb natural monopolies shows no tendency to absorb all business.

We live in a time of expanding industry, and government business has grown, as has all other business ; but there is no cause for alarm. While there has been an absolute growth in government business, such statistics as we have tend to show that, as compared with the amount of private business, there has been a relative decrease.

Another false alarm has been raised by the cry " central·

ization." The truth is, we are apparently living in a time of
relative decentralization. During the last sixty years in Ohio,
the expenses of the local political units, such as county, city,
school district, have increased far more than twice as rapidly
as those of the state ; and investigation in the countries of
Europe, as well as in the American States, shows very generally that during the past thirty or forty years local expenses
have increased twice as rapidly as those of the central state
governments. Now, as expenses are a tolerably fair measure
of functions, we can safely say that local business increases
faster than central state business ; and that we live in a time
when government is not extending its business as rapidly as
private persons, and when the business of central governments is not increasing so rapidly as the business of local
governments.

One other objection is increased political " patronage."
In itself, " patronage " for members of legislatures is not a
good thing, but in the purchase of the telegraph, rather than
in attempted control of it, the removal of opportunities for
fraud and oppression and the simplification of government
business would more than counterbalance the evils of increased patronage. Secondly, patronage can be remedied
by better civil service rules, and the very increase in the civil
service staff would strengthen existing civil service rules,
and would force the importance of civil service reform upon
the attention of the country. Thirdly, the telegraph business would be combined with the post-office business, and
as in many offices the same man could attend to both, there
would not be so large an increase in government employees
as one would at first imagine. The number of presidential
appointments would increase only slightly, and the number
of post-offices brought under the civil service rules as they
exist even now would be increased, because many more

offices would have the necessary number of employees.
Fourthly, as the business of government increases, there is,
in modern times, a constant tendency to improvement, and
this tendency is so marked that few exceptions to it can be
adduced.   Why was civil service reform introduced into the
United States?   Precisely on account of the growing importance of government business, and on this very account civil
service regulations were introduced in Philadelphia.[1]

One reason why our government has been so poor is the
indifference of upright men of intelligence and means ; but
this tends to disappear as they realize the importance of
government.   When government really amounts to something, it offers a career to men of talent.   On all these
accounts there has been a remarkable improvement in the
art of government throughout the civilized world during
the past twenty years.   I believe no assertion is safer than
the prediction that the purchase of telegraph lines would
improve our civil service immediately, and soon lead to
measures which would diminish the " patronage " of elected
office-holders, such as senators, representatives, President.
I think also that the wire-pullers appreciate this.   There is
not one of the worse class of " spoils " politicians who does
not oppose an extension of the business of government.
The shrewdest of them must see that to make government
an important business agency will mean death to " practical
politics."

In conclusion, we must ask the testimony of experience,
and this in all countries where a government telegraph has

---

[1] Another reason may be given for the expectation that the purchase
of the telegraph would improve our civil service.   A very large proportion of post-office employees would be obliged to be telegraphers,
and this would raise the standard of qualifications and lessen the number of qualified applicants.

been tried is unanimous in favor of public telegraph service. In none of these countries would the people even consider the subject of replacing public telegraphs by private telegraphs, and everywhere the experience of the United States is regarded as a warning against private telegraph companies. England's experience is instructive. Private companies were there tried until they proved to be intolerable; then they were purchased. Elsewhere in Europe the telegraph was from the start a public institution, and this is the result: while the estimated cost of telegraphs in all other states of Europe is 282,000,000 francs, the estimated cost to England of her telegraphs is 272,000,000 francs; in other words, owing to unsuccessful attempts to secure a good private telegraph system, England paid nearly as much for her telegraphs as all the other countries in Europe put together.

The following statistics show the increased facilities offered the public and the resulting increase of business. In 1868 private lines connected about 1000 cities. In 1870 the telegraph became a state institution; in 1882 there were 5595 telegraph stations, and in 1888, 6810. The telegrams forwarded in 1868 numbered six millions; in 1882, 31,500,000; in 1888, 53,403,425. It is said that technical improvements have not recently been introduced in England, but this is false. While American telegraphs are resisting improvements, and, according to uncontradicted newspaper reports, are buying important inventions of Edison and locking them up lest they should benefit any one, the English telegraph has made wonderful progress. In an address before the British Association for the Advancement of Science, at the meeting held in Bath, 1888, Mr. W. H. Preece, the best authority in England on the subject, said : "The telegraphic system of England has been brought to the highest pitch of perfection." He mentions also the fact that American newspapers chronicled it as a " big thing " when 500,000 words were sent by our telegraphic system over the wires in one night at the time of the last Republican Convention in Chicago, when President Harrison was nominated ; whereas the English telegraph sent 1,500,000 words from the central telegraph office in London in one night, when Mr. Gladstone introduced his Home Rule Bill on April 8, 1886. Moreover, we can judge our telegraphic managers " out of their own mouth." They declare themselves incompetent to place their wires underground, whereas of 1745 lines of wire entering the central station in London not one is open, and some wires extend underground for distances from twelve to twenty-two miles from that office.

The government telegraphs of Europe have made rapid strides in improvements, and much progress has been due to the *Journal Télégraphique,* the organ of the international union of government telegraphs. On the whole, in the way of supplying conveniences, forming international combinations, and in leading in cheap rates, government telegraphs have done far more than private lines, and their service to-day is for the ordinary private individual — one is almost tempted to say — incomparably better. Quite as much inducement for improvement is offered as in private telegraphy ; in fact, even more. First, each state takes a pride in establishing low rates, and so there is a kind of international competition. Secondly, each man at the head of the telegraph service wants to make a better showing than others. The people call for low rates and bring pressure to bear, and at the same time the administration dreads to apply to the public treasury to make good a deficiency ; thus the officials must be alert and active. The public demand for good and efficient service is more powerful with a public telegraph than with a private company.

The experience of both England and the United States shows that a few great centres are tolerably well served by private companies, but other places miserably. A few years ago I wanted to send a telegram of importance from Richmond, Va., early on Monday morning, but the telegraph office was locked until seven o'clock in the morning. This could have happened, I believe, in no city of seventy-five thousand inhabitants in Western Europe. During the summer of 1887 I sent a telegram from Baltimore to Fredonia, in New York State (about forty miles from Buffalo), on Saturday; on Sunday I sent a second — both of great importance; and on Sunday, receiving no answer to either, started for Fredonia, to arrive on the same day on which the telegrams came — namely, Monday. That could scarcely have happened in any country in Western Europe; and it is to be noticed that post-offices with us offer better facilities than telegraph offices; for even in small places they are open at least once on Sunday, although there is less call for it. These concrete illustrations are given because they are merely typical. As to poor quality of service, as seen in frequent mistakes, it is needless to speak. Every one knows that.

There has been an attempt to make it appear that prices are low in this country, but this results either from ignorance or from wilful intent to deceive. They are as high as they profitably can be. It is ridiculous to compare the charge for telegraphing a mile here and a mile in Europe, because the cost of service is not greatly influenced by distance. Some claim that it is not at all influenced thereby, while others even maintain that, on an average, the actual outlay for a domestic telegram to a remote part of the country is less than to a nearer point. This is going too far, but without entering into technical details, it can readily be seen on reflection that a great part of the labor and expense of sending a domestic telegram is absolutely independent of distance. This matter of distance is so subordinate that all European countries except Russia and Turkey neglect it altogether, and have one uniform price for all domestic telegrams, as for letters. The average price in the United States should be compared with this. Let us place the average price in the United States at fifty cents, and as it is so much more to many distant points, it will be conceded that sufficient allowance has been made for the legitimate added costs of long distances and sparsely settled districts. If, then, this average charge, with due allowance for great distances, is fifty cents for ten words in the United States, we have a basis for comparison.

England charges twelve cents for twelve words ; Germany, twelve cents for ten words, a recent reduction of five cents in the rate for ten words ; Belgium, nine cents for ten words ; Italy, eighteen cents for fifteen words ; Switzerland ten cents for ten words. It will be perceived that the charges for telegrams are higher in the United States than elsewhere. On the other hand, letters are actually carried, and notwithstanding long distances our government sends letters as cheaply as any country and more cheaply than some countries.

Many of these countries, it should be further remembered, derive a net revenue from the telegraph, which enables them to lessen taxation by so much. The English telegraph has not yielded net revenue because the policy of England has been to reduce rates and improve service rather than to seek profits.[1] It now about pays expenses ; and if the recent

[1] During the summer of 1889 I travelled several thousand miles in Europe, and gave an account of my observations in a series of papers published in the *Christian Union*, entitled " Social Studies in Europe." The following is an extract on the telegraphs of Europe : —

rapid increase of revenue continues, the English telegraph will also soon yield net revenue to the public treasury.[1]

It has been urged that a private telegraph company is responsible for errors, but business men say that this nominal legal responsibility is actually a farce. Moreover, government can, if it is desired, make itself responsible for

"As I visited and passed through city after city, I noticed that no telegraph poles in any city, not even the smallest, disfigured the streets and endangered the lives of the firemen while obstructing their work with street wires. Here is a marked superiority over our cities, for even in our greatest city, New York, telegraph poles still advertise to all the world corporate domination among us. In Europe no difficulty is found in burying wires, and otherwise getting them off the streets. Wires run out of London for twenty miles and more underground, and in Germany wires run underground for even hundreds of miles. We can say to those who supply electric services of one kind and another to us, 'Either you proclaim your own incompetency or you tell falsehoods when you say that electric wires cannot be buried.' Where electric services are rendered by government, no difficulty seems to be experienced in removing wires from streets.

"My friends and I had several times occasion to use the telegraph, which is everywhere except with us a branch of the post-office, and I cannot refrain from expressing my admiration for the superiority and cheapness of the European service. A man in any European country would be set down as worthy a place in a lunatic asylum, I think, who would want to turn over the telegraph service to private corporations. England is satisfied with her costly experience with private corporations.

"Let us first take up charges. We all know the large pamphlet in which the Western Union tariff is kept, and which must be consulted by the operator each time before you know what your telegram is to cost — for the tariff, as a whole, is kept secret, and you are not allowed to see it. Contrast with this the English tariff, the whole of which is printed on every blank. Here it is: 'Twelve words sixpence, every

---

[1] It does not require the gift of prophecy to enable one to predict that when that time comes, we will see far less than we do at present about the financial results of the English telegraph service.

errors. On the continent of Europe the post-office pays damages if a registered letter is lost.

Finally, a world telegraph union has been discussed, and it would bring great advantage, as has the Universal Postal Union ; but the chief obstacle in the way has been the private telegraphs of the United States. If we, in this country,

additional word one halfpenny.' This is the whole. You write your telegram, put on the postage stamp in the corner, paying for every word in address and text, and that is all. As elsewhere in Europe, for domestic telegrams distance is so small a matter in cost that it is neglected, as with us for letters. Of course, for international telegrams higher charges are made, because cables must be used, and receipts must be divided between two or more countries. Those who say you can send a telegram cheaper in the United States a thousand miles than elsewhere presume on the ignorance of the American public. A thousand-miles telegram in Europe is, of course, an international telegram, and in many cases requires the use of submarine cables, and the receipts must be divided between two or more countries. Yet the assertion itself is not true. Some people among us who write on telegraphs are, curiously, several years behind the times in their information about European services. If you enter an English telegraph office, you may read this notice, dated March 28, 1889: 'GOVERNMENT CABLES. — Charges from Great Britain to Germany, Holland, Belgium, and France, twopence a word, minimum (for a telegram) tenpence.' One reason why the business can be done so cheaply is the economy effected in combining it with the post-office. In most countries the business yields a profit; but in Great Britain the aim has been to give low charges rather than to strive for a profit; yet so entirely successful is the system that recent reports indicate that shortly the government telegraph service of Great Britain will yield a profit unless further reductions are made. Of course it must be remembered that England tried competition; that, by a familiar process, companies always consolidated, with increased capitalization, and that, as a result, the telegraph cost England nearly as much as it cost all the other countries of Europe put together. The high interest charges on purchase money are thus one of the results of admitting the principle of private business into an unsuitable field. The increase in telegrams sent in Great

buy the private lines and establish a public service, a world telegraph union will soon be formed, and that will be another one of those bonds which unite nations and make for international peace.

Britain in 1888–89 was 8.5 per cent. over the previous year, and, excluding interest on capital, the net returns to the government were about half a million dollars. It must be remembered that to this we ought to add what the government would pay out for telegraph services for its own administration if the wires were private property, and we shall find that quite a large profit accrued to the British government in the last fiscal year from government ownership of telegraph lines. The test of experience has decided the question for everybody in England.

"But some other things must be noticed. In Baltimore I quite often have occasion to visit a dingy and uncomfortable telegraph office in a basement, and one must often have noticed how consumptive, poorly cared for, underfed, and oppressed many of our telegraph operators look. I noticed that in England the offices were high and airy, that the operators, men and women, were fine-looking, well-cared-for people, apparently well educated and intelligent, and always polite and attentive. The quality of the service was excellent, telegrams being promptly sent and promptly delivered, and, were not space too limited, I could give many interesting contrasts with our Western Union service."

APPENDIX.

THE following tables and extracts are taken from the Report of the English Postmaster-General for the year ended the 31st of March, 1889, and show the activity of the telegraph department and the brilliant results achieved.

The deficit is obtained by adding to other expenses the interest on the money paid for the plant. It should also be remembered in addition to what has been said that England has spent large sums in improving and extending the telegraph plant which has been charged to expenditures, although they are really investments of capital.

" The financial position of the Telegraph Service, which, since the introduction of the reduced rate for Inland Telegrams, has given rise to some anxiety, has shown a satisfactory improvement in the past year, due to some extent, no doubt, to the general revival of trade as well as to the increased facilities offered. Excluding Foreign, Press, and Free telegrams, the returns show a total number of 46,816,711 Inland Telegrams, being an increase of 3,684,965 telegrams, or of 8.5 per cent. as compared with the number for the preceding year. The average value was 7.92*d*. as compared with 7.96*d*. in 1887–88, giving an aggregate value £1,545,592, as compared with £1,431,266. A large and growing amount of local business is conducted in London, and it would seem that the wants of the metropolis can only be satisfied by the transmission of nearly five million telegrams a year, an increase of some 11 per cent. on the number for the preceding year. The Foreign, Press, and Free telegrams occupy a considerable portion of the Telegraph System. Foreign telegrams numbered 4,828,228, showing an increase of 360,355. Press telegrams, which are received at exceptionally low rates, numbered 4,760,891, as compared with 4,609,308 for the previous year; but the receipts under this head were £411 less than those of 1887–88, owing probably to a diminution in the number of single messages, and to the growth of the practice of sending copies of the same telegram to several newspapers. Free telegrams, *i.e.* Official telegrams sent on Her Majesty's Service and telegrams relating to the business of various Railway Companies, figure at 1,359,516, as compared with 1,194,497 sent in 1887–88. A comparative statement relating to these three classes is given below.

Nature of Telegrams.	Year.	Number.	Increase.	Receipts.	Increase.
Foreign telegrams	1888–89	4,828,229	360,355	£174,477	£10,584
" "	1887–88	4,467,874	——	163,893	Decrease.
Press telegrams	1888–89	4,760,891	151,583	111,159	411
" "	1887–88	4,609,308	——	111,570	
Official telegrams	1888–89	254,323	36,213	} Nil.	
" "	1887–88	218,110	——		
Railway telegrams	1888–89	1,105,193	128,806		
" "	1887–88	976,387	——		

" The following table gives a comparison of figures for seven years, bringing out the expenditure by this Department, and also the amounts paid by other Departments, on account of the Telegraph Service, and also shows the deficit on each year : —

Year.	Receipts.	Expenditure.			Annual Interest on Capital.	Deficit.
		By Telegraph Department.	By other Departments.	Total.		
1882–83 . . .	£1,768,070	£1,504,204	£79,673	£1,583,877	£326,417	£142,224
1883–84 . . .	1,789,223	1,709,644	99,276	1,808,920	326,417	346,114
1884–85 . . .	1,784,414	1,731,040	89,724	1,820,764	326,417	362,767
1885–86 . . .	1,787,264	1,733,104	99,297	1,832,401	326,417	371,554
1886–87 . . .	1,887,160	1,939,764	92,868	2,032,632	326,417	471,889
1887–88 . . .	1,992,949	1,928,345	70,688	1,999,033	326,417	332,501
1888–89 . . .	2,129,669	1,969,096	73,298	2,042,394	326,417	239,142

" New Telegraph Offices have been opened at 181 Post Offices and at 40 Railway Stations in the United Kingdom. The total number of Telegraph Offices, which are also Post Offices, was at the end of the year 5410, and the total number of Telegraph Offices at Railway Stations 1621, giving a total of 7031 Offices at which Postal Telegraph business is transacted.

" The concessions held by the Submarine Telegraph Company expired in January, but were extended to the 31st March, 1889. It was evident from representations made in Parliament, and by Chambers of Commerce and other bodies, that a strong feeling existed that the opportunity should be taken to establish between England and the neighboring Continental States a direct system of International Telegraphic communication, without the intervention of a private Company; and the opinion of your Lordships and myself was entirely in harmony with this feeling.

" Due notice was therefore given to the Company that this country could not agree to the renewal of their concessions, and negotiations were entered into with the German, French, Dutch, and Belgian Governments. The various, and in some cases opposing, interests which had to be considered rendered these negotiations both difficult and delicate; but at length agreements were made which provided for the direct transmission of telegrams between the Telegraph Department of this country and the Telegraph Administrations of the other countries concerned, and admitted of a reduction in the charges for telegrams to three of those countries, viz., France, Germany, and Holland.

" The Cables purchased from the Submarine Company jointly by France and England were those between the following points: Calais and Dover, Boulogne and Folkestone, Dieppe and Beachy Head, Havre and Beachy Head, and Piron (near Coutances) and Vieux Chateau (near St. Helier, Jersey). The cables between Ostend and Ramsgate, and De la Panne (near Furnes) and Dover were purchased from the Company jointly by Belgium and England. The two cables to Holland and one of the cables to Germany were already the property of this country; and the German Union Company's cable to Germany was purchased by the German Government. The offices of the Submarine Com-

pany in Throgmorton Avenue and at Dover, Ramsgate, East
Dean, and Jersey had to be purchased by this Department, as
well as the cable ship " The Lady Carmichael "; and 370 of the
staff of the Company were taken over by the Department.

"The capital amount expended by England was £67,163, and
on the 1st April the new business was commenced with a uniform rate to France, Germany, Holland, and Belgium of 2*d*. per
word, with a minimum of 10*d*. for a message."

TELEGRAMS.

TABLE showing the TOTAL NUMBER OF TELEGRAMS forwarded from TELEGRAPH OFFICES in ENGLAND and WALES, SCOTLAND, and IRELAND, in each Year since the transfer of the TELEGRAPHS to the STATE.

| Year. | NUMBER OF TELEGRAMS. | | | | | |
| | England and Wales. | | | Scotland. | Ireland. | TOTAL. |
	Provinces.	London.	Total.			
1870–71 . .	5,299,882	2,863,821	8,163,703	1,080,189	606,285	9,850,177
1871–72 . .	6,594,590	3,612,772	10,207,362	1,388,434	878,000	12,473,796
1872–73 . .	8,022,151	4,577,015	12,599,166	1,761,298	1,175,316	15,535,780
1873–74 . .	9,233,854	5,254,547	14,488,401	2,009,893	1,323,236	17,821,530
1874–75 . .	10,124,661	5,652,033	15,776,694	2,132,787	1,343,639	19,253,120
1875–76 . .	10,883,282	6,350,714	17,233,996	2,287,359	1,452,180	20,973,535
1876–77 . .	11,232,704	6,561,930	17,794,634	2,402,347	1,529,162	21,726,143
1877–78 . .	11,392,098	6,700,504	18,092,602	2,490,776	1,588,489	22,171,867
1878–79 . .	11,592,899	8,830,019	20,422,918	2,477,003	1,559,854	24,459,775
1879–80 . .	12,392,996	9,854,566	22,247,562	2,704,574	1,595,001	26,547,137
1880–81 . .	13,456,555	11,176,459	24,633,014	3,042,291	1,736,677	29,411,982
1881–82 . .	14,204,479	12,071,034	26,275,513	3,207,994	1,862,354	31,345,861
1882–83 . .	14,554,015	12,374,707	26,928,722	3,244,202	1,919,102	32,092,026
1883–84 . .	14,920,413	12,686,433	27,606,846	3,299,428	1,936,846	32,843,120
1884–85 . .	15,195,618	12,930,376	28,125,994	3,257,546	1,894,919	33,278,459
1885–86 . .	18,029,008	15,081,433	33,110,441	3,812,173	2,223,669	39,146,283
1886–87 . .	24,044,077	18,276,108	42,320,185	5,106,774	2,816,680	50,243,639
1887–88 . .	26,052,717	18,872,554	44,925,271	5,430,623	3,047,531	53,403,425
1888–89 . .	28,269,130	20,263,539	48,532,669	5,991,223	3,241,455	57,765,347

The figures for each year since 1877–78 include the number of certain Press Telegrams not previously included in these Returns.

Prior to 1883–84 the returns were made to the end of the last complete week in the year. Since that time they are, in each case, to the last day of the year inclusive.

On the 1st October, 1885, the minimum charge for an inland telegram was reduced from one shilling to sixpence.

LIBRARY OF ECONOMICS and POLITICS.

MESSRS. T. Y. CROWELL & CO. take pleasure in announcing that they have completed arrangements for a series of volumes dealing with timely topics in a fresh, interesting, and instructive manner. The series will be entitled "Library of Economics and Politics," and will be under the editorial control of Professor Richard T. Ely, Ph.D., LL.D., Professor of Political Economy and Director of the School of Economics, Political Science and History at the University of Wisconsin.

It is proposed to issue volumes at irregular intervals, and to supply only the best literature. A standard of excellence will be maintained, which it is hoped will give to this series a leading rank in this country and abroad.

The volumes for which arrangements have thus far been made are: —

First, "THE INDEPENDENT TREASURY SYSTEM OF THE UNITED STATES." An historical and critical examination of this important institution; a work which will prove valuable to bankers and financiers generally, as well as to scholars. The author of this volume is Mr. DAVID KINLEY, A.B., Assistant and Fellow in Economics in the University of Wisconsin.

Second, "AMERICAN CHARITIES: A STUDY IN PHILANTHROPY AND ECONOMICS." By AMOS G. WARNER, Ph.D., Superintendent of Charities for the District of Columbia, and Professor-elect of Economics in the Leland-Stanford, Jr. University. This work will be the first exhaustive treatment of the subject. It will be a careful presentation of theory and of practical experience, making it an indispensable hand-book for all those who are theoretically and practically interested in charities.

Third, "REPUDIATION OF STATE DEBTS IN THE UNITED STATES." By WILLIAM A. SCOTT, Ph.D., Assistant Professor of Political Economy in the University of Wisconsin. This is a work which deals with one of the most important phases of American finance. Perhaps there is no field of financial investigation in the United States which has been so neglected. The work will be of practical importance to all those who are concerned with investments, as well as to scholars interested in our financial history and institutions.

The editor of the series promises two volumes. One on Socialism, which will be considered descriptively and critically. The work will be divided into four parts: Part One treating of the Nature of Socialism, Part Two of the Strength of Socialism, Part Three of the Weakness of Socialism, and Part Four, the Golden Mean, or Practicable Social Reform. The other volume which the editor will contribute, will be called "Suggestions on Social Topics," dealing with social classes, legal inequality, labor organizations, the eight-hour day, the widening and deepening range of ethical obligation, etc.

ALBERT SHAW, Ph.D., American Editor of the "Review of Reviews," is engaged in the preparation of a work suitable for the series, the title of which will be announced subsequently. The publishers, however, venture to assure the public that the work by Dr. SHAW will be one of the most popular and useful volumes in the series.

THOMAS Y. CROWELL & CO., NEW YORK and BOSTON.

www.ingramcontent.com/pod-product-compliance
Lightning Source LLC
Chambersburg PA
CBHW031400270326
41929CB00010BA/1269